THE GREAT BOOM
AND PANIC

THE
GREAT BOOM
AND PANIC
1921-1929

Robert T. Patterson

HENRY REGNERY COMPANY
CHICAGO

To

WEBSTER COXE PATTERSON

Preface

THE PURPOSE OF THIS BOOK, besides that of diversion, is to go at least a little of the way toward answering two questions: (1) Just what did happen during the boom and the panic of the 1920's? and (2) What were their causes? Complete answers to these questions are, of course, impossible. With respect to the first question, selection, emphasis, and interpretation of relevant facts can show what was significant in these two large episodes and bring them to life for the reader; but why the boom and panic occurred is still a controversial subject, and may continue to be so forever. There are many hypotheses to explain them, and this study offers a simple, realistic one that combines monetary influences and human impulses, neither of which is as yet fully understood.

The old truism that "hindsight is better than foresight" should serve to caution us, because as this story of an epoch unfolds many of us may be tempted to assume—all too easily—that in such times we, unlike the many who were beguiled in the 1920's by the rise of stock prices and bereft by their fall, would know better and react differently. A few would, of course, but most of us would not, if history is any guide to future human actions.

In going forward with this work I have become indebted to many. Members of the staff of the Library of Congress and of the New York Public Library, in its Main Reading Room, the Division of Economics, and the Division of History, as well as at the Annex on West Forty-third Street, have been very helpful. In gathering material I have had access to hundreds of sources of information, some of which more or less duplicate others. Those that have contributed significantly to this book are acknowledged in the Bibliography and throughout the text. Credits for photographs, drawings, and the chart appear on the respective pages. Several of my colleagues at the American Institute for Economic Research read the manuscript at different stages of its development and made wise and useful suggestions. My special thanks go to Lieutenant Commander James T. Gibbs for his help in the chapter on causes and for many worthwhile criticisms, and to Mr. William S. Peirce and Mr. Alex S. Perry, Jr., for their valued comments and suggestions. I am grateful to Catherine F. Noble for putting into readable form the semi-legible handwriting that she had to cope with.

I alone am responsible for the limitations, interpretations, and conclusions of this study.

ROBERT T. PATTERSON

Great Barrington, Massachusetts
July 19, 1964

Contents

Prologue

WITH THE STOCK MARKET CRASH late in 1929 the world seemed to collapse for hundreds of thousands of buoyantly hopeful Americans. As wave after wave of selling beat down security prices, great fortunes and small savings alike vanished before the unbelieving eyes of those who followed stocks on the ticker tape and in the daily newspapers. The great boom of the 1920's was over.

This marked the end of one era and the beginning of another, although no one knew that at the time. Perhaps it was better that no one did, for there lay ahead hard, bitter years of misery and despair. The panic ushered in one of the deepest and most severe depressions that the nation had ever experienced.

Many still remember the golden, turbulent years of the 1920's, that fantastic period of inflation and mounting speculation; of boosters and Babbitts, sports records and fads; of bootlegging and speakeasies, racketeering and gang wars; of flaming youth, flappers, and the language of Freudian psychology; of cynicism, idealism, and reform.

It was a decade of high-pressure advertising and selling in which the automobile, the radio, electric power and electric appliances of many kinds, cosmetics, cigarettes, and many other products came into almost universal use. The movies prospered, the chain-store movement accelerated, and consumer instalment buying became an important part of the national way of life. Great gains in industrial technology and managerial efficiency, and here and there the strengthening of monopoly power, multiplied business profits. The number of individuals having million dollar incomes increased manyfold.[1]

As the decade advanced it seemed as though prosperity was everywhere; and the vision of the future was of a utopia of ever-expanding profits—in business and in the stock market. In the most prosperous country of the world, millions believed that they were destined for wealth. All one had to do, apparently, was to buy stocks and watch them go up. And as people bought, prices soared. Paper profits were pyramided with money borrowed on margin from the brokers, who in turn borrowed from the banks and other big lenders. Practically every town had its stock market *nouveaux riches*. Those who became millionaires reached out for more millions.

Then came the reckoning as the stock market turned to rend its bedazzled followers. In the late summer and the autumn of 1929 the great boom sickened and died. The decline in prices in the securities markets in New York and across the country, which had begun undramatically in early September, accelerated in a mad panic of selling from mid-October to mid-November. One crisis of liquidation followed another until there seemed no bottom for the market, no surcease for those who owned stocks and clung to some last shred of hope that they would recover their losses.

The worst of the panic occurred on October 24, 28, 29, and from November 4 through 13, after which a temporary recovery set in. Later the decline resumed, continuing until the middle of 1932. By that time stock values had been whittled to a small fraction of what they had been.

---

[1] According to the Bureau of Internal Revenue, 513 individuals reported income of a million dollars or more for 1929. Even by 1961, the next best year thereafter, the number of individuals having income of that magnitude was only 398.

NEW YORK STOCK EXCHANGE	1929 HIGH	PANIC LOW	1932 LOW
American Telephone and Telegraph	310¼	197¼	70¼
Anaconda Copper	140	70	3
Auburn Auto	514	120	28¾
Chrysler	135	26	5
Du Pont	231	80	22
General Electric	403	168⅛	34*
General Motors	91¾	33½	7⅝
International Telephone and Telegraph	149¼	53	2⅝
Johns-Manville	242¾	90	10
Montgomery Ward	156⅞	49¼	3½
New York Central	256½	160	8¾
Pennsylvania Railroad	110	74	6½
Radio Corporation of America	114¾ †	26	2½
United States Steel	261¾	150	21¼
White Sewing Machine	48	1	¼
Woolworth	103⅞	52¼	22
Zenith Radio	52¾	10⅛	½

NEW YORK CURB EXCHANGE			
Aluminum Company of America	539½	180	22
Cities Service	68⅛	20	1¼
Electric Bond & Share	189	50	5
Goldman Sachs Trading Corporation	121¼	32	1

* This figure represents an adjustment to take account of a four-for-one stock "split."
† It had been "split" five shares for one earlier in 1929.

Every so often, it seems, humankind almost *en masse* has a compulsion to speculate, and it yields to that compulsion with abandon. Yet many who succumb do not perceive that in the excitement of a boom much of what is called "investment" or "speculation" is merely gambling. In some individuals the propensity to speculate is always present. And it seems to be characteristic of almost all who are attracted to speculation that when they win they try to win some more; and when they lose, they try again. Unlike the burnt child, the singed speculator is likely to return to the attractive flame. Few learn from their elders' painful experiences or from their own.

But this human inclination is not the sole explanation of booms and of the panics that have been their aftermath. The time must be ripe for a boom. In business and finance conditions must be developing in such a way that they provide a rationale for the spreading and heightening of optimism. An abundance of historical evidence suggests that one of the necessary conditions is a plenitude of currency and credit, that is, considerably more than enough purchasing media to meet the needs of industry and commerce. In every great boom, apparently, an excessive amount of such means of exchange has helped to foster the delusion that a "New Era" of ever-increasing gains will last forever. This was the situation during much of the 1920's.

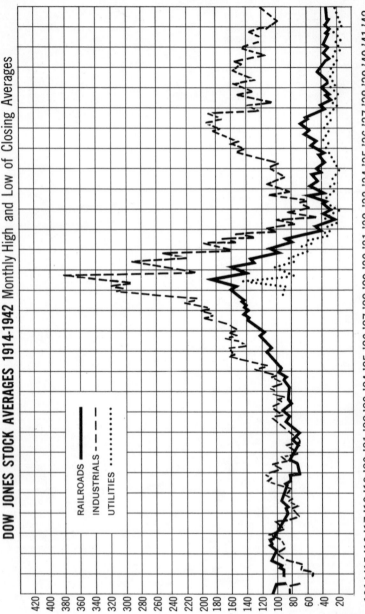

DOW JONES STOCK AVERAGES 1914-1942 Monthly High and Low of Closing Averages

RAILROADS ———
INDUSTRIALS – – –
UTILITIES ·········

420 400 380 360 340 320 300 280 260 240 220 200 180 160 140 120 100 80 60 40 20

1914 '15 '16 '17 '18 '19 '20 '21 '22 '23 '24 '25 '26 '27 '28 '29 '30 '31 '32 '33 '34 '35 '36 '37 '38 '39 '40 '41 '42

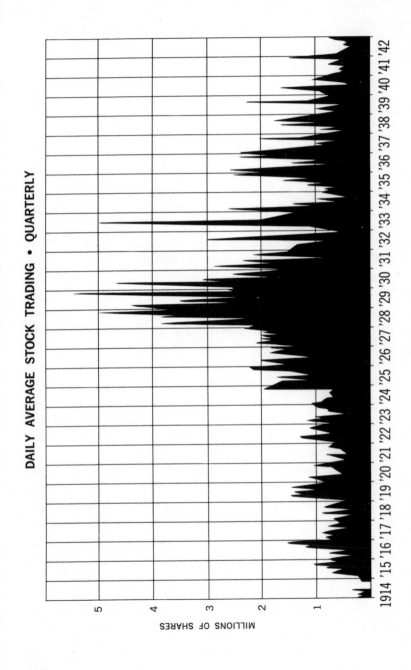

DAILY AVERAGE STOCK TRADING • QUARTERLY

MILLIONS OF SHARES

1914 '15 '16 '17 '18 '19 '20 '21 '22 '23 '24 '25 '26 '27 '28 '29 '30 '31 '32 '33 '34 '35 '36 '37 '38 '39 '40 '41 '42

1

A Brief Perspective

THE PANIC OF 1929 was history repeating itself, but on a tremendous scale. As far back as 1720, the bursting of the Mississippi Bubble in France and the South Sea Bubble in England had brought an end to a period of inflation and wild speculation in each of those countries. In the United States, dating from the beginning of the Republic, panics or crises had occurred at irregular intervals, taking the nation by surprise, often with a violence that prostrated all business. There had been a severe panic in 1920, and still vivid in many memories were the panics of 1907, 1903, and 1893. Some oldsters even bore scars from the great debacle of 1873. The crises of 1857 and 1837 were, of course, far in the past, but the devastation they had wrought was known even to the casual reader of history. However complex their causes, each one was associated with excessive speculation of some kind or other.

What became the roaring boom of the late 1920's began quietly in the summer of 1921. And for eight years the trend of common stock prices was upward, although it was subject at times to sudden, sharp reversals and periods of stagnation. Until the latter part of 1924 the advance appeared to be nothing more than a strong cyclical upward movement. But it fed on its own progress, each new upsurge creating more paper wealth that could be used to buy more shares of stock. Public participation grew continually, and again and again the volume of trading on the exchanges broke previous records.

4

Stock prices rose from the summer of 1921 to the spring of 1923. From then until the summer of 1924 they declined, rallied, and declined again. But in the autumn of 1924 prices exceeded their high point of 1923, and by the end of the year they had passed the peak reached in 1919, continuing upward with only moderate reactions until February, 1926. The severe but short-lived decline that ensued was followed by a recovery during the summer of 1926 and another sharp but less severe decline in the autumn.

Early in 1927, the great upswing in stock prices began that was to carry them, with some brief but sharp reactions, to their 1929 peak. From the beginning of the boom until the panic, the low point of each major reaction was well above that of the preceding reaction. Between August 24, 1921, and September 3, 1929, the Dow-Jones industrial stock price average increased from 63.90 to 381.17, and between June 20, 1921, and September 3, 1929, the Dow-Jones railroad stock price average increased from 65.52 to 189.11. To an uncritical eye, the curve of stock prices for the whole period would appear to be one long upward, accelerating streak.

Studies of cyclical fluctuations show that in the period extending from the trough of business activity in 1921 to the trough in 1933 three distinct business cycles were completed. These cyclical movements are dated as follows[1]:

TROUGHS		PEAKS	
July,	1921	May,	1923
July,	1924	October,	1926
November,	1927	August,	1929
March,	1933		

[1] Geoffrey H. Moore, "Measuring Recessions," *Business Cycle Indicators*, Volume I, a study by the National Bureau of Economic Research (Princeton: Princeton University Press, 1961), p. 121.

But these were lesser cycles within the larger one, throughout which the movement of stock prices was sometimes nearly coincident with business recessions and recoveries, sometimes not.

The demand that had accumulated for all kinds of producer and consumer goods during the wartime scarcity of materials and manpower gave impetus to business activity in the earlier phase of the boom. Later, stock market profits augmented demand. During most of its course the boom was supported by phenomenal growth in the automobile, construction, and electric power industries. Although many industries besides these grew and prospered, agriculture, coal mining, textile manufacturing, shipbuilding, and some others did not.

Shaping the whole economic situation was the "easy money" policy of the Federal Reserve Board and its twelve regional banks. From 1921 onward, and especially after 1924, the Federal Reserve System made bank credit so liberally available that there was a sufficiency not only for the needs of business but also for the speculative purchasing of securities and real estate that, by 1925, was developing on a large scale. Except for a short period of time early in 1924 and again early in 1927, when reserve bank credit was substantially reduced,[2] the Federal Reserve continually followed this easy money policy. Although in 1928 the Federal Reserve Bank of New York raised its rediscount rate in steps from 3½ to 5 per cent, total reserve bank credit available to the commercial banks was greatly expanded.[3] When the Federal Reserve Board, in February, 1929, sought by "moral suasion" to restrain the use of credit in the stock market, it was unsuccessful.

Monetary expansion by way of the stock market was a comparatively simple process. Loans on securities were made by the banks to brokers and others, and the brokers in turn loaned

---

[2] *Annual Report of the Federal Reserve Board*, 1931, p. 29.
[3] *Ibid.*, pp. 30, 74.

the funds to their customers who bought stocks "on margin." As speculators profited from rising stock prices they spent part of their gains on various goods and services, and as businesses raised capital through the sale of their securities to those who borrowed from the brokers and the banks, the proceeds entered circulation through disbursements for business purposes. Thus the money supply increased.[4]

The long inflation was followed, however, by an extended and painful deflation, of which the panic of October and November, 1929, was only the beginning. Thus, booming prosperity of the 1920's gave way to deep depression in the early 1930's, and to a new political and economic order. The marked recovery in business and in the stock market that took place between 1933 and 1937 was followed by another severe decline and more depression. The outbreak of war in Europe in 1939 and the subsequent entry of the United States into it and into one in the Far East brought the economy out of stagnation but led to strict economic controls. Wartime and postwar inflation, due to the monetization of government debt on a vast scale, became a major problem. Between 1942 and 1946 stock prices more than doubled. For three years thereafter they moved in a comparatively narrow range and at a somewhat lower level. The long upward sweep of the market that began in 1949, although subject to setbacks associated with mild recessions and "rolling readjustments" in the economy, carried the Dow-Jones industrial, railroad, and utility averages far above their peaks of 1929 to levels unthought of then in all but the wildest imaginings.

No one can know in advance to what high level stock prices will have risen before the next great break in the market occurs. Perhaps even then many individuals' expectations will have far exceeded those prices. In the spring of 1929 a cynical cartoonist depicted a comic little man bending over a stock ticker

[4] For further explanation of the money-credit underpinnings of the boom, see Chapter 12.

and opining, "Everything's going to 5000."[5] Under certain dire circumstances, of course, a great many stocks could go to $5,000 a share, or far more than that. A panic due to inflation, or the prospect of inflation, with a flight away from money and into goods, real estate, common stocks, and other equities, could have that effect. Few investors and speculators, however, would wish for that kind of bull market![6]

Without attempting to predict the future course of the stock market, let us see what lessons there may be in the story of the great boom of the 1920's and the panic that followed it.

[5] H. I. Phillips, "My Stock Market Operations," *The American Magazine* (March, 1929), p. 54.

[6] Panics of this kind have occurred in many countries at various times in the past because of the degradation of the monetary unit through long-continued, unwarranted increases in currency and credit. One of the many instances of a "panic on the upside," due to extreme inflation, occurred in Germany after World War I. As it ran its course, common stock prices rose to astronomical heights. The once sound and stable mark depreciated so rapidly and so far that prices of almost everything were multiplied by billions. The denouement of that tragic episode was a revaluation of the mark, one new mark being made the equivalent of one trillion old marks. Under similar, although not necessarily as extreme circumstances, in whatever country they developed, stock prices could rise far beyond even the most hopeful expectations. For an excellent description and analysis of the great German inflation that culminated in 1923, see Constantino Bresciani-Turroni, *The Economics of Inflation* (New York: Barnes & Noble, Inc., 1938).

2

Various Aspects of the Boom

DURING AND AFTER WORLD WAR I, the Liberty and Victory Loan drives had taught people to buy securities. More than 22 million individuals had discovered the magic of coupon-clipping and the desirability of bonds as a form of wealth in the safe deposit box, or their usefulness as collateral at the bank. For those with surplus funds, then, it was an easy step to the purchase of bonds and stocks of corporations, especially common stocks, which could grow in value and pay attractive dividends. As the boom developed, however, there was less concern for dividends and much more for price appreciation. Some individuals came to regard their profits in stocks as recurring income, and they spent lavishly.

As the good word about the stock market spread, and as the public's appetite for securities grew, it became profitable to cater to that appetite. News services, which earlier had furnished editors with a few paragraphs of market generalities, began daily to pour forth thousands of words of investment and financial information for an eager public. Newspapers, even those in small cities, published tables of stock quotations with a commentary on the market's action. From Maine to California large and small speculators, as well as many conservative investors, avidly turned to the financial page each day to note the fluctuations of "Big Steel," "Motors," Montgomery Ward, "Radio," and many other popular issues. The Paris edition of the *New York Herald* brought stock prices to almost every city in Western Europe.

This was good for newspaper circulation and for advertising too. Conservative, long-established bond houses were adding common stocks to their lists of offerings, and the larger banks were underwriting and selling stocks through their investment subsidiaries. Advertising in the financial section of the nation's newspapers was a good way to bring each new stock issue to the attention of the stock-buying public.

Other media also helped to meet the demand for news of the stock market and for information and opinions on particular stocks. Popularized financial journals enjoyed a wide circulation. Forecasting services found subscribers in even the remotest rural areas, and tipster sheets were mailed to every likely prospect. Tickers, quotation boards, and brokerage services were installed on some ocean liners. Radio stations adopted the practice of broadcasting stock prices at intervals throughout the day. In one factory, prices were posted on a blackboard from hour to hour to please the workers. On a western ranch a radio blared quotations for the help. Over one network "The Old Counselor," a professional actor who talked earnestly about the market in an unctuous voice, was a popular advertisement for Halsey Stuart & Company, a prominent investment underwriting firm.

Although the stock exchanges were too dignified to advertise their services, it was done for them anyway. Their member firms, the brokerage houses, discreetly let the availability of their services be known—that they would buy and sell securities for a modest commission. Their partners and employees kept a weather-eye out for business, at first mainly among the wealthy, but later on a broad and democratic front.

Old customers brought in new ones as the "sure thing" of the market seemed ever surer. Most of the earlier participants made no secret of their profits; instead they urged their relatives and friends to get in on the "game." To buy and sell shares of stock was easy; in fact, it was hard not to do so once you had established a brokerage connection.

The brokerage firm kept an account for you. All you had to do was telephone the "customers' man" assigned to service your account and tell him what to buy or sell. Often he called you and suggested what to do. When you bought some shares of stock you could, if you chose, pay for them in full and in ten days or so receive the certificate. That way you bought outright; you were regarded as a conservative investor.

If you preferred, however, you could deposit 20 per cent of the stock's value with the brokerage firm, and it would "carry" you by lending the difference. Some firms would carry favored customers on a 10 per cent margin. Thus you could buy "on margin" five or ten times as much as you could pay for, and—of course—make five or ten times as much profit if the price advanced. You paid interest on the loan from the broker, but all dividends from the stock were yours.

The customers' man, now more suitably known as "account executive" or "registered representative," was the link between the customer and the broker. His business was to earn commissions for the firm, and his salary was in proportion to them. He had to watch closely both the action of the market and the status of his customers' margin accounts, keep in touch with the customers, and avoid any infraction of the Stock Exchange rules and the policies of his firm. Some customers gave him full discretion to buy and sell for them as he deemed best. Typically, he was a younger man of good family, graduated from one of the Ivy League colleges and endowed with relatives or friends of means. The social pleasures were a source of business for him, and urbanity and charm were his capital. But he worked hard, was continually harassed by the emotional reactions of his clients, and endeavored to maintain the illusion for himself and for them that he comprehended the fundamentals of the market's action and perhaps could even foretell its future. He was not allowed to buy on margin for his own account. If he was experienced and well situated he could earn upward of $20,000 a year, a much more significant sum then than now.

When the customers' man received an order it was immediately transmitted by wire or telephone to the floor of the Stock Exchange, where it was delivered to the firm's representative there, the broker himself. The broker immediately went to the post where the stock was traded and bought or sold as directed by the customer. Orders above or below the prevailing price were left with a specialist in the stock. Orders for less than a full hundred shares were passed on to brokerage firms that specialized in "odd lots" and charged an extra eighth of a point for their service.

By 1925, the volume of trading on the New York Stock Exchange had broken all records. From the 173 million shares traded during 1921 the volume increased to 920 million in 1928, and to 1,125 million in 1929. On September 1, 1929, more than 1,200 stock issues, comprising more than a billion shares, were listed for trading. The total market value of these shares exceeded $89 billion.

Anyone so fortunate as to be a member of the New York Stock Exchange at this time had a highly lucrative as well as socially approved occupation. On a busy day practically every broker on the floor shared in handling the deluge of orders that poured in. The brokers with "big" connections enlisted the aid of any others who could be found to help them. Obscurity was in some ways an advantage to a broker, because when large operators and "pools" wanted to conceal their purchases or sales they enlisted floor brokers who were not known to be associated with them. Individual traders like the fabulous William C. Durant and other large operators who bought and sold millions of shares a year, along with discretionary accounts that traded a million shares or more in a month, made the stock brokerage business a lush one. Every purchase of stock was also a sale, and each party's broker took a commission. It is said that the average earnings of a broker on the New York Stock Exchange in 1928 was $367,000, not including profits from personal speculation.

In October, 1929, there were 1,375 members of the New York Stock Exchange. The number had been increased earlier in the year by a 25 per cent "dividend." Each member received a "right" to an additional fourth of a seat[1] on the Exchange. These fractional rights were sold to qualified men who combined four of them in order to obtain a membership. On an ordinary business day 700 or 800 members would be present on the floor of the Exchange to carry out their firms' commissions or to buy and sell for their own accounts. Older members who were partners in the larger firms could remain in their offices on most days and let the younger and more energetic partner-members do the floor work. When the market became especially active, however, the older members went on the floor too.

During the later years of the boom, employment on the major stock exchanges and in brokerage offices, even in the most menial capacity, came to have honorific value. The page boys on the floor of the Exchange who had little more than a grammar school education and who tended to resent the uniform they had to wear were gradually outnumbered by those who had high school and even college diplomas. Some of the latter wore the uniform with the kind of pride associated with the uniforms of West Point and Annapolis. They, and others like them in minor jobs with brokerage firms, thought

[1] A membership in the Exchange is called a "seat" because at one time the members sat at desks. In 1929, a seat on the New York Stock Exchange sold for as high as $625,000, compared with a low of $17,000 in 1942. The highest price paid for a seat on the New York Curb Exchange was $254,000 in 1929, the lowest price since then being $650 in 1942.

little of starting at $15 a week. Often, away from their work, they were treated with deference and their opinions on the market were sought; but more important, they felt themselves at the center of the financial world with boundless opportunity ahead.

Before the panic shattered many a Horatio Alger dream, some of the young newcomers to the world of stock trading and ticker tape did achieve wealth and high position. Quite a number of memberships on the New York Stock Exchange were acquired by younger men, a few in their early twenties, who had earlier held subordinate positions but who, with ability (and often the right connections), had risen in rank and fortune along with the rising price level. In 1929, for example, three former telephone clerks in brokerage houses purchased seats on the Exchange for $550,000 and upward. One of the seats was acquired from a broker who had bought it for about $80,000 in 1908. Another seat, which sold for $580,000, had been bought in 1896, when the price ranged between $14,000 and $20,000.

A few blocks from the New York Stock Exchange was its lusty little brother, the New York Curb Market, where less seasoned stock issues and those of less prominent companies were traded in the same way as on the "Big Board." During the later part of the boom, and for a while afterward, the New York Produce Exchange listed about a hundred stocks for trading. In some of the other large cities also there were stock exchanges, but most of them listed comparatively few issues, mainly those of local interest. In Chicago and Los Angeles, however, the stock exchanges grew and prospered during the boom, and brokers who held memberships in them were kept busy and prosperous. A nationwide "over-the-counter" market flourished for stocks and bonds not traded on the exchanges. In it your broker could buy or sell for you the bluest of "blue chips" (U.S. government securities and New York City bank stocks, for example) and also the meanest of "cats and dogs," some of which in actuality were worthless from the moment they were issued.

From the visitors' gallery of the New York Stock Exchange or the New York Curb Market you could view the milling and churning multitude of brokers, note a flurry of activity here or there in some particular stock, and witness pandemonium everywhere when the market surged forward or sold off sharply. Whatever occurred on the floor of the New York Stock Exchange was quickly reflected in every brokerage boardroom in the country. There some of the brokers' customers sat in rows of chairs or stood about to watch the endlessly unfolding story told by the ticker tape. High at one end of the typical boardroom was the illuminated reflection of the moving tape, projected from below by the Translux, an innovation of the later 1920's. Board boys chalked a running record of stock prices on huge blackboards along one or more sides of the room. On days when the market was especially active, crowds packed in to watch. The atmosphere might register jubilation or dejection as prices rose or fell. The speculating public, with few exceptions, was on the buying side of the market. It was "long" in stocks and was chronically "bullish."

Despite the long-term upward movement of stock prices, there were many uncertainties. To do well you had to pick the right stocks and "stay with them" as long as they were "hot." For considerable lengths of time prices would fluctuate at random, no overall trend being discernible. Sometimes, in a burst of selling, prices would fall back sharply, creating widespread anxiety as well as chagrin on the part of those who had bought near the top of the preceding rise. The old Wall Street ditty was still appropriate:

> Sell them and you'll be sorry,
> Buy them and you'll regret,
> Hold them and you'll worry,
> Do nothing and you'll fret.

As stock prices advanced, speculative profits augmented the general demand for goods and services, including luxuries of every kind. For those who wanted such things, and managed to stay with the right stocks, the market yielded country estates, Park Avenue apartments, butlers and chauffeurs, oriental rugs, mink coats, diamond tiaras, rare first editions, old masters, yachts, private airplanes, Hispano-Suizas, and innumerable lesser luxuries.

The difference between investment and speculation was often discussed. The cynical view was that if you made a profit you had invested, and if you took a loss you had been speculating. It was far from agreed that margin trading was speculative. Many regarded it as a "dynamic" form of investment. People who "played the market" seldom spoke of themselves as speculators, although they might refer to others in that way.

There was a ready explanation of the difference between speculation and gambling: Speculation provided an economic service, and so was in the public interest; gambling, of course, did not. At best, gambling might yield some pleasurable excitement for those who indulged in it, and this could be found at the gaming tables and the race tracks. Speculation was useful, serious business, so many people said.

The justifications for speculation were that it made the securities markets broader and more active, thus facilitating the flow of savings to industry and rendering the vast capital of the nation more liquid; that it enabled the market to absorb large purchases or sales with comparatively small price changes; and that the judgment and foresight of speculators led them to support prices when prices were too low, and restrained them from doing so when prices were too high. The conclusion drawn from all this was that because speculators performed an economic service by assuming the risks of the market place, their reward should be commensurate with the risks. Underlying this reasoning seems to have been the assumption that on the whole the judgment of the speculators was correct. And for a long time that seemed to be the case. Less was said of those who misjudged the future course of the market and were penalized for being wrong. In all this theorizing, one of the important lessons of financial history was generally forgotten, namely, that the great majority in their long-run judgment could be wrong but not have to pay the penalty for quite a long time.

Women—"Ladybulls," Will Rogers called them—as well as men understood the symbolism of the tape and spoke the jargon of Wall Street and the boardrooms. Earlier in the boom some brokers had refused their accounts, fearing hysterical scenes if the market went against them. But that soon changed as women became a powerful force in the market and an important source of commissions. Some brokerage firms even had elegantly furnished and decorated boardrooms exclusively for the use of their women customers. In March, 1929, for example, a branch office for women only was opened on East Fifty-seventh Street, in New York City, by the Stock Exchange firm of Muir & Loomis. Well-bred customers' women served the patrons, taking their orders and giving information, although board boys were employed to post the quotations. And there were women brokers as well as customers. At the peak of the boom, at least twenty-two New York Stock Exchange firms had one or more as partners. Some of them merely owned an interest in their firms, but others took an active part, although none of them were members of the Exchange. One woman, Mrs. Ethel G. Rich, was the head of the firm of Rich, Clark and Company.

Many women played the market for thrills, but only the rare few bought stocks of corporations because of their cute names or photogenic officers. Some of them carried over to stock trading their household marketing attitudes, were picayunish, and made themselves nuisances. Perhaps a few had prejudiced the case for the majority when one writer, a woman, reported that brokers regarded most women speculators as "hard losers, naggers, stubborn as mules, suspicious as serpents, and absolutely hell bent to have their own way. . . ."[2] Other observations, however, indicated not only that some women were astute traders and that most could take a loss without tears, but that altogether, throughout the boom and panic, they were just as good winners and losers as the men.

While women's opinions about the market, and the tips they passed on, apparently did not carry as much weight as the men's, most women seemed not to mind this. In some families the women did better with their speculations than the men did with theirs, especially those who simply held on to their purchases while their menfolk were in and out of the market, making short turns and jumping from one stock to another. Where both husband and wife speculated, the rivalry was good-humored as long as all went well for both. According to folklore, in one happy and well-to-do family the wise husband periodically transferred from his own account to his wife's the stocks that showed a profit.

By 1929 everyone, it seemed, was in the market: rich and poor, bankers and bootblacks, dowagers and scrubwomen, teachers and students, nurses and barbers, clergymen and taxi-drivers, and even the corner newsvendor. It was a new kind of democracy. The ten-share plunger and the multimillionaire operator were brothers under the skin. Many business and professional men neglected their occupations to dabble in the market and hang around the boardrooms. They were seldom too busy at their offices to phone their customers' man at least once or twice a day for quotations. Professional men were supposed to be especially credulous, readily believing any information that came their way. Like many other people, some were the

---

[2] Elizabeth Frazer, "The Lady and the Ticker," *The Saturday Evening Post* (March 8, 1930), p. 12.

victims of peddlers of worthless and near-worthless securities. Others, relying on their own initiative or the advice of conscientious customers' men, multiplied their capital.

Everyone, it seemed, talked "stocks"—at the dinner table, at business conferences, at cocktail parties, in the locker room at the country club, in billiard parlors and barber shops, on streetcars and in country stores, and sometimes, surreptitiously, even in church. "The market" became, like baseball and the weather, a prime topic of conversation. A New York City bus driver who overheard one passenger telling another that he intended to sell his U. S. Steel is said to have exclaimed, "Don't do it. It'll cross 200 before the end of the month." And, so the story went, it did.

Superficial financial knowledge became widespread, and it found expression in the technical language of the market. If only in self-defense, one learned to talk with a wise air of "split-ups," "rights," "call money," "the short interest," "car loadings," "the Fed," "Big Steel," "brokers' loans," "the rediscount rate," "the technical position," "margins," "new issues," "bulls and bears," "pools," "professionals," "tipsters," "forecasts," "insiders," "over-the-counter," "the tape," "yields," "earnings," "the Big Board," and—especially—the ubiquitous and sempiternal "they."

Here and there were skeptics, but they were a small minority of the millions whose awareness of the stock market ranged from just the bare knowledge of its existence to a fascination with every aspect of it. Between these poles of market interest were many people who occasionally bought and sold shares of stock, as well as many others who merely held on to what they had. There was continual flux in the great mass of individual participants. Always there were the newcomers, many of whom knew little or nothing about securities; the recidivists, returning to speculation after having been forced out or having withdrawn voluntarily; and the chronic bears who episodically "bucked" the market, took their losses, and waited for the next "opportunity."

But the large hard core of the speculating mass consisted of those professional traders who were persistently "long" in stocks or who were bullish enough of the time to survive; and of those of the general public, rich and not so rich, who held on to their shares of stocks and perhaps added to them, either refusing to take profits or replacing whatever they sold with something else. Many of the latter owned their stocks "outright," and so were less sensitive to sharp and deep price reactions; others were securely enough "on margin" to maintain their "positions" unscathed through the setbacks that forced out those who traded on too thin an equity.

"Characters" and "odd balls," attracted by the long upward trend of stock prices, haunted the boardrooms. Superstition, covert and open, influenced many who bought and sold stocks. Astrology, numerology, spiritualism, and various other methods of prophesy were employed to divine the market. Some individualists found unique ways of selecting the issues they would purchase. One thrifty individual, apparently obsessed with the principle of diversification, set out methodically to buy one share of every stock listed on the New York Stock Exchange, from A to Z. Another bought only shares of corporations with names that began with his initial, the letter K. For guidance in buying and selling, one boardroom habitué relied on an elaborate system of counting the dots that appeared between quotations on the ticker tape.

Some small speculators, probably despairing of the cross fire of tips and "advice," were said to select their stocks by closing their eyes and punching a pin through the financial page of a newspaper. Perhaps this procedure produced, on balance, results as good as those obtained by many of the thousands of "tape readers" and "chartists" who believed they had a scientific method for beating the market. Many seemingly unsuperstitious individuals arduously studied business and financial conditions and the technicalities of the market, and they amassed tremendous amounts of information on various corporations. Some devoted most of their free time to this. The idea seemed to be that the harder one worked at "playing the market," the greater and more justified would be the reward. Perhaps this was superstition too.

It was considered easy to make money in stocks, especially if you bought the speculative leaders. One sage of the financial district observed that it required something like genius to lose money in the market. A joke was current about a gentleman who called on the manager of a leading brokerage firm and inquired, "Does William Jones have an account here?"

"What right have you to ask?"

"I am attorney and guardian for William Jones. He is in an insane asylum."

"His account shows $180,000 profit."

One prospering market operator was supposed to have complained, with some exaggeration, that to keep a good cook he had to install a ticker in the pantry, that his valet refused to come on duty before the market closed, and that street cleaners in the Wall Street district would pick up only financial papers.

At least one criminal character of the era, Al Capone, had no use for the stock market. Said he, scornfully: "It's a racket. Those stock market guys are crooked!"

The widespread interest in the stock market had a conservative political and social influence. A few shares of stock may not have been a cure-all for radicalism, but anyone who owned them was "in the market" and a "partner in industry." This was socially creditable and carried a certain prestige. "Wall Street," "big business," "corporation," "financier," and other such terms lost much of the odium they had had for many people. Some parents bought stock for their children, often just a few shares and perhaps with the children's savings. Thus many youngsters, pleased to cash their little dividend checks and often conscious too of their stocks' price fluctuations, acquired the attitudes and language of their stock-market-minded elders.

In a measure, contemporary mores were made over to accommodate the propensity for stock speculation that appeared among members of the straighter-laced element of society. Before the boom ended, many a clergyman thought nothing of phoning his broker's office or of appearing in a boardroom. Bishop Cannon, that ardent prohibitionist and great expounder of morality, himself helped matters along when he defended his own trading on margin as merely buying stock on the "partial payment plan."

No Securities and Exchange Commission at this time regulated the markets and set standards of conduct for brokers, manipulators, and promoters. The various exchanges made their own rules and policed their own members. The codes of ethics of the New York Stock Exchange, the New York Curb Exchange, and many of the smaller exchanges were high, but outside of these, various long-established practices reflected a philosophy of dog-eat-dog and devil-take-the-hindermost.

Rumors, tips, and the market advice of self-styled experts, at least a few of whom were in the pay of promoters and behind-the-scenes manipulators, led some stock buyers from one issue to another. Hearsay, often groundless, of earnings, prospective dividends, stock "split-ups," new financing, and the activities of big operators spread with uncanny speed from person to person throughout the country. For many it was enough just to hear that the maid who worked for J. P. Morgan's secretary liked Auburn Auto or Zenith Radio. As H. I. Phillips, a contemporary humorist, commented in the *American Magazine* of March, 1929:

Of course, I ought to know very well that the pants presser's boy hasn't the inside track on a big bull movement in International Horse Collars, Common, just because he has a distant cousin who is married to a man who is a close friend of the brother of a Wall Street traffic cop who is popular with a broker who is 'just like that' with the Fisher brothers.

In almost every broker's office was a quantity of market literature, free for the taking. One could readily obtain bulletins, form-letters, tip sheets, and the advice of bureaus and services that were better rewarded by touting the public than by following their own hunches. Almost invariably they were bullish, urging the stock dabbler to buy. Beyond the pale of the stock exchange firms and the established underwriting houses were the promoters of new security issues that were worth no more than "a piece of blue sky." "Boiler rooms" with long batteries of telephones beguiled the gullible with high-pressure calls followed up by persuasive, mendacious letters. Salesmen sold unlisted stocks, often of doubtful value, from door to door.

Frequently an officer or a director of a large corporation took advantage of "inside information," buying or selling his company's stock before the information was made known to the rank and file of the stockholders or was openly publicized. During the boom, when most corporation news was favorable, such a person could buy before the news was out and then take a profit when the stock rose in response to it. Later, in the depression, this procedure was reversed. Some corporation officers would sell, and perhaps even go short of their company's stock, before the announcement of poor quarterly earnings or a dividend reduction. The president of one large corporation was reported to have made more than $7 million by selling out his holdings early in 1930 at around $64.00 a share and buying them back, after the company had omitted its dividend, for about $15.00 a share.

The speculating public, which often was left "holding the bag" for the "insiders," was also up against shrewd and ruthless operators who acted both individually and in groups to use every means they dared to for furthering their own interests. One method of price manipulation, which was legal and also a generally accepted fact of stock market life, was the "pool" or "syndicate." During the later years of the boom, probably at least one pool was operating in every major issue listed on the New York Stock Exchange. Many pools were organized by insiders, directors, officers, major stockholders, and sometimes the bankers of the corporation whose stock was to be subject to the operation. Others were organized by outsiders, usually professional market operators; these were sometimes referred to as "bob-tail" pools. The general method of pool operation was to "accumulate" a "line" of stock while bidding up the price, and then to "distribute" the stock at what was hoped would be a higher average price than had been paid.

Some pools were fabulously profitable, while others sustained losses (a pool might make only a few points on a 20 or 30 point rise, because of commissions, taxes, and day-to-day trading losses). To be profitable a pool had to go with the trend. Because its purpose was to "buy cheap and sell dear," the price fluctuations engineered by the pool's manager were intended to induce outsiders to sell when the pool was accumulating stock and buy when it was distributing its accumulation. Ordinarily, the distribution would cause a substantial decline in the price, but at times during the boom the market was so strong that after a pool had sold out its holdings the stock continued to advance.

The following is a description of a profitable pool operation in the stock of Radio Corporation of America. Sixty-three people participated.

Among these were the late Nicholas F. Brady, William F. Kenny, John Jacob Raskob, each down for 50,000 shares and a deposit of a million dollars. Percy A. Rockefeller, William C. Durant, Walter P. Chrysler, Herbert B. Swope, and the Fisher brothers were also listed, and several, including Eddie Dowling, comedian, made no deposit. The presiding genius of the pool was Michael J. Meehan, the Radio specialist on the floor. . . . With him were associated the Pool Manager, Bradford Ellsworth, and Co-Manager, Thomas E. Bragg, later to attain fame as a great bear.

On the day before the pool was formed, Radio sold at 74 with a total turnover of 98,000 shares. The market was upward, and the price rose to $91.75, even before the pool got started. On the first day of pool activity 392,000 shares were bought, and 246,000 shares were sold. With trading at a terrific pace, the price was pushed up to $109.25 a share. The tremendous activity at mounting prices brought the public into the market. On the last two days of the pool's active life, only 210,000 shares were purchased, and 449,000 were sold as excited small traders scrambled for the stock. In those two days 931,-000 shares were traded in. The pool represented an investment of 13 million dollars, and in this short period its profits totalled five million dollars or thirty-nine per cent. The price dropped to 101 immediately after the pool ended its activities, and five days later was back to 87.[3]

Until the panic few bear pools operated, and scarcely could any have been successful.

Corporations put on campaigns to sell their stock to employees and customers. This not only brought them new capital, but it was supposed to inspire customer and employee loyalty. Some of the largest companies sold their shares to employees at attractive discounts, and some even contributed a percentage of the employees' payments on the stock allotted them. Management seems to have had a benign and even generous motive in most employee stock ownership plans, but it could not fore-

[3] Barnie F. Winkelman, *Ten Years of Wall Street* (Philadelphia: The John C. Winston Company, 1932), pp. 290–91.

see the time some years later when stock values had shrunk, dividends had been reduced or passed, and the employee, out of a job, had to sell his stock for what little he could get, perhaps realizing bitterly that he had had "too many eggs in one basket."

Investment trusts, especially those of the "closed end" variety, which were traded on the stock exchanges and in the over-the-counter market, became extremely popular in the last year or so of the boom. Those who owned shares in such corporations were in effect letting the investment trusts' managers speculate for them. The portfolios of most of these companies were made up almost entirely of common stocks. Diversification and the supposedly superior knowledge, "connections," and "scientific" trading skill of their sponsors were believed to make them an especially desirable way of participating in the stock market. Their shares became widely distributed and were owned by every class of stock buyer from the wealthiest to the poorest.

Commonly the market price of investment trust shares was more than their liquidating value. This disparity was taken for granted, and it had the effect of whetting the public's appetite for the shares of newly formed companies. It became a privilege to be invited or allowed to subscribe to new issues. In 1929, hundreds of these financial companies were formed and their shares sold to the public. Sometimes two or three new ones appeared in one day. A professor of economics was reported to have declared that because of the investment trusts the risks in common stock investment had been largely removed. But the great increase in their popularity was regarded by more conservative observers as an unwholesome sign. An editorial in the *Annalist*[4] that emphasized the possibility of drastic "speculative deflation" said of them:

[4] (October 18, 1929), p. 732. © 1929 by The New York Times Company. Reprinted by permission.

An unfavorable feature in the stock market situation is the huge volume of new securities issued by investment and financing companies—$643 million in September; $707 million in the two dull Summer months of July and August; and a total for the first nine months of the year of $2,239 million.

So great was the enthusiasm for the investment trusts, however, that by August, 1929, the shares of some were selling at about twice their book value. When, on July 26, 1929, a million shares of the Shenandoah Corporation were offered at $17.50 a share, the whole amount was immediately purchased, and before the day was over the price was quoted at $42.00. When a million shares of the Lehman Corporation were offered on September 17 at $104 per share, dealers were allotted only 12½ per cent of their subscriptions, and the first freely quoted price that day was $120. Three days later the price was $136. On September 19, while an offering of Marine Midland Corporation at about $60.00 a share was still in prospect, $85.00 was being bid for it in the over-the-counter market.

As the boom developed, mass psychology took hold. In some speculative circles it became a kind of heresy to question whether stock prices might be too high, and a kind of treason to sell unless you intended to buy something else. Business and financial leaders continually talked of "prosperity," and many urged their employees and the public to buy common stocks. Practically all of the financial and investment periodicals were obdurately bullish. Some professors of economics proclaimed from their ivied towers that this was truly a new era, that stock prices were on a plateau from which they would rise to far greater heights, and that a panic could never again occur. It became fashionable to believe this, and easy, especially if you and your friends owned stocks.

Typical of the outlook of many business leaders of the time was that of John J. Raskob, who was chairman of both the

General Motors Corporation and the Democratic party. In an article in the *Ladies' Home Journal*[5] Raskob claimed that if a person saved $15.00 a week and invested the savings in good stocks, he could accumulate $80,000 or more in twenty years. Raskob's use of the word "everybody" was unrealistic, for many people earned little more than the amount of savings he prescribed. That the future of common stocks would prove to be quite different, Raskob had no inkling.

The editors of the more popular investment periodicals were apparently just as susceptible to the boom psychology as anyone else, and perhaps the subtle social pressure to give the reading public the opinions it wanted also influenced them. Although they could not ignore the panic when it came, they did not foresee it, and when the decline in prices had come to a temporary halt they again urged their readers to buy.

The financial editors of the staid *New York Times* and its weekly adjunct, the *Annalist,* and those of the less "popular" *Commercial and Financial Chronicle* saw the situation differently. They and their assistants understood, explained, and criticized the "orgy of speculation," the unjustifiably high prices of many stocks, and the widespread abuse of credit. But their views were widely disdained because the action of the market for a long time seemed to disprove them, and some readers who took their words of caution seriously complained of missing the opportunity for large profits.

Most of the economists who served the larger banks and industrial corporations, as well as many economists in academic life, helped foster the New Era illusion. Perhaps the most remarkable of them was Professor Irving Fisher of Yale, who became almost an oracle of the stock market during the boom, but lost whatever remained of his reputation for prophecy on October 24, 1929, a day of severe panic. On October 22 he

---

[5] Samuel Crowther, "Everybody Ought to Be Rich" (an interview with John J. Raskob), *Ladies' Home Journal* (August, 1929), p. 9.

had announced in a widely publicized address that "in my opinion current predictions of heavy reaction affecting the general level of securities find little if any foundation in fact." Another academic economist declared at the height of the boom that buyers of stock "are among the best informed and most intelligent people in America." Another averred that "old standards are not only futile; they are childish." These statements are more or less representative of those made by other, less publicized economists.

After 1926, as the boom expanded and speculation ran wild, stock prices seemed to have only one direction—up! Astonished old-timers in Wall Street shook their heads in amazement that the market could rise so far, apparently defying all the time-tested axioms of speculation. Reactions, inevitably followed by recoveries, became recognized as part of the bull market pattern, and some speculators waited for them as "bargain days" for buying. But they occurred when least expected. Often, after an upsurge in prices, a dull and narrow market was the equivalent of a corrective setback, so strong were the underlying forces ready to push quotations higher. At one time, when public participation was increasing rapidly, a certain broker said he was sure that it was a bull market because when his firm's weekly letter to customers advised them to take profits they responded with more buying orders.

After the Dow-Jones industrial and railroad stock averages broke into new high ground on October 3, 1927, the *Wall Street Journal*, in discussing the Dow theory of market performance, made the following observations:

> Reading the Dow-Jones averages in the manner formulated a quarter of a century ago by the late Charles H. Dow, the indication is plainly bullish. . . . All this is irrespective of the fact that stock prices are relatively very high and have now been advancing for a full four years. Beyond offering the somewhat trite reflection that no tree grows to the sky, there is no need to

moralize about it. The stock market is saying, in so many words, that the business outlook is good and likely to continue so for as far ahead as general information can calculate, assuming that Wall Street is the reservoir of all that everybody knows about everything connected with business. The assumption is fully justified and that is why the stock market averages reflect so much more than any individual can possibly know or the wealthiest combination can manipulate.[6]

The movement in the stock of Radio Corporation of America was a dramatic example of the effect of the boom on stock values. When it was listed on the New York Stock Exchange on October 1, 1924, having been transferred from the New York Curb Market, it sold for as low as 26⅝ per share. It soon became one of the most active issues, and fluctuated widely. On the first day of trading in 1925 it reached a high of 77⅞, but by March, 1926, it had declined to 32. From a new high of 101 in 1927 it receded to 85¼ in February, 1928. Thereafter, however, its rise was sensational. Early in December, 1928, it reached 420, having gained as much as 33 points in one day. During that year more than 16 million shares of "Radio" were traded. After the stock had been "split," five new shares for one old share, the price of the new shares rose as high as 114¾ in 1929.

Even before the great upward movement of prices in 1929, the market overvalued the common stocks of most American corporations, according to any previously accepted standards. Many a corporation officer must have gasped at the mounting price of his company's stock, knowing as he did firsthand the limits of its earning power. Although it was not financially or socially acceptable for a high officer of a corporation to question publicly the value set in the market for his company's shares, some did so, especially during the last year or so of the

[6] *Wall Street Journal* (October 4, 1927), p. 1.

boom. When, in 1928, A. P. Giannini, the head of Bancitaly, made a statement to the effect that the high price of the company's stock was not justified, it dropped about 100 points in two days. But when Brooklyn Edison shares surged upward, and its president warned the public that they were not worth so high a price, the public's answer was to push the price still higher.

Few dared to address their stockholders with the frankness of the chairman of Canadian Marconi, a company of moderate size whose stock was traded on the New York Curb Market, paid no dividends, was highly speculative, and had sold as low as $3.00 a share early in 1928. When, in late November of that year, after it had risen to $28.50, the chairman asserted in a plain, blunt statement that the market overvalued the stock and that it was even "too high at $3," it immediately dropped twelve points and a few days later sold for $7.25. But this occurrence adversely affected the market as a whole for only a day or so, and many of those who had protested against "inflated values" and "overcapitalized earnings" in 1927 and 1928 were to marvel and go on protesting throughout the first nine months of 1929.

3

Titans, Moguls, and Tycoons

"RAGS TO RICHES" STORIES became the folktales of the boom period of the twenties. Many of them were true. With each upward surge of prices some new millionaire opened a bottle of champagne for his friends and celebrated a milestone in his progress. Fortunes of $10 and $20 million were not uncommon. One trader was supposed to have run a million dollars up to $30 million in eight months. At the pinnacle of his success he dealt with nineteen brokerage firms and had a telephone for each. A midwesterner, almost unknown before he had come to New York during the boom, built up profits of $80 million in one stock, $30 million in another, and $10 million or more in several others. According to boardroom gossip, an operator in public utility shares had amassed more than $800 million before the crash. One important trader was said to have expressed chagrin that he could not get his profits above the $500 million mark.

Hero worship during this time was reserved not for generals and statesmen, or even the great captains of industry, but for stock operators and large-scale promoters. Their names were magic, and the public hearkened to every tale and rumor of what these wizards did and said.

The Rockefellers, Morgans, Mellons, Du Ponts, Fords, and other families of great entrenched wealth were hardly of this ilk, though various members doubtless plunged, dabbled, and took flyers in the market. While during the boom the wealth of such families was largely augmented by the general prosperity and the great increase in value of their many properties and interests, and during the panic and depression it was diminished, in general the role played by this "upper crust" of wealth during this period was not spectacular or flamboyant. Although surely not untouched by the madness of the times, they remained essentially different from the great plungers, the new "empire-builders," the manipulators, and the super-salesmen of high finance.

Probably the biggest of these great plungers was William C. Durant, whose various abilities distinguished him at different times as a builder, organizer, promoter, super-salesman, and speculator. In whatever he attempted he showed brilliance of imagination and prodigious energy. He had charm, audacity, and a remarkable talent for salesmanship. His power of persuasion was so great that it was said "he could coax a bird out of a tree."

As a young man, Durant had first been fascinated by the building of wagons and carriages, and then by the manufacture of automobiles. The first car he marketed was the Buick. His greatest achievement, from an historical point of view, was the organization of the General Motors Company (predecessor of the present General Motors Corporation) in 1908. But speculation was his first love, and when the stock market turned against him in 1910 he lost control of the company. Undaunted, he began manufacturing a car that he called the Chevrolet, and as he prospered he again acquired so much stock in General Motors that he regained control. In the panic of 1920, however, when he attempted to support the price of General Motors stock as it plummeted from about 40 to 12, he lost $90 million and again his control of the company, this time for good. Still undaunted, he organized a company to manufacture a car named for himself, the Durant, but this attempt to make a comeback in the automobile field was unsuccessful.

Yet Durant's best years were still ahead, for the long bull market was just getting under way and he, of all people—with his flair for speculation, his congenital optimism, and his skill and daring—appeared ideally qualified to make the most of it. He was a chronic bull, and as prices advanced he multiplied his holdings of various stocks, many of them fast-moving market leaders. The slim margin of equity on which stocks could be carried enabled him at times to augment his profits at an almost geometrical rate of progression. Evidently there was also in his makeup a sensitivity to price movements, a timely prudence that protected him in the sharp reactions that occurred from time to time, wiping out many others who were playing the market for all it was worth.

Durant's power in the market was augmented by the dealings of others who relied on him for guidance. He was also an influential participant in many pool operations. Like practically every other large operator in the market, he saw nothing wrong in manipulating prices in order to fool smaller speculators and to profit at their expense. His fame as a speculator became such that his comments and opinions, whenever he cared to offer them, were widely publicized and generally respected. Merely a rumor that he was buying a particular stock was enough to send the price up. By 1929, he had acquired an enormous fortune—at least $100 million, and perhaps much more.

Jesse L. Livermore's career, like Durant's, was especially spectacular because of its extreme ups and downs. In his earlier years he was known as "the boy plunger," but unlike most of the other great traders in the stock market he was not a case-hardened bull. Although not committed solely to the bear side of the market, he seemed to prefer it. In his heyday he was reputed to have had a better understanding of price movements than any other speculator. To him statistics and other "fundamental" information about a company whose stock might interest him were important, but how the stock acted was especially so. He once stated that he hoped to be "right 60 per cent of the time."

As a boy of fifteen, well before the turn of the century, Livermore had played the market in "bucket shops,"[1] where he developed such aptness in foreseeing short-run fluctuations that finally the bucket shop proprietors refused his business. At twenty-one he came to New York with a stake of $2,500, which he promptly lost. He had to learn the hard lesson, he later admitted, that dealing through a legitimate brokerage firm was quite different from dealing with a bucket shop, and that the big profits necessary to offset numerous small losses had to be made on extended price trends. He made his first million in the stock market by selling short during the panic of 1907, but within a year he had lost it in the cotton market. He went bankrupt for the first time in 1915, but brokers were willing to let him trade in a limited way without capital of his own. During the war he rode upward with Bethlehem Steel in its dizzy ascent, and, through that and other transactions, his capital increased to $5 million in a few years.

How much larger Livermore's fortune grew is not clear, but when the market was going his way he traded on a very large scale and lived magnificently. His suite of offices was believed to be the most luxurious in New York City. There, at times, he employed as many as twenty people. A private quotation board was kept posted for him, and an array of telephones gave him quick access to his various brokers. He maintained several residences staffed with servants, was fastidious in his tastes, and

[1] A "bucket shop" was a pseudo brokerage house that did not actually execute its customers' orders. The purchase or sales price was the most recent one that had appeared on the ticker tape when an order was placed by the customer. The firm "bucketed" the transaction by taking the chance that the customer's judgment would prove to be wrong and his loss would become the bucket shop's gain. Because the brokerage commissions for both buying and selling were deducted from the customer's margin, which was ordinarily only a dollar per share, an adverse fluctuation of more than three-fourths of a point would wipe out the customer's commitment. Thus the odds were tremendously in favor of the bucket shop. Well before the boom of the 1920's such firms had been outlawed and had disappeared from the scene.

relished luxury. He was said to be superstitious; some of his important market operations were rumored to have been based upon his interpretations of the purring of a cat named Nanny.

Superstitious or not, Livermore was keenly aware of the inflated nature of the great bull market. As the upward trend progressed, he became more and more skeptical of it. From time to time he tested the market with short sales in stocks that he thought might be vulnerable. Sometimes, when the market was reacting, he seemed, briefly, to be right. But soon, as the upward trend was resumed, he sustained fresh losses. These repeated forays against the trend eroded his fortune. At almost the peak of the boom he had taken a long position in the market, but he soon abandoned it.

Not until the autumn of 1929 did he come into his own once again as a great bear operator. Boldly selling short large quantities of many different stocks as the market declined, he became known and feared as the most aggressive of the bears. As prices fell his fortune rapidly increased. How much money he made during the panic is not known, but it was probably many millions.

Arthur W. Cutten differed in personality from Livermore in many ways, but they had some things in common, notably their keenness in appraising market situations and the boldness of their trading operations. Each, when he believed himself right, would proceed fearlessly to back up his conviction on as large a scale as his capital or the limitations of the market permitted. But while Cutten was calm, slow-spoken, deliberate, unconventional, quiet, and unassuming—a "country storekeeper" type, as one journalist described him—Livermore was high-strung and excitable. Also, Cutten was perennially a bull, while Livermore tended to favor the bear side of the market. At one time there even was supposed to be a feud between the two men.

Cutten, who had come from Canada to Chicago, began his career in the Chicago wheat pit as a "scalper," trading in and out of the market in an endeavor to catch short-run price fluctuations. From this he went on to larger, longer-term operations in the grain markets. Livermore also sometimes speculated in those markets, and there were times when he dogged the steps of the often successful Cutten, buying and selling when Cutten did so. At other times, however, he took the opposite position. Once, so the story goes, when he knew that Cutten was heavily long in wheat and in Florida for a time, Livermore "raided" the wheat market with sudden huge sales that knocked down prices and endangered Cutten's position. Whether there was actually bad blood between them is not clear, but their opposite positions in the stock market during the panic were dramatized by the press as an implacable feud.

Cutten had made a large fortune speculating in grain before he sought an even larger harvest in the stock market. In the mid-1920's he had engineered what was practically a corner in wheat, and his income tax for 1924, when such tax rates were comparatively low, was nearly half a million dollars.

Cutten's first big foray in Wall Street occurred when he joined with the Fisher brothers to gain control of the Baldwin Locomotive Company. As the price of the stock increased greatly, this was a highly profitable operation for them. He was sometimes associated with the Fisher brothers, Durant, and other big operators in pools organized from time to time to accumulate certain stocks, put up their prices, and then unload the holdings they had acquired. Nevertheless, he was a great trader in his own right and a source of large commissions for about a dozen brokerage firms. Several of the biggest of these kept a private room for his exclusive use.

Primarily, Cutten played the market for the "long pull." In 1927, he acquired large holdings—100,000 shares or more —of Radio Corporation and Montgomery Ward at about

$80.00 per share. He had other large commitments as well. His practice seems to have been to sell some shares of his holdings after a substantial rise in prices, and then to repurchase them when the market reacted—all the while, however, maintaining the greater part of his position in the issues he favored.

Although Cutten was an astute speculator, the principal reason for his enormous financial success during the boom was his apparently absolute conviction that stock prices were bound to rise even far higher than the high level they finally attained. He was a whole-souled bull who, seemingly, could neither imagine nor countenance any other view of the market's prospects than his own thoroughly bullish one.

The seven Fisher brothers (Fred, Charles, Lawrence, William, Edward, Albert, and Howard), usually thought of as a unit, were a powerful influence in Wall Street throughout the greater part of the boom. Although they were associated with other big operators in pool manipulations, and the extent of their operations in the market was regarded with awe by many of the speculating multitude, they seem, nevertheless, to have been of a different breed from speculators like Durant, Livermore, and Cutten. Their background and outlook, and even their long-run purpose in the market, were different. They were, first of all, industrialists, and they brought to the market the vast fortune—$208 million—that General Motors had paid them for their business, the Fisher Body Company, which they had founded in 1908.

The brothers were practical, realistic men, and most of them had worked with their hands in their early days. They were large holders of General Motors stock, but needed to find other investments for their collective fortune. For this purpose they organized the Fisher Company, Inc. Customarily, before buying into a corporation they made an elaborate study of it. How much of their activities in the stock market, especially in the later years of the boom, was speculation and manipulation, and how much was simple and deliberate investment is not clear. At any rate, as titans in the great bullish contingent they were far from anonymous. If the Fisher brothers were believed to be buying a certain stock, that was recommendation enough for thousands of smaller followers of the market.

Perhaps the most mysterious of the great plungers was Louis W. Zimmerman, reputed to be the "biggest trader on the West Coast."[2] To his brokers in New York he was little more than a voice on the telephone. His judgment of the market and the timing of his orders seemed almost uncanny. A short time before the panic, for instance, he sold out his holdings, taking profits of as much as 300 and 400 points on certain stocks. What his profits totaled is unknown, but estimates run from $10 million to $75 million. Like Durant and Cutten, he too was a perennial bull, but evidently he did not share their blind faith in perpetually higher stock prices.

Harry F. Sinclair also was one of the great plungers in the stock market, as well as a gambler on other things besides stocks. He was the founder and highly successful developer of one of the nation's great oil companies, the Sinclair Oil Corporation. As a young man working in his father's drug store in Independence, Kansas, he was fascinated by the oil drilling activities in that area. Owing to an accident while rabbit hunting (he shot off his toe), he received a $5,000 insurance payment, and with this he began his "wildcatting" in the oil fields, bringing in the successful wells that provided the means for expanding his interests. By combining other companies with his own he became a major figure in the oil industry.

In the early 1920's, Sinclair was involved in the Teapot Dome oil reserve scandal that blackened the Harding administration. Although acquitted of the charges against him, he was later imprisoned for about six months for contempt of court

[2] Earl Sparling, *Mystery Men of Wall Street* (New York: Greenberg Publisher, 1930), p. 191.

and contempt of the Senate. This seemed to make no difference in his aggressive business operations and his love for taking a chance, for apparently he played the stock market with a relish of the risks it offered. He was sometimes involved with other big operators in pools organized to push up the prices of certain stocks. He was said to be ready to bet anyone $10,000 that a stock's price would move up or down. Sinclair's attempt to organize a third major baseball league was costly, and the string of race horses that he maintained was probably costly too, though one of his horses, Zev, won the Kentucky Derby in 1923. One of the most colorful men of the times, Sinclair was more than just a large-scale plunger in the stock market; he was a strange combination of gambler and able businessman.

The long uptrend in stock prices was conducive to corporate empire-building. The holding company was a perfectly legal means by which such an empire could be held together and controlled by one or a few individuals, with the investing or speculating public supplying by far the greater part of the capital involved. In its simplest form, a holding company is a corporation that owns the securities of other corporations in order to control their operating and financial policies.

The holding company today is subject to many restrictions that were unknown in the 1920's, when it was generally looked upon with approval as the means by which many operating companies, usually within one industry, could be subject to a common management policy and presumably benefit through various advantages and economies. That it had become subject to many abuses and had in many cases been the means for outrageous exploitation of investors became clearly apparent during the depression.

In many instances holding companies were placed one on top of another in several tiers to form a pyramid of corporations, at the base of which were the operating companies. A holding company had to have only a majority (sometimes much less) of the voting stock of a subsidiary company, which might be either another holding company or an operating company, in order to control it. The minority of the voting stock and all other securities issued by the subsidiary—nonvoting common stock, preferred stock, bonds, debentures, etc.—ordinarily were sold to the public. An important feature of the usual holding company complex was that it gave tremendous leverage to the earnings of the parent company. It was an elaborate means of "trading on the equity," and in an institutionalized way it was similar to owning stock on margin. When the subsidiary operating companies could pay large dividends the holding company prospered; but when, as in the depression, most could not and some even failed to meet interest payments on borrowed funds, the leverage was reversed.

So keen was the appetite of the public for securities that a great variety of them was spawned by holding company managements and sold, usually with ease if one of the many well-established investment underwriting firms offered them. Thus individuals and small groups acquired fortunes and great power by building corporate empires that drew their capital from the booming market for securities and their strength from the prevailing high level of prosperity.

The railroad empire-builders of the 1920's were two brothers, Oris Paxton and Mantis James Van Sweringen, the former being the elder by two years. They were practically inseparable throughout their lives, and as a team they rose to national prominence together. Of modest origin, and with grammar school education, they worked at making a living during their teens, seeking to improve themselves in every way they could. When only of college age they were in the real estate business, and in time they prospered greatly through their development of a Cleveland suburb.

In 1916, while seeking to provide a rapid-transit line between the city and their suburban development, they learned that a run-down railroad, the New York, Chicago, and St. Louis ("The Nickel Plate"), could be bought from the New York Central, which had been pressured by the Interstate Commerce Commission to sell it. The brothers bought the "Nickel Plate" with a down payment obtained by selling preferred stock in a holding company that they formed, the Nickel Plate Securities Corporation, and instalment payments. They obtained excellent management for their newly acquired railroad, and its earnings rapidly increased. Because the Nickel Plate Securities Corporation thus prospered, the Van Sweringens were able to buy, partly on credit, three other small railroads.

Then in the 1920's, as prosperity increased the earnings of their railroads and strong securities markets absorbed the new issues of stocks and bonds that their holding companies offered the public, the Van Sweringens aggressively pushed forward, buying the Père Marquette Railroad and acquiring control of the Chesapeake and Ohio, as well as the Erie. Later the Missouri Pacific came under their influence. With J. P. Morgan & Company aiding them, they built a pyramid of holding companies that seemed to assure their control.

At the apex of this pyramid was the Vaness Corporation, 80 per cent of which was owned by the two Van Sweringens. Below this was the General Securities Corporation, which controlled the Allegheny Corporation, which in turn controlled the Chesapeake Corporation and the New York, Chicago, and St. Louis Railroad, which controlled the Wheeling and Lake Erie. The Chesapeake Corporation controlled the Chesapeake and Ohio, which controlled the Hocking Valley, and (in conjunction with the Allegheny Corporation) the Erie and the Père Marquette railroads. The Allegheny Corporation also held a large interest in the Missouri Pacific.

At the pinnacle of their success, before the panic, the Van Sweringen brothers were worth an estimated $120 million, and the 23,000-mile railroad system that they had pieced together and controlled had an aggregate value of perhaps $3 billion.

During the boom and even preceding it, empire-building by means of holding companies and the sale of all manner of securities to the public was a dominant feature of the rapidly growing electric power and light industry. The 1920's saw the remarkable development of quite a number of such "systems," which embraced scores and even a hundred or more corporations. Among the most prominent of these were the Electric Bond and Share system, the Associated Gas & Electric system, the Insull system, the American Waterworks & Electric system, the American & Foreign Power system, and the Cities Service Power & Light system. The Insull system, which flourished under the control of Samuel Insull, and the Associated Gas & Electric system, which was controlled by Howard C. Hopson, are dramatic examples of what was possible under favorable conditions.

Samuel Insull, an Englishman who had come to the United States in 1881 to take a position as private secretary to Thomas Edison, was soon assisting in the management of companies in which Edison was interested, and while still a young man he became president of the Chicago Edison Company. Brilliant, ambitious, and hard-working, he had a gift for industrial organization and development. Throughout his life he was to be devoted to the economical production and distribution of electric power. By seeking technical advances in every possible direction, by expanding the market for electric light and power through both salesmanship and rate reductions, and by centralizing the power supply for many communities, he was able to reduce the cost per kilowatt-hour of electricity to a small fraction of what it once had been in the areas served by his companies.

His empire-building began gradually, first with the strengthening of the original Chicago company and then the establishment of the Commonwealth Electric Company. In time he acquired the other electric companies in Chicago and began acquiring companies outside the city. In 1912 he organized the Middle West Utilities Company to obtain investment funds for financing the further expansion of his system's holdings.

As the system grew, Insull gained prominence as one of Chicago's leading businessmen. He was respected and honored, and his reputation made the sale of the securities of his various companies easy. He became such a powerful figure in the Chicago financial world that it was said, facetiously, to be worth a million dollars just to be seen talking with him in front of the Continental Illinois Bank. He was noted for his generosity to individuals and to institutions. His civic interest was genuine, and he gave lavishly to many good causes.

By 1926 the pyramid of Insull companies, some of them outside the electric power field, was growing rapidly. By 1929 the proliferation of corporations within the pyramid had gone so far, and the relationships of the individual corporations to each other and to the system as a whole had become so complex, that the organization was beyond most people's comprehension. At the peak of Insull's success his personal fortune was estimated at perhaps $170 million. The empire that he had built represented billions of dollars of invested capital.

Howard C. Hopson, also a public utility tycoon, built an empire that in magnitude and complexity of structure greatly resembled Insull's. But the two men were different personalities, with different outlooks and different motives. While they both had a desire for power, Insull was a builder and producer, whereas Hopson appears to have been primarily an exploiter. A strange man, short, fat, and bald, and sometimes jovial, he was believed to have been deeply and permanently affected by the tragic death of his wife soon after their marriage. He was devoted to his three sisters. It was said that in the early days of Hopson's empire Franklin D. Roosevelt had called on him and asked for an administrative position with one of his companies, and that Hopson had responded by laughing in his face.

Hopson had gotten into the electric power business in a modest way early in the 1920's. Little by little, and then more rapidly, he had expanded his interests into what became the massive Associated Gas & Electric System, in which more than half a million people had invested about a billion dollars. When the system was at the height of its expansion its "Chart of Corporate Ownership" was unbelievably complex, involving 179 corporations.

At the top of the pyramid were the Associated Gas & Electric Company (Ageco), which Hopson and an associate controlled, and its wholly owned subsidiary, the Associated Gas & Electric Corporation (Agecorp). Beneath these holding companies were as many as six layers of smaller holding companies, all dependent upon the earnings of the system's operating companies. Hopson had devised a great variety of securities to be sold to the public, and at one time the Associated Gas and Electric Company had three classes of common stock and ten classes of preferred and preference stock outstanding, as well as many different interest-bearing obligations.

Fortune said of Hopson's amazing career, "Hopson caught the most easily promoted type of enterprise at the bottom of the greatest promotion market in history, rode it for all it was worth to the Pike's Peak of October, 1929, and then nearly rode out the depression through some of the most amazing financial broncobusting ever witnessed."[3]

Ivar Kreuger, a native of Sweden but "Match King of the World," towered above the other empire-builders. His business and financial interests and his influence, even on governments, extended throughout the greater part of the civilized world. In the words of T. G. Barman, Kreuger was "acclaimed on all sides as the greatest constructive financial genius of our genera-

[3] "Through the Wringer with A.G.&E.," *Fortune* (December, 1945), p. 168.

tion; praised by statesmen and bankers as the apostle of en-
lightened capitalism . . . a man whose views were quoted by the
most distinguished economists in support of their own."[4]

Almost shy, somewhat boyish-looking, and a bachelor, he
reached the pinnacle of success at the age of forty-nine. The
image he created was that of a modest man, almost Spartan
in his disregard for the material things of the world. There was
an element of mystery about him. Despite this image, he was a
dominating personality who knew the art of ruling and com-
manding. The great system of corporations that he built was
veritably a one-man organization. "Nobody dared move a
finger without Kreuger's specific authority. . . . Some of Kreuger's colleagues have related how he cut short their objections
at board meetings. He would listen to no views counter to his
own. . . . [Sometimes] he talked pettishly of plots against him."[5]

The top holding company of the worldwide match trust
pyramid that Kreuger created was Kreuger & Toll, the two
great subsidiaries of which were the Swedish Match Company
and the International Match Corporation. This trust produced
more than three-fourths of the world's matches, and was probably better organized than any other international monopoly.
Its operations were carried on through 225 subsidiary companies located in every country except Russia. Its various
securities were highly regarded everywhere as investment
media. Some $250 million of them were sold to American in-
vestors, and twice that amount was sold in other countries.

Because of the tremendous financial power that Kreuger had
acquired, he was able to make large loans at various times to
nearly a dozen European and South American governments in
need of financial aid. His "bonus" for such a loan was the match
monopoly of the country involved. He took a special sort of

[4] T. G. Barman, "Ivar Kreuger: His Life and Work," *The Atlantic Monthly*
(August, 1932), p. 238.
[5] *Ibid.*, pp. 241, 242, 247–48.

pride in lending to governments, and it increased his prestige in a way that great business success or great wealth alone could not have done. Consorting with rulers of nations and their ministers opened many doors for him and cleared the way for projects he was fostering.

Kreuger made it a practically inviolable rule not to be interviewed by journalists. One of the rare exceptions was when Isaac F. Marcosson was preparing an article about him for the *Saturday Evening Post*. The article was merely a human interest story, and did not delve into the intricacies of Kreuger's financial operations. In the course of the interview he remarked: "Whatever success I have had may perhaps be attributable to three things: One is silence, the second is more silence, while the third is still more silence."[6] For many years, throughout the world, there was complete confidence in the financial genius and the probity of Ivar Kreuger.

The boom fostered other kinds of titans besides the plungers and empire-builders. While they cannot all be dealt with here, or neatly classified, they all are characterized by a dominating faith in the upward trend of stock prices, a faith that led each to make the most of the boom in ways that seemed best to suit his own personality and capabilities, as well as his business and social environment. In their different fields of activity they served the public, or so they claimed and doubtless believed. But they served themselves first of all and were richly rewarded. Their names became known to practically every boardroom habitué, and their opinions as to the condition of the national economy, and more particularly the stock market, were greatly respected.

John J. Raskob is thought of favorably even today by many who remember the 1920's, not so much perhaps for the part he played in the stock market as for his roles as a leading industrialist and a national political leader. The son of a cigar-

[6] "The Match King," *Saturday Evening Post* (October 12, 1929), p. 238.

maker, he began to earn his living as a stenographer at the age of nineteen. The turning point of his life was when he became secretary to Pierre S. Du Pont. The Du Ponts recognized in Raskob the exceptional qualities that even long after the panic and depression caused him to be referred to as a "financial genius."

It was Raskob's interest in the stock market, and particularly in General Motors, that led him to bring what he was convinced were the golden prospects of that company to the attention of the Du Ponts. E. I. Du Pont de Nemours & Company, which prospered greatly during the war, had a plenitude of free funds to invest, and the Du Ponts, persuaded by Raskob and through arrangements worked out by him, in 1917 acquired for their company a large interest in General Motors, which eventually gave them a 26 per cent interest in it. The cost of this investment was approximately $57 million. (In 1962, after a federal court had ordered the distribution of the company's 63 million shares of General Motors to Du Pont shareholders, the value of this investment was approximately $3 billion.)

The Du Ponts and the other shareholders in their company could indeed be thankful to John J. Raskob for his foresight and persuasion. Many others and their wealthy or affluent descendants could be too, for he was a maker of millionaires—scores of them, perhaps hundreds. And, of course, he himself became a millionaire many times over. As chairman of the Finance Committee of General Motors, Raskob played an important part in the great expansion of that company. Before the bull market was well under way he had induced eighty of the company's executives to join together in acquiring a large amount of the company's stock by means of liberal credit arrangements. The $5 million thus invested by the participants became worth about $250 million in 1929.

Raskob's formula for acquiring great wealth was utterly simple: Buy stock in General Motors and hold on to it. Like many of the great plungers and the hordes of lesser speculators, he was chronically a bull in the whole stock market. Raskob did some plunging on his own and also in some large pool activities with Cutten, Durant, the Fisher brothers, and other big operators. Nevertheless, General Motors was his first love, and his fidelity was richly rewarded.

Raskob became a national figure in politics also. A Republican and ardent antiprohibitionist, he turned Democrat in order to help his friend Al Smith, who was running against Hoover for the presidency. As chairman of the Democratic National Committee, Raskob, who was something of a symbol of big business and high finance, no doubt somewhat increased the total vote for Smith, who was considered the ordinary man's candidate. Although he helped Roosevelt in the 1932 campaign, he became disgusted with the New Deal and eventually left the party.

Michael J. Meehan was probably the most colorful figure on the New York Stock Exchange, and his rise to fame and wealth had dramatic qualities that appealed particularly to the speculating multitude. Because he was right there on the floor of the Exchange as a broker and a specialist, buying and selling for thousands of his and other brokers' customers, many people seemed to think that he played an important part in making the market go up.

Before Mike Meehan came to Wall Street he had been manager of McBride's Theater Ticket Agency, and many of the people he had met in this occupation had stimulated his interest in the stock market. By 1918 his savings were enough to buy him a membership in the New York Curb Market, and in 1920 he was able to pay $90,000 for a seat on the New York Stock Exchange. His career advanced with the advancing stock price averages, and by 1929, at the age of thirty-seven, he was one of the most important brokers in Wall Street. His firm, M. J. Meehan & Company, owned eight New York Stock Exchange memberships, the most held by any member firm. At the peak of the boom it had numerous branch offices, three of which were on trans-Atlantic liners.

On the floor of the Exchange, Meehan acted as specialist in three important stocks, Radio Corporation of America, International Match, and Utilities Power & Light. Of these, Radio was by far the most heavily traded and the most spectactular, when its price was rising and even when the price declined. Meehan kept the "book" on Radio, executing standing orders to buy and sell as the price of the stock fluctuated. He also sometimes participated in pool operations in which a group of speculators, using shrewd trading tactics, would accumulate and distribute large amounts of Radio. On busy days his brokerage commissions ranged to $15,000. Like Raskob, who was devoted to General Motors, Meehan was enamored of Radio, almost to the point of obsession. He is said to have urged anyone and everyone to buy it. Through commissions, trading profits, and gains on his stock holdings, Meehan's fortune increased to perhaps as much as $25 million before the panic.

Redhaired, high-strung Mike Meehan, sometimes witty and sometimes profane, was known for both his generosity and his superstition. For example, the color green was anathema to him. Once, at someone's suggestion, and perhaps to end the superstition, he wore a green necktie for several days, later disposing of it in disgust, claiming that he had suffered heavy losses because of it.

Charles E. Mitchell, a banker by profession but by temperament a super-salesman, outdazzled all other bankers in the sunlight of public esteem that shone even on bankers if they were bullish and told the public what it wanted to hear—that stock prices would go ever higher, ad infinitum. He was a big man physically, and his strong, stern features brooked no nonsense and discouraged doubt. He kept in trim by walking each morning the seven miles from his home to the financial district. The physical vitality that reinforced his expressions of complete confidence in the market's great destiny gave many the impression that here was a man who could not be wrong.

In 1916 Mitchell became president of the National City Company, a wholly owned affiliate of the National City Bank. By 1921 he was president of the bank itself, but this did not reduce his interest in the security-selling activities of its affiliate. Legally, the company was distinct from the bank, and the purpose of its separation was to permit the latter to profit from security dealings that a bank could not legally engage in.

Mitchell brought to the company a combination of qualifications that, given so perfect an opportunity to apply them, made him a genius in a sense. He could organize and he could sell; he organized securities salesmen and high-pressured them into high-pressuring their prospects, who, potentially at least, were every man, woman, and child who had savings enough to buy a bond or a few shares of stock. His "vital personal force," his driving, dynamic optimism, his occasional arrogance, and his veiled threats kept the salesmen constantly striving to sell more stocks and bonds.

From a small beginning, the National City Company grew under Mitchell's determined direction into a network of offices in every fair-sized city, and it had as many as 350 salesmen. Until the boom in the stock market was well under way the company underwrote and sold only bonds, but selling stocks to the public proved to be highly lucrative. Other banks, in New York and throughout the country, became infected with what came to be called "Mitchellism," and they formed their own selling affiliates as the public's avidity for securities increased.

The National City Company distributed, in addition to many other stocks, more than a million shares of its parent corporation at prices that in retrospect proved to have been fantastically high. Altogether, over a period of ten years the National City Company sold more than $15 billion of stocks and bonds.

Mitchell himself became a multimillionaire through salaries, bonuses, and opportune investment. In 1928 alone his bonus from the "management fund" of the National City Company was three-quarters of a million dollars, and in 1929 his fortune was estimated at $30 million.

"Charley" Mitchell was indeed influenced by his circumstances and the times, as well as by his own temperament, to be continually bullish. Like many other moguls, titans, and tycoons of the New Era, he could see only one direction—upward, ever upward—for all the economic and financial indexes, including the stock price averages.

Those whose careers during the years of the great boom have been sketched here are only a few of the many whose personal qualities collectively did much to form the psychological warp and woof of the bull market. There were many thousands of others, from the great and near-great to the middle-class and small speculators and promoters.

4

The Last Year of the Boom

THE MAJOR CHANGES in the level of stock prices and in business activity throughout the boom of the 1920's already have been outlined. It is not necessary to record every advance and setback in the securities markets that occurred in those years, the vacillations between hope and fear that various developments aroused in the stock-minded public and the professional speculators, or the mounting evidence of an expanding illusion. All this is epitomized in the last twelve months of the boom. During this fantastic period the Dow-Jones average of industrial stock prices increased again as much as it had in the preceding six years, and the railroad stock-price average increased almost as much.

From early in 1927 until late in the spring the market advanced. In July this advance was given new impetus by the Federal Reserve Board's resumption of the "easy" money policy that it had applied in 1925, again primarily to aid England and continental European countries by causing U.S. gold to flow to them, thereby increasing the basic reserves of their monetary systems. Another consequence of the resumption, however, was a long-extended stimulation of stock speculation in the American securities markets. Through liberal lending and open market operations, and by reducing the rediscount rate, the Board encouraged a further expansion of bank credit for speculative purposes.[1]

[1] See Chapter 12.

After a setback toward the end of 1927, and again after a reaction from a higher level, in the summer of 1928, the market moved into new high ground. Through September, 1928, stock prices remained high, but buyers were reluctant to bid aggressively. In October the upward trend was resumed, despite seasonal pressure upon the loan markets for funds to harvest and move the crops and stock goods for the heavy retail buying of the holiday season. The rates for call money and for thirty- to ninety-day loans ranged around 7 per cent. Seasoned followers of the securities and commodities market knew that a credit strain in the autumn sometimes had led to panic.

The high interest rates, however, attracted funds from Europe. To ease the credit situation further the Federal Reserve banks bought bankers' acceptances (short-term credit instruments that financed commercial transactions). Nevertheless, during October some wary brokerage firms raised their minimum margin requirements from the more usual 20 per cent of the value of the securities in customers' accounts to 25 per cent.

During the greater part of the decade, speculative interest had centered on common stocks to the neglect of commodities. In the autumn of 1928 prices of the major staples seemed neither high nor low. Wheat ranged around $1.15, corn 80 cents, and oats 43 cents a bushel. Cotton sold at about 20 cents, lard 12 cents, and copper 16 cents a pound. What appeared to be a "normal" level of prices for wholesale commodities, which are likely to become the center of excited speculative attention during an inflation, was considered reassuring, and often was pointed to as evidence of monetary stability. Few people realized that without the inordinate expansion of credit commodity prices probably would have been much lower.

During the autumn of 1928, betting in the New York financial district heavily favored a Republican election victory. By early November, the odds favoring Herbert Hoover over

Alfred E. Smith were about five to one.[2] Altogether, perhaps $5 million was wagered. On the Thursday before Tuesday, November 6—Election Day—the pleasurable expectation of Mr. Hoover's victory came to the fore in the stock market. An exuberant bullish enthusiasm sent prices bounding upward. During the following two days, however, they settled back somewhat, probably because of the announcement that brokers' loans had increased by $135 million to a record high of $4.9 billion. This small, brief reaction in the face of a development that ordinarily would be considered distinctly bearish suggested that a large potential demand for stocks underlay the market; for ordinarily, a large increase in brokers' loans meant that on balance stock was passing from stronger to weaker hands—from outright holders to buyers on margin—and that the "technical position" of the market had deteriorated accordingly. It was soon apparent, however, that buyers subordinated this latter consideration to others that they believed far outweighed it. The market's strength was in fact revealed even more dynamically on Monday, November 5, as prices moved rapidly upward.

The election was a landslide for Hoover. State after state that the Democrats had counted on went over to the Republicans. Even the "solid South" was split. Although the exchanges were closed on Election Day, orders to buy poured into brokers' offices, piling up for the opening Wednesday morning. Wednesday was the second busiest day up to then in the history of the New York Stock Exchange, transactions approximating 4.8 million shares. Almost every issue rose as the enthusiasm

---

[2] *Wall Street Journal* (November 5, 1928), p. 18. Wall Street betting in 1924 had made Calvin Coolidge a 10 to 1 favorite over John W. Davis, and in 1920 it had made Warren G. Harding an 8 to 1 favorite over James M. Cox. In the 1916 election, the Republican bias in the New York financial district was indicated by odds that favored Charles Evans Hughes over Woodrow Wilson by as much as 6 to 1.

mounted, gains in some stocks ranging from a few points to as many as fifteen. Brokers on the floor were hard pressed to handle the orders, and the stock ticker lagged far behind the market. The bulls had the upper hand, and the bears were in full flight. The next morning jubilant headlines told the story. Already people were referring to the "Hoover Market," and extravagant predictions were being made for it.

On Thursday the rise continued on large volume, with the ticker tape running late, although a substantial reaction occurred in the final hour. On Friday the advance was resumed, with especially large gains in many of the railroad stocks. Saturday's volume of transactions was the greatest on record for that day of the week, and many large gains were made throughout the list. On Monday, November 12, large blocks of stock were transferred at the opening, and during the day prices rose markedly, Radio Corporation of America gaining a sensational 25¼ points. The trading set a new record at more than 5.7 million shares, and at one time the stock ticker was nearly an hour and a half behind transactions on the floor of the Exchange. On Tuesday the tremendous trading activity, the excitement, and the confusion continued, but deceptively. Although certain favored stocks advanced rapidly and substantially, prices on the average scarcely changed, and Radio lost 9 points.

To the older and more experienced traders this gave pause. So rapid and violent a rise surely called for a considerable, if merely technical, reaction. Some of the more prudent speculators took profits and some of the more daring sold short, among them unregenerate bears who somehow had survived with means enough to test their convictions once more. To many of them this must have seemed the point at which a reversal would begin that could yield quick and substantial profits on the down side of the market.

At about this time the conservative *New York Times* commented somberly:

> The gambling spirit that has developed since election has never before been exceeded. There have been bull markets before, but the present one surpasses them all, having been taken up at a time when stocks were already high, when all warnings had been disregarded, when brokers' loans had been swollen and when stocks selling at $200, $300, and $400 a share had multiplied tremendously.[3]

Stock prices moved downward for only one day. To the chagrin of those who had confidently expected a marked sell-off, this proved to be merely a brief pause in the post-election upsurge. On November 16 the market again boiled over. Prices moved violently upward, and the number of shares exchanged exceeded 6.6 million, another new record. The renewal of the advance was ascribed to the report that brokers' loans had increased during the preceding week by less than $2 million, although an increase of $100 million had been expected.

During the next two trading days the market rose moderately. But on Tuesday the twentieth it moved sharply upward, led by the high-priced stocks. Despite a reaction just at the close, which was ascribed to "profit-taking," some stocks showed tremendous gains. Radio was up 26½ points, Du Pont up 52 points, Case Threshing Machine up 45¾ points, and International Harvester up 43¼ points.

After this day of especially rapid advance one financial writer expressed the thoughts of many of the more experienced market observers:

> That the stock speculation had reached an exceedingly dangerous stage was a conclusion that no one of sense or experience

[3] (November 13, 1928), p. 1. © 1928 by The New York Times Company. Reprinted by permission.

could escape after the performances of yesterday's market. Wall Street itself was left in a state of astonishment, not unmixed with consternation, at the bidding up of prices. . . .

.   .   .   .

. . . the recent action of the stock market, supplemented by yesterday's wild extravagances, should emphasize the belief that this sort of thing cannot possibly be continued much longer. . . .[4]

From the beginning of the post-election upsurge, the volume of trading had continually been so large that most brokerage firms could not keep up with it. Their office staffs labored far into the night and sometimes until dawn with the masses of paper work that had to be attended to promptly and accurately. Some brokers petitioned the Governing Committee of the Exchange to declare a holiday so that the situation might be eased, but others—especially those whose firms' operations entailed large overhead costs—were opposed to this. Finally, however, the Committee decided to suspend trading for the short session on Saturday, November 24.

For a week after the sharp rise on the twentieth, there were alternate waves of heavy selling and aggressive buying, with a small net gain in prices. This "churning" movement on large volume was especially marked on the twenty-third, when nearly 7 million shares were traded with practically no change in the price level. Again, it seemed to market technicians that an upper limit had been reached and that a climax must be at hand. On the twenty-eighth, the day before the Thanksgiving recess, however, prices rose despite pre-holiday profit-taking sales, which professionals had expected to be large. Selling was readily absorbed by buyers who apparently were glad to be long in stock over the holiday. On the day after Thanksgiving, the averages declined slightly.

[4] *Ibid.* (November 21, 1928), p. 37.

In this post-election speculative frenzy, the public's awareness of the stock market and its exciting possibilities for profit increased. Superficially at least, it seemed as though almost any kind of stock was "a good buy." Humorist Will Rogers remarked in his newspaper column:

> If the Democrats had had the party incorporated and listed on the Exchange as "Democratic Hopes and Aspirations, Inc.," then let somebody buy ten shares to get it started, millions would have bought it on the Exchange that wouldn't think of taking it at the polls. They buy anything there worse than Democrats.
>
> You can't buy a pair of shoes in New York, without its done through the Stock Exchange. I got an order in with a broker for ten subway tickets.[5]

During this strongly upward phase of the boom, as in other such phases yet to come, brokers' offices were focal points of the excitement stimulated by the market's rapid advance. Of all those who crowded into the many hundreds of boardrooms throughout the country, almost all were jubilant, some even entranced. Good feeling was contagious and pervasive, and the little five- or ten-share traders were close kin emotionally to those who dealt in thousand-share blocks. To the former, a few hundred dollars profit was more than most of them could save from hard-earned wages in two or three years. Many, from small trader to large, were quickly becoming richer than they had ever seriously expected to be. The daring and agile pyramided their profits by using them to buy more and more stock on the basis of the very thin margins that most brokers were glad to accept.

Those who bought the more sensational market leaders—such as Radio Corporation of America, Wright Aeronautical, Du Pont, International Harvester, Case Threshing Machine,

[5] *Ibid.* (December 7, 1928), p. 29.

Montgomery Ward, Adams Express, and International Nickel —were able, within a month or so, to make enormous profits. Radio, for example, which had sold at 85¼ earlier in the year, rose from 225½ to 420 in this short period, and Wright Aeronautical, which had sold as low as 69 that year, rose from 159 to 289. Wright Aeronautical had come into prominence more recently than Radio, but it had many enthusiastic followers.

Off in a corner of one boardroom during the post-election advance, three of these followers—well-dressed gentlemen and respected members of the community—would lounge in the leather-upholstered chairs, hats on back of head, cigars tilted upward. They were long in Wright Aeronautical and enjoying the experience tremendously. When a string of quotations at successively higher prices followed the ticker symbol WAC as it moved across the Translux, or when a single quotation for WAC at a point or so higher appeared, they would break into a joyous chorus of quacking sounds—"Wac, wac, wac, wac, wac!" Others in the boardroom would laugh happily and sometimes join in, for most of them also were making money in one stock or another.

In November the volume of trading was so large that on many days the stock ticker ran far behind. Although the operators of the ticker worked with the greatest possible speed, an hour was sometimes required to record perhaps forty minutes of trading. This was a serious matter for the more active speculators, whose decisions to buy or sell were sometimes made from one moment to the next on the basis of the latest prices. Ordinarily these were transmitted almost immediately over the ticker, and became known simultaneously to all who watched the tape in every part of the country.

The first attempt to solve this problem was to print on the tape merely the last whole figure and the fraction of a stock's price. The final two zeros in the number of shares involved in a trade were already being omitted. Thus, instead of a 200-share transaction in U. S. Steel being reported as X 2. 174¾, under the new method it was reported as X 2. 4¾. When the indication of the number of shares was omitted entirely to help speed the process there was some objection, but this was done only during the longer periods in which the ticker lagged behind. Omitting the dots that were ordinarily used to separate prices in a sequence also helped somewhat. A 300-share transaction in U. S. Steel at different prices might then appear as X 4½ ⅝ ¾. Another resort when the tape was late was to transmit the most recent prices of a dozen or so of the market leaders over the bond ticker. Although these expedients reduced the problem of delayed quotations, they did not solve it.

Thanksgiving Day marked a turning point in the post-election upsurge. Thereafter, until December 10, prices declined, gradually at first and then precipitously in waves of urgent selling on December 6, 7, and 8. The proximate causes of the rapid acceleration of the decline on those three days were an increase in the call money rate to 12 per cent on the sixth, the first time so high a rate had been reached since July 1, 1920, and an increase in the rate for sixty- to ninety-day loans to 7¾ per cent on the seventh, which was the highest obtained for that kind of credit since mid-November, 1920. On the second of these near-panic days, bull operators attempted to bolster the market. Radio Corporation of America, for example, was forced upward more than 20 points for a brief interval. The attempt failed, however, and the liquidating movement was resumed in the later hours of trading. Urgent distress selling of the speculative favorites appeared. During the day, Radio lost 27 points, Du Pont, 27¾ points, and Montgomery Ward, 26 points.

On Saturday, December 8, with a record volume of 3.7 million shares for the short trading session, stocks again fell sharply as many of those who could not meet margin calls were forced to sell. Radio dropped 72 points to close at 296, its low for the day. International Harvester was down 61½ points, Wright Aeronautical, 26 points, and Montgomery Ward, 24 points. A considerable number of stocks showed declines of from 5 to 10 points.

Many who were long in stocks had followed them up with stop-loss orders. (Such an order could be placed below the current market price of a stock, and it would become a "sell-at-the-market" order if and when the designated price was reached. A similar order to buy could be entered above the prevailing price.) As the decline set off these selling orders they added to the pressure upon the market from the forced liquidation of margin accounts and from the persistent short selling of the bears. Thousands of thinly margined accounts, some of whose paper profits had been used to "pyramid" holdings, were sold out by the brokers to protect themselves from loss.

This was not the first or the last of the severe reversals that the market experienced during its long upward trend. As during previous setbacks, while this one lasted no one could know whether it was merely an adjustment, such as the more experienced market operators expected from time to time, or whether it marked at last the end of the boom. The break was severe enough to cause concern on the part of even the chronically optimistic. One broker commented sadly, "The bulls had the Thanksgiving turkey, and it looks as if the bears will have the Christmas stocking."

Many professional followers of the market believed that considerable time would have to elapse before public enthusiasm could revive sufficiently to sustain another advance. One journalist averred that "the economic mirage has evaporated." Financial leaders in European capitals commented pessimistically. In London, the Wall Street decline was expected to continue until prices no longer would "discount real business conditions so extravagantly." In Amsterdam there was fear of a Wall Street crisis and a belief that there were "dangerous risks for the near future in American finance." In Berlin, "at some time in 1929, a further general decline in prices" was expected. In Paris, however, some well-informed financiers believed that "although the great Wall Street boom seems to be definitely ended, there still remain numerous American securities worth picking up with a view to future appreciation."[6]

In June, 1928, somewhat the same situation had confronted speculators and investors. A rapid decline in prices then shook confidence in the market's future, and apprehension clouded the boardrooms. But it lasted only seven or eight trading days, and the ensuing rise, which continued until the December break in the market, carried the stock price averages much higher than they had been at their preceding peaks. The recovery from the June reaction and from others before it had convinced many people that they should ignore the reversals and hold on to their stocks. They had learned how difficult it was to get out of the market and back in again to any advantage, and that in selling out they risked losing for good their bull market positions.

Although the sudden, sharp decline in early December jolted the financial community and the stock-conscious public, it was no worse than might have been expected after the violence of the advance. After a sharp two-day rally the market drifted irregularly downward for most of the following week; but as the days passed and the urgent selling was not renewed, the purveyors of optimism lifted their heads and looked around. Letters and comments on Wall Street began to mention the "greatly improved technical position" of the market. Elimination of the weakest margin traders was presumed to have made it less vulnerable. The bolder forecasters, who came out from under cover to suggest that the major trend was still upward, proved to be right. On December 18 and 19 prices rose deci-

[6] *Ibid.* (December 16, 1928), p. 40.

sively, and from then until the Christmas holiday they advanced substantially. The prudent and cautious who were waiting for "bargain day" found that stocks were hard to buy at prevailing prices. Just at that time the exceptionally large volume of pre-Christmas shopping was taken to be a very favorable sign by those who thought of consumer demand as the basic support of the great prosperity.

On the day after Christmas and on the two succeeding days, in spite of call money at 12 per cent, prices moved upward vigorously. In the final trading session of the year various of the market leaders gained several points or more. Thus 1928 ended with a flourish of bullish enthusiasm. For most of Wall Street's functionaries and devotees it had been the best year ever, one of new high records in both the price level of common stocks and the volume of trading.

One important change that had come about in the financial scene was the high "price" of money. Borrowable funds were no longer abundant and cheap, as they had been from the 1920–21 deflation through 1927. Interest rates had risen markedly along with the enormous increase in borrowing by brokers to finance their customers who bought and held stocks on margin. Loans to brokers had increased by $2 billion during 1928 and by $3.2 billion since the beginning of 1927. At the end of 1928 the total amount of Federal Reserve bank credit outstanding was "at the highest level in seven years."[7]

The new year began with a rapid rise in stock prices and a large volume of transactions. With the year-end pressure on the money market past, the rate for call loans was, nevertheless, 10 per cent. Attendance in brokerage offices, which had fallen off greatly after the reaction in early December, was increasing, although some brokers reported a large number of inactive accounts. The recovery in the three weeks since then was a powerful attraction to many who had been temporarily disillusioned and had sworn "never again."

[7] *Federal Reserve Bulletin* (January, 1929), p. 9.

This was perhaps the most rapid and extensive upward movement following a severe break in the market that had ever occurred on the New York Stock Exchange, exceeding even the remarkable recoveries that took place after the Northern Pacific panic in May, 1901, and the severe decline set off by the San Francisco earthquake in April, 1906.[8] Among the more sensational performers on the New York Stock Exchange, Radio Corporation, which had declined from 420 to 275 during the reaction, was back to 394¾ on January 2; Wright Aeronautical, which had declined from 289 to 196, rose to 270.

After the first trading day in January the market sold off, and by the middle of the month prices were at just about the same level as they had been at the end of December. Three influences restraining bullish activities were the high rates of interest, apprehension that an investigation of brokers' loans and perhaps of the securities markets in general would be undertaken in Washington, and a rumor that the New York Federal Reserve Bank would raise its rediscount rate. Whether or not the rediscount rate would be increased was the subject of substantial betting each week in the New York and out-of-town financial districts.

These restraining influences were soon overcome, however. On the sixteenth a strong upward movement began. While some stocks fluctuated in a narrow range, others became very active and attracted an aggressive following. Many traders came to believe that only those promising "fireworks" merited their attention. Leading the advance were the so-called "rich men's stocks," issues that sold at several hundred dollars or more per share. There was supposed to be great significance in the fact that these, rather than low-priced stocks—the so-called "cats and dogs"—were leading the market.

Speculative enthusiasm and stock prices mounted together. When brokers' loans reached a new high during the third week of January, this was bullishly construed, the rationalization

[8] *The Annalist* (January 4, 1929), p. 2.

being that the increase might have been much larger. Supporting the bulls was a decline in the rate on call money for a brief period to 6 per cent, a figure that the brokers and their customers no longer regarded as excessive. The speculating public and even many professional traders were determined, so it seemed, either to interpret business and financial news favorably or, when that was impossible, to ignore it. Toward the end of January, however, price movements had become confused, some stocks rising while others declined. On some days prices swung rapidly upward and downward, making little or no progress, but on the thirty-first the market was generally strong. Financial commentators and customers' men shifted their opinions uncertainly. Sometimes they urged their followers to sell and soon after would suggest buying.

Early in February, prices moved upward and then fluctuated irregularly. Some observers thought they recognized the manipulative tactics of large professional operators. Also, an unusually large volume of odd-lot purchases, many of them outright rather than on margin, was noted, as well as a considerable amount of "switching" from stocks that seemed to have reached their peaks to others with supposedly better prospects.

At this time, a new influence became apparent. Its full significance, however, was not to be comprehended until later in the year. A change in attitude had been developing within the Federal Reserve Board, owing in part to the death in October, 1928, of Benjamin Strong, who had been governor of the Federal Reserve Bank of New York since its establishment in 1914. Strange as it may seem that the demise of a man who was not a member of the Board should significantly affect its policies, that appears to have been the case. Strong's forceful personality, energy, understanding of the Federal Reserve System, and position as head of the largest and most powerful of the twelve Federal Reserve banks made it so. As his contemporaries have noted: "He was just a natural-born leader; no one else was in his class"; "In all situations he was dominant, but never domineering"; "Wherever he sat was the head of the table."[9]

Internationally minded, Strong was sympathetic to the problems of the European central banks, especially those of the Bank of England, whose governor, Montagu Norman, exerted considerable influence on him. Throughout a great part of the 1920's, Strong endeavored with great determination to aid England and other European countries by means of a continuously "easy" money policy that would prevent a drain of gold from Europe to New York. President Hoover, in his *Memoirs*, has referred to Strong as a "mental annex to Europe."

Although the rediscount rate was raised during 1928, the Federal Reserve Board did not then take a determined stand against the excessive use of credit in the stock market. Its changing attitude, due partly to Strong's disappearance from the scene, was influenced as well by the earlier resignation of its governor, Daniel Crissinger, who leaned toward the New Era way of thinking, and his replacement by Roy Young, who was clearly aware of the dangerous credit situation.

On February 6, after the close of the market, the Federal Reserve Board issued a forthright statement to the effect that too much of the country's bank credit was being absorbed by speculation. Its purpose was to discourage the commercial banks from borrowing at the Federal Reserve banks while making loans that supported stock speculation. Although the Board took no direct action to tighten credit, the possibility that it would do so was implied.

While earlier and milder warnings had had no more than passing effect on the market, this one indicated that the Board was thoroughly in earnest. Moreover, the warning was apparently timed to coincide with the action of the Bank of England in raising its discount rate from 4½ to 5½ per cent. England's

---

[9] Lester V. Chandler, *Benjamin Strong, Central Banker* (Washington, D.C.: The Brookings Institution, 1958), p. 47.

international financial position had again worsened, and her central bank was attempting to stanch the outflow of funds to foreign countries. Higher interest rates in England than in the United States would help to do this. If the Federal Reserve Board's warning and its implied threat of more drastic action should cause a substantial decline in stock prices, the volume of credit thereby released from speculative use, and so available for other purposes, would tend to lower interest rates in the United States.

On the following Monday the United States Senate adopted a resolution requesting the Federal Reserve Board "to give to the Senate any information and suggestions that it feels would be helpful in securing legislation necessary to correct the evil complained of and prevent illegitimate and harmful speculation."[10] And a few days later the Federal Advisory Council of the Federal Reserve System, at its quarterly meeting, approved the Board's desire "to prevent, as far as possible, the diversion of Federal Reserve funds for the purpose of carrying loans based on securities."[11] Although moral suasion could induce most of the member banks to follow a policy of restraint, the Board could not stop the flow of funds to the call loan market from wealthy individuals, large corporations, investment trusts, and other sources that found the high rates of interest there attractive.

On February 6, prices began to decline even before the Board's statement was publicized, and on the following day they broke badly. Many buying orders that rested below the market were cancelled, and some frightened bulls sold out all their holdings. Others held on grimly. The "bear clique," supposed to be operating from Palm Beach and selling short on a large scale, was said to be so jubilant because of the turn in the market that there was "dancing in the streets." But the bears'

10 *Federal Reserve Bulletin* (March, 1929), p. 175.
11 *Ibid.*, p. 176.

rejoicing was short-lived. The steep decline, which was interrupted occasionally by uncertain rallies, lasted only about ten days.

During the second half of February the market regained its vitality, and a strong upward movement occurred. Highly reassuring to many brokers and speculators was the fact that leading the broad recovery were the so-called "Morgan stocks," issues that had been underwritten or were sponsored by the powerful banking firm of J. P. Morgan & Company, and that were in a measure protected by it and its many influential allies in Wall Street and throughout the country. The more prominent of these stocks were U. S. Steel, General Motors, Du Pont, General Electric, Johns-Manville, Montgomery Ward, and Radio Corporation.

Nevertheless, once again the public had had a small taste of panic. The Federal Reserve Board's favorable attitude, which had given strength to the market for such a long time, had changed, and investors and speculators alike were now highly conscious of the possible effect on the market's action of changes in the credit supply and interest rates. A financial writer, musing on this and other problems that beset the stock-minded public, commented:

> The life of the speculator in stocks, particularly if he be on the long side of the market, is no downy bed of ease these days. There is something for him to worry about in almost every day of the week. On Monday he can worry about the size of the over-Sunday accumulation of orders and whether the volume will be sufficient to pull the market into a brisk rally; on Tuesday he can worry about the statement of individual banks in the twelve Reserve Districts; Wednesday's particular worry is whether the Bank of England will make any changes in its re-discount rate; on Thursday he has the double worry of a possible change in the [New York Federal Reserve Bank's rediscount] rate, also the size of brokers' loans; on Friday he

can worry about the Chicago rediscount rate. In former days and in less troublesome times, Saturday was the day practically free from worries and the one in which he could now and then get away for a round of golf. With the Reserve Board holding impromptu meetings on Saturday mornings, the life of the speculator is just about filled with things to worry about. Sunday, of course, is out of the calculation. He can spend this holiday in worrying about what the market will do on Monday.[12]

Temporarily offsetting the uncertainty that the Federal Reserve Board's warning had created was President Coolidge's statement to the press shortly before he left office early in March that the nation's economic condition was "absolutely sound," and that stocks were "cheap at current prices." Perhaps partly as a consequence of this, stock prices, although they fluctuated widely, showed a fair gain for the first three weeks of March. On the fifteenth, however, a statement by Secretary of the Treasury Andrew Mellon, advising investors to buy bonds, made newspaper headlines. Mellon pointed out that the relatively low prices and high rate of return on bonds made them an especially attractive form of investment. His advice had no apparent immediate effect on the stock market, although it may have contributed to the severe decline that began on March 22.

On this date followers of the market again had a foretaste of panic. The break in prices was worse than the one in February, although it lasted less than a week. On Monday, March 25, one of the severest daily declines in the history of the Stock Exchange, up to that time, occurred. Large blocks of stock were thrown on the market, and ninety issues made new low prices for the year. Most pools and banking interests that might have supported their favorite stocks apparently stood aside as the liquidation increased. The mystery of the day, however, was the action of Radio Corporation of America and International

[12] *New York Times* (March 24, 1929), p. 11. © 1929 by The New York Times Company. Reprinted by permission.

Telephone and Telegraph, both of which moved against the downward trend and made substantial gains. In other parts of the market frantic selling was intensified as the decline touched off stop-loss orders and brokers sold out the weakened accounts of traders who failed to meet margin calls. Call loan money had become scarce, the rate rising to 14 per cent, and there was no indication that the banks would relieve this tight situation. As the day wore on, no sign of a rally appeared. Again, those who were bearishly inclined averred that the back of the bull market had been broken.

Throughout most of the session of March 26 the rapid decline in prices continued. The credit situation now dominated the scene; funds for speculative use were scarce, both because of the increasing seasonal business needs and the commercial banks' reluctance, in light of the warnings of the Federal Reserve Board, to make loans in the call money market. As the call loan rate rose in successive jumps from 12 to 15 to 17, and then to 20 per cent, the panicky selling increased. Just as the 20 per cent rate was posted on the Stock Exchange's new electric announcement board, a fuse blew out. According to one observer, "even the worst crippled of the bull operators were able to get a laugh." Suddenly, however, late in the trading session prices turned about, and there was a rapid recovery on heavy volume. Some stocks regained all their losses of the day, others half or more. Transactions set a new daily record of well over eight million shares, and final quotations were not printed on the stock ticker until after five o'clock. This recovery continued strongly for the remaining days of the month.

The reason for the sharp reversal of the downward movement on March 26 soon became known: A substantial amount of funds suddenly had been offered on the call loan market. With stock prices declining and call money at 20 per cent, it had looked as though the Federal Reserve Board's attempt to halt the boom by means of "moral suasion," rather than by direct, blunt action, was about to succeed. At that point, however, several New York banks came to the aid of the market by discounting collateral at the Federal Reserve Bank and offering the proceeds to eager borrowers. Charles E. Mitchell, president of the National City Bank of New York and also a director of the Federal Reserve Bank of New York, was the only banker to acknowledge publicly his part in helping to meet the emergency: "So far as this institution is concerned, we feel we have an obligation which is paramount to any Federal Reserve warning, or anything else, to avert, so far as lies in our power, any dangerous crisis in the money market."[13] On the following day his bank offered $25 million in the call loan market, $5 million at each percentage point above the 15 per cent level. Other bankers also made funds available, and consequently on March 27 the call loan rate remained at 15 per cent. These measures reduced the pressure on the money market and stimulated the sharp recovery in stock prices. While other bankers cooperated with the Federal Reserve Board in its policy of restricting the use of bank credit for speculation in order to hold the boom in check, Mitchell and a few others, by apparently thwarting that policy, created the impression among many speculators that the Board could not have an important influence on the course of stock prices.

Many people supposed that Mitchell had defied the Federal Reserve Board. But that was not so, although his published statement seemed to indicate defiance. When the call loan rate reached 20 per cent, several New York bankers had inquired of the governor of the Federal Reserve Bank of New York whether he wanted them to offer sufficient funds to keep the rate from rising further. After telling them to use their own judgment, the governor reported his advice to the Board in Washington, which almost immediately approved it.[14]

[13] *Commercial and Financial Chronicle* (March 30, 1929), p. 2014.
[14] Benjamin M. Anderson, *Economics and the Public Welfare* (Princeton: D. Van Nostrand Company, Inc., 1949), p. 206.

Senator Carter Glass, who had helped to frame the Federal Reserve Act in 1913 and who was an authority on the purposes and functions of the Federal Reserve System, roundly denounced Mr. Mitchell for this "challenge to the authority and the announced policy of the Federal Reserve Board" and demanded that he resign from his Federal Reserve directorship. Some members of Congress and prominent men in business and finance came to Mitchell's defense. The great bull trader William C. Durant and others of his persuasion insisted that the Federal Reserve authorities had no business attempting to control the flow of credit for speculative purposes. Soon after this the National City Bank stated in its *Bulletin* that it recognized the dangers of overspeculation and favored the Federal Reserve's policy of restraining credit expansion for that reason, although it also noted the desirability of avoiding "a general collapse of the securities markets."

Many experienced bankers must have been concerned about the extremes to which stock speculation had been carried, but they did little to call the public's attention to it. Paul M. Warburg, prominent in New York banking and respected for the work he had done in bringing about the establishment of the Federal Reserve System, was, however, an exception. Early in March he vigorously attacked the "orgies of unrestrained speculation," pointing out that the increase in stock prices was "quite unrelated to respective increases in plant, property, or earning power." He predicted that unless the speculation were halted it would "bring about a general depression involving the entire country."[15] This warning caused some alarm, but it was soon ridiculed and forgotten.

On April 1, following a three-day Easter recess, stocks sold off sharply in what proved to be a "secondary reaction." During April, the continuing dispute over Federal Reserve policy, fear that the Board would take more decisive action, and the rise

---

[15] *Commercial and Financial Chronicle* (March 9, 1929), p. 1444.

of the interest rate on thirty- to sixty-day loans to 9 per cent contributed to the uncertainty. Those who understood money, credit, and interest rate relationships realized that the Federal Reserve banks' rediscount rate of only 5 per cent was far out of line with rates set by the free play of supply and demand for lendable funds. Call loan rates, which ranged from about 7 per cent to as high as 16 per cent, were most of the time between 8 and 10 per cent. According to a joke that passed about the boardrooms, when call money reached 30 per cent it would be split on a three-for-one basis.

Although there were fairly sharp declines and rallies during April, values registered an overall gain of about 4 per cent. The market had quieted down. A measure of conservatism crept into brokerage and banking circles. Some brokers raised their margin requirements, and one prominent firm announced that after May 1 its minimum margin requirement would be 40 per cent on all stocks selling for more than ten dollars a share. There was also some effort to discourage small traders from buying on margin. Here and there bankers cautioned their customers about buying stocks.

A month after the March reaction, however, tipsters were again active, and almost all of them were bullish. The old Wall Street maxim, "Never sell a dull market short," was being quoted. Over and above the day-to-day matters that influenced stock trading was the impressive fact that business conditions throughout the country were very good. Except for some decline in building construction, most industrial and commercial activity was at a high level and increasing.

In May, stock prices declined somewhat. Although the expectation of an increase in the Federal Reserve rediscount rate continued, and the Board let it be known that its attitude toward the use of credit for speculation had not changed, the Board took no action. About the middle of the month some apprehension was caused by the revelation that the Federal Reserve

Bank of Chicago had sought the Board's permission to raise its discount rate. But when the Board failed to act on this and a similar request made by the New York Federal Reserve Bank a few weeks before, the apprehension was relieved, although some traders expressed the wish that the Board would raise the discount rate and "get it over with."

In May, the average rate for call loans was lower than it had been earlier in the year. Toward the end of the month bond prices reached new low levels. A substantial decline occurred in the price of wheat in Chicago late in the month, only to be followed by an equally substantial rise early in June. These fluctuations in the grain market drew a little speculative attention away from the stock market, but only briefly. A vigorous rally in stock prices late in May was cut short by a brief but sharp reaction that was ascribed by some to the decline in the price of wheat. On Friday, May 31, after the close of the market, a large reduction in brokers' loans was announced. An ironically amusing example of the forecasts being made at this time was that of a veteran Wall Street operator, who confidently declared for publication that "we will get a big bull market in the fall with many stocks making new highs."[16]

After a short but sharp advance at the beginning of June the market turned dull and irregular, although pools and large individual operators were rumored to be taking renewed interest in certain stocks. Most commentators were noncommittal and anticipated a period of "quiet trading." It was reported that among professional traders the watchword had become "Wait until August." The continuing tight credit situation was reflected in the U.S. Treasury's sale of an issue of 9-month certificates at 5⅛ per cent. About the middle of June the New York Curb Market received some special publicity when its name was changed to New York Curb Exchange and when, on Saturday, June 15, an especially slow day on the New York Stock Ex-

[16] *Wall Street Journal* (May 22, 1929), p. 2.

change, the volume of transactions on the "Curb" exceeded that on the "Big Board" for the first time in history.

Business news continued to be favorable. There appeared to be no slackening in industrial and commercial activity, although a seasonal slowing-up was to be expected. Some notice was taken of the increase in the monetary gold stock, which was about $200 million larger than it had been twelve months earlier. The return of gold from abroad was ascribed primarily to high interest rates in the United States. The trend of member bank borrowing at the New York Federal Reserve Bank, which had been downward for several weeks, was reversed in mid-June. Brokers' loans increased rapidly throughout the remainder of the month and into early July. The character of the buying, which especially favored high-quality stocks, impressed financial writers sufficiently for them to resume their bullish predictions. Some observed that in each of the four preceding years stock prices had advanced during July and August. And as the month of June came to an end the market was rising.

In July, August, and at the very beginning of September the long boom reached its climax. From the first part of July the stock price averages were higher than at any time before. The upward progression in that month was substantial, but it was to prove small in comparison with the rise during August. Although the rate for call money was 15 per cent on the first two days of July, by the third it had dropped to 6 per cent. Soon it was apparent that the bulls were again in the ascendency. On July 2 the advance broadened, with stocks in practically every category moving up decisively. The high-priced shares of certain industrial companies and those of many of the railroads received particular attention as their prices were rapidly swept upward. Marked strength in U.S. Steel and General Electric was interpreted to mean that powerful banking interests and certain very wealthy operators had resumed their activities in the market.

In Wall Street, and in brokerage offices throughout the country, people talked once more of "a roaring bull market." The business news behind the market was generally good, and the report on steel production was exceptionally so. According to the Iron and Steel Institute, daily output in June was almost equal to that of May, the month for which steel production had until then been the greatest on record. The general optimism was enhanced by President Hoover's comment that a tax reduction was possible.

In the second and third weeks of July the market was very strong, with public utility and railroad stocks leading the advance. Rumors of stock splits floated around. The breakthrough of many issues to new high price levels caused market commentators to predict still higher prices on the premise that this was the direction of least resistance. It was observed that some market favorites, the "high-steppers," did not sell off, as often occurred after publication of favorable news items concerning them. Again, the strength of the market was attracting the attention of people in all parts of the country, and buying from the far West had increased considerably.

At this time followers of the securities markets, as well as many others, were diverted by the new-sized currency being issued just then by the Treasury and the Federal Reserve banks. It seemed like paper money in miniature, compared with the "horseblanket"-sized currency that it replaced. A curiosity of the moment was the public's demand for the new bills in larger denominations. The temporary increase in circulation due to the currency transformation caused a reduction in bank reserves and perhaps some increase in the call money rate, but this was of no great significance.

After the third week of July the market alternated between strength and irregularity, with an occasional sharp flurry of selling. There were indications that a fairly large short interest had developed, and rumors circulated to the effect that some big operators, in opposing the advance, had suffered large losses. On the other hand, certain "experts" believed that the market's "technical position" had been weakened by the advance, and that a "shakeout" was overdue. The threat of war between China and Russia seemed to be ignored. A rise in grain prices—especially in the price of wheat, which had increased by 50 cents or more a bushel in two months—was regarded as a source of more wealth that indirectly would support stock prices.

During July, brokers' loans reached new high levels without markedly affecting the call loan rate. Corporations, wealthy individuals with excess cash, and foreign bankers were supplying the extra short-term funds that were needed to support the new extension of the boom. This was taken to mean that the Federal Reserve Board had failed in its attempt to prevent the increased use of credit in the stock market. There was some awareness of the problem that the Federal Reserve would encounter in the autumn, when the credit needs of agriculture and business would be greatest, but the booming market seemed to be saying, "Don't worry about that." Some brokers' weekly letters suggested taking profits, but at the same time they recommended various stocks for "the long pull." At the end of July, when U. S. Steel reported its earnings per share for the first half of the year at $11.72—a peacetime record—the market was strong, with "Big Steel" leading the advance.

The strength of the market in July, however, was just a prelude to what occurred in August. The stock price averages show that the only rise for any monthly interval throughout the boom that was comparable in magnitude to that of August, 1929, was the rapid upward sweep of prices during the preceding November. A résumé of stock market activity during August can be divided conveniently into two parts, the first of which runs through Friday, August 9. On that day prices reacted violently to the announcement made on the preceding afternoon, after the close of the market, that the Federal Reserve Bank of New York was raising its rediscount rate from 5 to 6 per cent.

During the first few days of August the market advanced substantially. For the next few days it was "nervous," "irregular," and "unsettled." On Wednesday, August 7, prices were quite weak in the late trading, with many of the utility issues declining sharply. On the following day, however, a strong upward movement was led by U. S. Steel and other high-quality stocks. This show of strength suggests that the New York Federal Reserve Bank's announcement of the increase in the rediscount rate must have been generally unexpected, despite six months or more of conjecture as to when it would occur.

Actually, the New York Federal Reserve Bank was very much a laggard in the procession of central banks that took measures to tighten up their credit systems. Early in February the Bank of England had raised its discount rate from 4½ to 5½ per cent, and this action was followed before long by other central banks, including those of Germany, the Netherlands, Austria, Hungary, and Poland.

Before the market opened on the ninth, news of the higher rediscount rate had spread to almost every part of the country and to Europe. It made headlines in some of the morning papers. A "severe jolt" for the market was generally anticipated. Some brokers hopefully expressed their belief that the market was in a good technical position to withstand the shock, and that customers' accounts were better margined than usual; but apparently all of them regarded the Federal Reserve's action as unfavorable for stock prices. Some speculators and investors, sensing the full significance of it, were profoundly disturbed and sold out their holdings at the market's opening or as soon thereafter as they could. As prices fell, the sale of many large blocks of stock was a feature of the day's transactions. Again, thinly margined brokerage accounts were wiped out. For a time trading demoralized, and the market was weak at the close. Yet the reaction lasted for just this one day.

On Saturday there was a brisk recovery, which began the final upward movement that carried stock prices to the highest point in the boom. On the following Monday, August 12, the market was strong. High-priced leaders moved ahead vigorously, and U. S. Steel advanced to new high ground. Many bears whose hopes had been aroused on the preceding Friday but dampened on Saturday hastened to cover their short sales. Prices continued irregularly upward until Friday, when they surged forward on a large volume of transactions. On Saturday trading was again heavy, but prices were somewhat erratic. During this week of advancing prices, leadership of the market shifted from U. S. Steel to American Can, Standard Oil of New Jersey, and American Telephone and Telegraph—all stocks of the highest quality.

During the week beginning August 19, the market followed much the same pattern as that of the week before, but with greater trading activity and larger price increases. On Monday a rapid advance in U. S. Steel set off frantic bidding for many other of the leading issues, and on succeeding days, although there were brief periods of irregularity, the course of the market was strongly upward. Again the leaders of the previous week made large gains, but they shared the limelight with the previously lethargic General Motors and Radio Corporation of America, as well as with such respected speculative favorites as General Electric, Johns-Manville, Du Pont, Montgomery Ward, and Westinghouse Electric. Friday the twenty-third was a day of rapidly advancing prices on a broad front and with a large volume of trading. The rise continued on Saturday as well, but more selectively.

During this period of hectic buying the call loan rate ranged around 6 and 7 per cent. When a substantial increase in brokers' loans was announced after the close of the market on the twenty-second, professional traders expected a sharp re-action. That, instead, the market was exceptionally strong the next day revealed the temper of the stock-buying public. In these two weeks that followed the raising of the rediscount rate, the sensational increase in prices caused many traders to suppose that the Federal Reserve authorities, by adding action to persuasion, had merely revealed their lack of power over the stock market.

Yet individuals who had not lost all sense of proportion must have wondered how much higher stock prices could go after having been bid up so violently, some to 50 per cent or more above what they had been a few months before. The rapid rise was explained in various ways. Some people believed that large investment trusts, some of them recently formed, were "mopping up" stocks to fill out their portfolios. Others thought that frightened short-sellers, sold-out bulls, and newcomers to the market were absorbing shares offered just above the market, and that many potential sellers were raising their asking prices.

The tape frequently recorded large blocks of high-priced stock changing ownership at advancing prices. Some pool operators, to their amazement, discovered that they could liquidate all of their holdings of a stock with little effect on its price. One pool was reported to have sold 60,000 shares of a leading stock within an hour, and within a price range of little more than two points. Again, it was the "rich men's" stocks—the respectable, high-priced "blue chips"—in which a great deal of speculative excitement centered. It seemed as though such stocks were bought at high prices merely to pass them on presently to new buyers at still higher prices. Many low-priced stocks were neglected. It was said to be harder for most low-priced stocks to go up a half a point than for a high-priced leader to rise twenty or thirty points.

In the first half of the last week of August there was profit-taking. Prices moved irregularly, and the market seemed "tired." On Wednesday the twenty-eighth railroad stocks became active and strong, although most other stocks did little. On Thursday, the general upward trend was resumed, and on Friday, in spite of a report of another large increase in brokers' loans, prices moved up vigorously on a large volume of transactions, many stocks gaining from 5 to 15 points.

Because Friday the thirtieth was the last trading day of the week, and the markets would be closed until the following Tuesday because of Labor Day, this marked strength was regarded as an exceedingly favorable portent. Also believed to be highly significant were the movement of the market into new high ground, after only a brief period of "consolidation" in which it declined very little from its previous high level, and the surpassing of previous record highs, on large volume, by many important individual stocks. Although a selloff just before the long weekend would have been considered natural, and had been expected by the more experienced traders, the fact that it did not occur was even more impressive than the strength of the advance. The action of the market was saying, in effect, that the majority of its followers preferred to hold more rather than fewer shares of stock over the three-day period when the market would be closed.

Current statistics and other news of industrial and commercial developments were exerting a strong influence on those who watched the market, and at this time the news was particularly good. In steel, the nation's key industry, output at about 90 per cent of productive capacity was remarkably large for the time of year. It compared with an output of about 75 per cent in August, 1928. Leaders in the industry were themselves puzzled by "the unbroken continuance of business on such a scale." Railroad freight car loadings were at a record high for the season, and railroad earnings in July had exceeded by more than 25 per cent those of the preceding July. Such data were indicative of extraordinarily good business throughout the country, but by the time they reached the public they had become history. In late August it was too soon for the statisticians to know that small downturns in various areas of industry and commerce were already being extended, and that steel production and railroad car loadings were about to recede from their peaks.

Influences close to the stock market seemed highly favorable. Investment trusts were said to be adding to their holdings. An enthusiastic officer of one of the larger trusts commented that often the profit on a stock purchase in one day exceeded the return on funds invested in the call loan market for a whole year. Some large pools were known to be actively buying stocks, and many new pools were being formed. A rumor that the Federal Reserve Board was taking a more tolerant attitude toward the market passed around the boardrooms. This was to be doubted, although the Reserve banks began in August to buy a substantial amount of acceptances in order to ease credit for the increased movement of goods through the channels of commerce in the fall.

There was evidence that European investors were buying American securities, especially railroad shares, in large amounts, and travelers returning from South Africa and even from India reported a keen interest in fluctuation on the New York Stock Exchange. American stocks were a continual topic of conversation in foreign financial circles, and many well-to-do foreigners were speculating in them.

Stock brokerage itself was a booming industry. This was emphasized late in August when the Chicago Stock Exchange, on which a seat had recently sold for $110,000, announced that it would double its membership of 235 in order to care for the greatly increased volume of business. On the New York Stock Exchange the number of shares traded during August was the largest for any month on record, brokerage commissions being, of course, proportionately large.

Nevertheless, during July and August, and up until September 3, as many important stocks (and also many lesser ones) pushed upward to price levels never before attained, there were thousands of disillusioned speculators on the sidelines, some hoping for a chance to get in again to advantage, some bitterly or philosophically ignoring the market. Many other followers of the market, merely through prudence, were content to stand aside and wait.

Not everyone who participated in this last upward thrust of the great boom, however, did so indiscriminately, recklessly, or on a wholly emotional basis. There were many sophisticates to whom the market's action kept repeating the old trading maxim, "Go with it." And they did, while at the same time they stood ready to reduce or reverse their long positions with little hesitation. To speak of the boom as a "frenzy of speculation," then, would be an overgeneralization. There was a frenzy of excitement and activity, of course, whenever a rapid upward movement of prices occurred. One could see something of it and sense it in the brokers' boardrooms. But it was an unmeasurable phenomenon; whether it too reached its peak along with the boom, or whether it had been more pronounced at an earlier stage of the advance, no one can say. Perhaps for the continually successful some of the excitement of profit-making had worn away by late summer, 1929.

But as August passed and September began, the credulity and the delusion, the "willing suspension of disbelief" on the part not only of the less seasoned public but even of the smart, long-time professionals, were at just as high a level as the stock prices recorded on the exchanges.

5

The Developing Crisis

IT IS EASY TO SAY now that in early September, 1929, the market was "ripe" for a fall. But on the surface of things, while prices advanced, it certainly did not seem so. With respect to what were called "technical factors," however, the market was vulnerable.

A great deal of stock was in comparatively weak hands, notwithstanding the effect of the year's deeper reactions in eliminating thinly margined accounts. In the final four weeks of the boom, as prices rose far above their previous highest levels, the number of new "shoestring" speculators, and of those who had extended their commitments to the limit of their credit with the brokers, must have increased considerably. Just a "normal" compensatory reaction would have been sufficient to force some of them to sell, and if an extended downswing were to carry prices below the low points of the August 9 setback, it would cause selling from accounts that had barely survived at that time. Also, at the prevailing high prices, and because of the rapidity of the advance, a considerable amount of profit-taking by the more cautious and less credulous seemed overdue.

More fundamental aspects of the situation could make one skeptical of the frequent and fulsome predictions of the market's future. Especially important among these aspects was the changed attitude of the Federal Reserve authorities, made clear enough months before in their warnings and confirmed by the increase in the rediscount rate in August. Why the panic did not begin in August, set off by that traumatic event, which to the knowing was only further evidence of a determined restrictive credit policy, instead of a month later at a higher level of prices, is one of the great mysteries of the boom.

Although interest rates were high, the amount of credit used to carry stocks on margin was the largest on record. Such funds were costing the borrowers nearly 1 per cent a month, while the average yield received from dividends was barely 3 per cent per annum. Various widely held stocks were selling at 20, 30, 50, and even 100 or more times a year's earnings. Before the early part of 1928, the percentage return on stocks had been larger than that on high quality bonds, this being the normal relationship between yields for the two kinds of securities. But as stock prices continued to rise, prices of bonds declined until the return on them was about 5 per cent. So large a differential in favor of bonds, especially when viewed in terms of the high cost of carrying stocks on margin, was an anomaly that must have seemed portentous to the astute fringe of the stockholding public.

At about this time, some stock transfer clerks were said to have remarked on the many old, high-denomination certificates that passed through their hands, the implication being that an extraordinary number of staid, wealthy people who owned securities outright were moving out of stocks.

The technical condition of the market, the credit situation, and the distortion of interest rates were phenomena closely associated with stock market activity. But beyond the somewhat self-centered world of speculative finance, in the overall national and international economic and financial situation, other influences, perhaps less clearly visible but nonetheless fundamental, were also at work.[1] Except for the current technical situation, none of these influences had arisen suddenly as the

[1] See Chapter 12.

boom pushed upward to its peak in August and September; all of them had been operating inexorably over a long period of time through the calculating minds of many thousands of people whose decisions to buy less than they might have, to delay buying, or to sell, changed the course of the market, though the burden that they placed upon it was hardly observable from day to day or week to week. Early in September, as we see in retrospect, the force of these influences offset, and thereafter it exceeded, that of the mania for speculation, which was no longer fortified by an increasing amount of inflationary bank credit.

On Tuesday, September 3, the boom reached its peak. The Dow-Jones average of industrial stock prices was 381.17, and that of railroad stock prices 189.11 at the close.[2] The prevailing rate for call loans was 9 per cent, and the day's volume of transactions approximated 4.4 million shares. The *Wall Street Journal* commented on the general situation and the day's activities:

> Wall Street entered the autumn financial season in a definitely optimistic frame of mind. With railroad traffic showing steady gains, and production in the major branches of industry continuing at a high rate, the earnings prospects of the principal corporations with shares listed on the Stock Exchange were looked upon as extremely promising.
>
> Sentiment regarding the credit outlook was reassured by the activities of the Federal Reserve authorities in placing funds at

[2] The *New York Times* combined average of the prices of fifty stocks did not reach its highest point until September 19. On that date the Dow-Jones industrial average was 11 points lower than it had been on September 3, and the railroad average was 6 points lower. The writer has not attempted to appraise the representativeness of the various stock price averages, and it would be practically impossible to ascertain the total value of all stocks, listed and unlisted, for September 3 and September 19. In retrospect, the market was plainly a "sick" one after September 3, although between the thirteenth and nineteenth it rallied and for a few days seemed to have stabilized, with some issues making new highs.

the disposal of business through bill purchases in the open market. With trade and credit conditions favorable, buying orders accumulated in large volume over Labor Day, and the forward movement in the main body of stocks was vigorously resumed in the early dealings.

. . . .

While irregularity cropped out from time to time during the day, due to profit-taking attracted by the sweeping character of the recent gains, the main upward trend was fairly well sustained throughout the session. Bullish enthusiasm was stimulated by the return of United States Steel to leadership of the industrial division.

Steel surpassed its previous high [reaching 261¾], while Union Carbide also pushed into record territory. Announcement that some dealers had increased the domestic price of copper to 18¼ cents a pound started another aggressive demonstration in the shares of the principal producers. Anaconda stood out prominently, rising to the best levels of the movement on a large turnover.[3]

On September 3, then, a panic was hard to imagine. Public utility common stocks were strong as a result of the expectation of more and bigger mergers, and the stocks of amusement companies were heavily traded on the strength of various favorable rumors. Radio Corporation of America was "tremendously active" around the 100 mark, although it sold off somewhat toward the close. Allegheny Corporation (the gigantic railroad holding company of the Van Sweringen brothers), shares of which had been offered for subscription at $24.00 earlier in the year, reached its all-time high of 56½ on a large volume of trading. Numerous other stocks made new highs for the year or longer. Although the marked strength in copper mining stocks was at levels below their highs for the year, the increase in price of that commodity was looked upon as a highly favorable sign. The saying "the market has to have a copper roof," which was to be heard later in the 1930's, may have had its

[3] (September 4, 1929), pp. 1, 26.

origin in the upward price movement of copper and the copper stocks at the crest of the boom.

On September 4 most stock prices receded in what was regarded as an overdue "technical correction." General Motors and Radio Corporation moved against the day's trend, however, the former gaining more than 3 points and the latter more than 10. The strength in Radio, which brought its price up to 108½, was considered something of a sensation, for the stock had gained almost 14 points in three days of trading. One small cloud did appear on the market's bright horizon, however, in the form of a rumor that the Bank of England might raise its discount rate.

In the early afternoon of September 5, following a general rise in the early part of the trading session, a wave of urgent selling struck the market. The day's volume of transactions was the largest since the severe break late in March. This sudden burst of selling apparently was caused by Roger Babson's speech that day at the annual National Business Conference at Babson Park, Massachusetts, in which he observed ". . . sooner or later a crash is coming which will take the leading stocks and cause a decline of from 60 to 80 points in the Dow-Jones Barometer."[4]

---

[4] *New York Herald-Tribune* (September 6, 1929), p. 9. According to this source, Mr. Babson had given the same warning at each of the two preceding conferences. A financial writer for the *Herald-Tribune,* in a paragraph headed "Well Timed," commented caustically on this prediction and at the same time provided an example of the bullish emotionalism that could be read between the lines of many reporters and commentators of the times: "If 'Wolf, wolf!' is cried with sufficient persistence the time will arrive eventually when the warning will have been justified. A New England prognosticator, who has been bearish on the market for two years, made a speech yesterday in which he complained again that stocks were too high, and during the afternoon at least he saw some liquidation that must have been soothing to his harried soul." *Ibid.,* p. 28.

About a year later, in recapitulating the panic in the *New Republic,* Burton Rascoe wrote; "Meanwhile one guesser, Roger Babson, who had gained a vast reputation for prophecy by hollering 'Panic' in the summer of 1929 . . . made another bid for fame as a prophet by predicting in September of this year [1930] a rapid business recovery." "The Grim Anniversary" (October 29, 1930), p. 288.

On the same page of the *Herald-Tribune* that carried the account of Mr. Babson's speech was the report of a rejoinder, apparently quickly elicited, from one of the elite of the academic world. Although not quoting directly, the article said: Stock prices are not too high and Wall Street will not experience anything in the nature of a crash, is the opinion of Professor Irving Fisher, of Yale University, one of the nation's leading economists and students of the market. Both of these prophets of the market place would be heard from again in October, at a critical juncture in the course of the market.

On Friday the sixth the market turned strong, but it did not fully recover the preceding day's loss. Although brokers' loans had been reported the day before at a new high level, the call loan rate had declined to 6 per cent. Some brokers said that investment trusts were still adding to their holdings, and that most stocks appeared to be going into strong hands. General Motors was up 5 points, although it was still well below its high for the year, and Radio Corporation of America rose 11 points to 113¾. On Saturday, despite conflicting price movements, some issues made new highs.

As prices recovered, Mr. Babson's gloomy prediction of the market's future was ridiculed, though it still contributed to a certain uneasiness here and there: "Many observers felt that the market's sensitiveness to the Babson prophecy indicated an impaired position. . . ."[5] That the market was vulnerable—although how much so no one could judge—would become more apparent as it was assailed by various items of bad news as the days went by. After reaching a new low for the month on September 10, the market was alternately strong and weak, with some days on which irregularity prevailed, until the eighteenth.

During the middle part of September some commentators noted a considerable amount of pessimism among professional

5 *Wall Street Journal* (September 10, 1929), p. 1.

traders. They remarked that there seemed to be more bearish people in the Wall Street brokerage office than there had been for a long time. Some thought that a good "shakeout" was overdue. The short interest was said to have become much larger than it had been a month before, and there were rumors that several bear pools had been formed to do some short-selling in certain "special situations." Such comments were countered by bulls who claimed that an attempt was being made to "talk the market down." The weekly market letters sent out by various brokerage houses were mixed in sentiment. One ascribed the decline in the price of U. S. Steel to 28 points below its high for the year to the determination of some large banking interests to prevent "a runaway market in the stock."

Buying by out-of-town brokerage offices was especially heavy, and one of the largest New York firms reported a record high in the number of odd-lot transactions handled. A peculiarity in the market for some of the leading issues was the unusually large spread, sometimes several points or more, between the "bid" and the "asked" prices at the trading posts on the floor of the Exchange. Some analysts believed that the high level of the stock price averages, which represented mostly the more actively traded issues, was deceptive and that sustained strength in a few score of "favorites" concealed extensive liquidation. They pointed out that many listed stocks had lagged behind the averages and some were far below their best prices of the year.

On September 18 and throughout the morning of the nineteenth a rally was led by the bellwether of the market, U. S. Steel, which at its high for the two-day period showed a gain of 13½ points. When, on the twentieth, Charles E. Mitchell, head of the National City Bank and dubiously renowned for his intervention in the call loan market the preceding March, sailed for Europe to spend a month's vacation with Mrs. Mitchell in London and Paris, he told the reporters who saw him off, "There is nothing to worry about in the financial situation in the United States." On that same day aggressive selling upset the market, weakness in U. S. Steel, General Electric, and Radio Corporation of America being particularly evident. This setback was variously ascribed to "an attack of nerves," to the "staleness" of the market, whatever that meant, and to a "raid" by emboldened bears.

Reports that the London market had sold off sharply and that a large British corporation was in serious financial difficulty received little attention, yet this was the start of an outpouring of bad news from England that was to add to the burden upon American securities markets. The Hatry defalcations were just coming to light, and as the magnitude of their repercussions became evident, a growing wave of liquidation swept the London Stock Exchange and other British markets, some of which carried over to the markets in New York and other financial centers.

Hatry, who was first and last a promoter of corporations and big deals, had suffered serious losses in his earlier ventures in high finance during the first half of the decade. In 1925, however, he had begun a comeback that by 1929 was sensational, at first because of his apparently magnificent success as a financier and later because of the magnitude of the swindle to which he resorted in order to support the complex structure of large corporations and their subsidiaries that he had pieced together. As his financial difficulties increased, he simply issued more bonds and shares in companies under his influence, forging the certificates so as to make them appear genuine. On these he borrowed money while keeping the markets for the securities active with "wash sales," purchases and sales that more or less evened out, but which made his false collateral seem highly liquid.

As the trickery was discovered and the securities of the corporations involved were removed from trading on the London Exchange, many individuals, suffering losses estimated around

$50 million or more, were obliged to sell other securities to meet their obligations. Soon the adverse effect of this scandal was communicated throughout the world.[6] Although this episode was not a fundamental cause of the panic developing in the United States, it was one of several "last straws" that helped to accelerate the decline in prices.

On Saturday, September 21, after absorbing a carry-over of selling from the preceding day, the market strengthened somewhat. On Monday the twenty-third, however, renewed selling forced various leading stocks to new low prices for the month, after which a considerable part of the day's losses were recovered. On the twenty-fourth a rally in the morning was followed by such a sharp break in prices in the afternoon that the Dow-Jones industrial average showed a loss of more than 6 points for the day.

On the morning of the twenty-fifth urgent selling marked prices down with a rapidity that almost demoralized those who watched from moment to moment. But in the afternoon, as the force of the selling was offset by aggressive buying, a rally set in that recovered much of the morning's loss. The day's transactions approximated 5 million shares, and the number of issues in which trading took place was 868, the largest on record up to that time.

Some of the selling had apparently been set off by news of

[6] To investors, bankers, and brokers, just the idea that the securities they might buy or hold as collateral could be forged, and therefore worthless, must have been profoundly disturbing. The high standard of integrity in the London financial community, as well as New York and other financial centers, permitted the mechanism of the organized markets to operate easily and quickly; the good faith of every member of the Stock Exchange was presumed to be back of every transaction. Accordingly, "so that no loss shall fall on the public as a result of the Hatry crash," members of the London Stock Exchange decided, on January 15, 1930, "to create a $5,000,000 subscription fund for the purpose of buying up all the worthless shares and delivering the good shares . . . to buyers." Many brokers who were in no way connected with the situation subscribed substantial amounts. *New York Times* (January 16, 1930), p. 2. © 1930 by The New York Times Company. Reprinted by permission.

further liquidation in the London market and false rumors that some New York brokerage houses had failed. Somewhat unfavorable reports of industrial activity and a rumor, confirmed the next day, that the Bank of England would raise its discount rate, were augmenting influences. The sudden sharp upturn in the afternoon was ascribed to large buying orders thrown hastily into the market by banking interests that were determined to keep the market in balance. Although this support centered on U. S. Steel, Anaconda Copper, General Electric, Radio Corporation of America, Standard Oil of New Jersey, United Aircraft, and certain other leaders, it imparted strength to many lesser issues as well. Some buying also by "bargain-hunting" investment trusts also was believed to have come into the market toward the close.

Another "last straw" forcing the decline was the increase in the discount rate of the Bank of England from 5½ to 6½ per cent on September 26. This action not only confirmed the propriety of the rise in the New York Federal Reserve Bank's rate in August, but it also revealed that the world's most respected central banking authorities recognized the seriousness of the worldwide credit maladjustment. An immediate purpose in raising the rate was to halt the outflow of gold from England to France, Germany, and the United States.

Almost at once the central bank rates were raised in Austria, Denmark, Norway, Sweden, and the Irish Free State. Before this action, the rate of the Federal Reserve Bank of New York had been half a percentage point higher than that of the Bank of England, and its influence on the general pattern of interest rates in the United States had made the New York money market a point of attraction for foreign funds. The Bank of England, however, was now reversing the situation in order to attract liquid capital away from New York and other financial centers, just at a time when the seasonal need for funds in the United States was increasing rapidly.

Other adverse developments late in September were a decline in the price of wheat to a new seasonal low; reports of reductions in steel production, automobile manufacturing, and other industrial activity; and the announcement late in the day on the twenty-sixth of an increase of $192 million in brokers' loans for the week ending September 25, bringing them to a new high of $6.8 billion. The increase in such loans was surprising in view of the decrease in stock prices, the usual supposition being that brokers' loans would decline along with a decline in the stock market. That they had not could be interpreted as meaning that stock was passing from stronger hands into weaker.

The recovery during the afternoon of the twenty-fifth continued on into the twenty-sixth, the Bank of England's action seeming to have no immediate effect on prices. On the next day, Friday the twenty-seventh, however, the market declined on heavy selling that was attributed primarily to news of the increase in brokers' loans. This break in prices was intensified by short selling and stop-loss sales. At the close, the Dow-Jones industrial average was down 11 points. On Saturday the market sold off sharply and then recovered to show a moderate gain for the day, but on Monday the thirtieth the decline resumed on reduced volume, numerous issues losing several points or more. The closing averages on this last day of September were the lowest for the month.

Just at this time Arthur Cutten, one of the most rampant bulls that Wall Street would ever see, famed for his enormously profitable speculations in both commodities and common stocks, casually remarked that "$12,000,000,000 in brokers' loans would not be unduly large." He added, with all the authority of his multimillions, that he was "a bull on stocks" because he was "a bull on the United States." This was neither original nor especially informative, and as the *New York Times* observed: "It was the commonplace of argument a year or two before the panic of 1907."[7] Mr. Cutten's comment was merely a hackneyed variant of a cliché attributed to the elder J. P. Morgan long before: "Don't sell America short." But many, no doubt, who wanted to believe in a perpetually rising stock market found in it a rationalization that suited them. They would have been better off to have heard the remark once made by a well-known floor trader to a young man who asked his opinion of the market: "This is a great country, but my advice to you is to forget that fact once in a while."[8]

By the end of September it was apparent that the stock market was suffering something more than "an attack of nerves." Although many professional commentators were less outspokenly bullish, and whereas signs of bewilderment could be detected in some of their opinionations, belief in the market's "manifest destiny," the inevitability of "a happy outcome," and a "silver lining" for the clouds that had gathered were still implicit in what many of them wrote and said. Toward the end of the month some brokerage house letters suggested that both the foreign and domestic liquidation and the resulting distress selling from other accounts was about completed, that the better quality stocks were "under accumulation," and that the heavy selling had greatly strengthened the market's technical position. It was supposed to be a favorable sign that the decline had evoked comparatively few margin calls. Little of the selling, apparently, had come from the investment trusts, which were believed to be adding, on balance, to the higher quality stocks in their portfolios, although the large paper profits that many of them had accumulated were considerably reduced by the September drop in prices.

Somewhat oddly, a source of hope for many who had decided to wait out the decline was the seasonal tightness of the money

7 *Ibid.* (October 1, 1929), p. 36.

8 Albert W. Atwood, "Men and Markets," *Saturday Evening Post* (April 27, 1929), p. 100.

market, which might last through October and have a temporarily bad effect on the market. Although the flow of funds to England that had set in was increasing this strain, it was expected to diminish after September 30, which marked the end of both a monthly and a quarterly settlement period there. For these and other reasons many speculators supposed—or hoped—that the break in the market on the twenty-seventh was a culminating movement, as sharp declines sometimes are, and that it would be followed by a general recovery, or at least a rapid and extensive rally. It did not prove to be that, however.

Buyers no longer had to "reach" for stocks. There was no need to bid up prices to get them. In fact, a buyer got whatever shares he wanted if he placed his order at a price somewhat below the market and waited. Some brokers even recommended that their customers lighten holdings whenever the market rallied. Various commentators observed the market's lack of "snap and buoyancy," the "tired" and "disgusted" nature of some of the selling, the anxiety of the boardroom crowds, the absence of bull pool activity, and the weakness that had developed in the "blue chips." One reporter quoted the words of a boardroom trader as representing the thoughts of many others: "Well, if they won't support Steel, they won't support anything!" Another averred that the market had lost "many of its recent friends."

A plain and disconcerting fact; one which could not be rationalized away, was that during the final week of September many issues listed on the New York Stock Exchange fell to new low prices for the year. During this extended reaction from the high point registered at the beginning of the month, the market closed at successively lower levels for the Dow-Jones industrial and railroad averages on September 4, 5, 10, 12, 23, 24, 25, 27, and 30. The industrial average also closed at new low levels for the month on September 20 and 21.

OCTOBER 1–23 ·

The writers of two columns that appeared periodically in the *Wall Street Journal* evidently were free to express their individual opinions, which at this time represented contrasting views of the market situation. Early in October, in the column "Broad Street Gossip," allegiance to the long bull market was stoutly maintained:

> Every time the market has a bad slump the bears start inflation talk.... In years to come you will hear inflation talk when some stocks are selling for ten times their present worth and brokers' loans are many billions higher than they are now.
>
> .   .   .   .
>
> Some traders selling stocks short and claiming the bull market is over, forget they said the same thing on every one of the half dozen or more big reactions the market has had over the last five years.
>
> .   .   .   .
>
> Don't get too bearish on the shares of the well managed, growing companies. Wise traders do not sell stocks after a decline running from 20 to 100 points or more.
>
> .   .   .   .
>
> The view of one large house is that the recent break makes a firm foundation for a big bull market in the last quarter of the year.[9]

In "Abreast of the Market," however, a caution that reflected the widely developing apprehension was clearly apparent. Of the rally that began on October 5 it said:

> Sentiment is cautious. . . . Leading observers were advising followers to take advantage of further advances to reduce long

[9] *Wall Street Journal* (October 3, 1929), p. 2; (October 5, 1929), p. 2; (October 8, 1929), p. 2.

positions because of the belief that the market again would suffer from bear attacks and liquidation.

. . . .

Most observers are recommending the use of rallies to reduce long holdings because they anticipate another set back in the next few days. However, at the moment no one is looking for any decided break. . . .

. . . .

A large number of conservative observers are strongly advising followers to accept profits on stocks purchased on a scale during the breaks.

. . . .

Conservative observers continue to urge customers to reduce long holdings on all rallies. Many believe that the market is not yet in a position where the groundwork can be laid for a new advance, and for that reason they are looking for irregularly lower levels from time to time.[10]

On Tuesday, October 1, prices moved downward throughout most of the trading session, many stocks reaching new lows. In the final hour, however, following the announcement of an unexpected and substantial increase in the rate of steel operations, there was some hasty short-covering and other aggressive buying of stocks. Although this reversal of a downward trend in steel production that was being taken for granted even within the industry proved to be only an aberration, it led many people to assess the business situation more favorably. Some commentators explained it as reflecting an increased demand from the railroads for steel rails, and the anticipation of an increase in their buying of new cars and locomotives, which, it was supposed, would more than offset the decline in demand for steel from automobile manufacturers and others.

[10] *Ibid.* (October 7, 1929), p. 14; (October 9, 1929), p. 17; (October 23, 1929), p. 15.

The upturn was extended to Wednesday, October 2, with gains in various issues that nevertheless failed to hold until the close. This rally, such as it was, could only be described as "feeble," in view of the extensive decline that had preceded it.

That the bullish enthusiasm of the market's followers had been tempered by the month of declining prices was humorously indicated in "Broad Street Gossip":[11]

In the last few weeks bull tips have been selling at a discount. . . .

. . . .

. . . in one of the super barbershops in Wall Street Wednesday—twenty barbers, four manicurists, and three bootblacks—and not a market tip in the crowd.

Some technicians who had observed the market under many different conditions held that a vigorous and substantial recovery was improbable until a further sharp selloff on heavy volume brought the downward movement to a climax. On Thursday and Friday, October 3 and 4, the market experienced a severe decline. Losses of from 5 to 10 points were widespread throughout the list, and there were others of from 10 to 25 points or more. Again the weakest speculators, many of them "small fry," were forced to liquidate part or all of their margined holdings. During the two days, the Dow-Jones industrial average lost more than 19 points, and the railroad average almost 6 points. Because the decline occurred on a very large volume of transactions, it had the appearance of being the selling climax that the more astute and patient were awaiting. And in the last few minutes on Friday, some of the more heavily traded issues did make a moderate recovery.

On Saturday the market rebounded, many of the opening prices well above those at Friday's close. In heavy trading during the remainder of the short session prices advanced rapidly,

[11] *Ibid.* (October 5, 1929), p. 2.

with many large gains throughout the list. At one time the ticker lagged forty minutes behind transactions on the floor of the Exchange. This turnabout was the swiftest and most dramatic that many stock watchers had ever witnessed. The Dow-Jones industrial average regained more than 16 points, and the railroad average regained almost 3 points.

During most of this first week of October, the question of whether the figure for brokers' loans, to be reported after the close of the market on Thursday, would show a substantial decrease was considered of major importance. A general belief that as prices declined stock was being transferred from thinly margined accounts to those where they would be secured by larger margins or held outright—that on balance stock was going from weak holders to stronger ones—caused widespread expectation of a significantly lower total for brokers' loans. By Thursday morning, October 3, however, this expectation had changed to fear that possibly such loans had increased. It had become widely known that the borrowings of several large Wall Street firms were greater than ever before. It was probably this fear that caused the severe break in prices that began on this morning. The announcement after the close that brokers' loans had increased by $43 million to a new high of $6,804 million, about $2,000 million above the total twelve months before, probably helped to accelerate the decline on Friday.

Throughout October and thereafter, the rate of interest on call loans was not an adverse influence on the market, as it had been during the brief but marked reactions earlier in the year. Although short-term funds continued to flow to England, as indicated by the strong market for pounds sterling, and the New York city banks refrained from adding to the credit available for stock market purposes, enough domestic funds were being offered from other sources to keep the call money rate comparatively low. Part of these came from corporations in strong cash positions, and part from wealthy people, some of whom had probably been liquidating their stock holdings. Thus from 10 per cent on October 1, the call loan rate declined to 5 per cent on the ninth, its lowest point since August 17, 1928. Although the rate fluctuated somewhat thereafter, it did not go high enough to be one of the proximate causes of the crisis that was developing. In fact, the easing of this rate to what seemed a modest figure was a deceptive influence of considerable magnitude, because it reassured the multitude who knew that panic conditions in the past had been closely associated with extreme "tightness" in the money market and extremely high rates for call loans.[12]

Early in October unfavorable attention was directed at Wall Street by the American Bankers' Association, which at its convention in San Francisco adopted a resolution that the Federal Reserve Board investigate the whole situation involving brokers' loans. The president of the association, asserting that many banks were overloaned, warned of the grave danger inherent in the massive use of credit for stock speculation. At about the same time, in England, Chancellor of the Exchequer Snowden laid the blame for financial troubles in Europe on the "orgy of speculation" in New York.

More palatable to the bullish contingent were scattered comments of optimistic import, such as that which appeared in *Dun's Review & Modern Industry*: "Nothing has occurred to indicate that widespread trade recession is under way, and statistics of railroad freight traffic show, week after week, that distribution of merchandise remains at a notably high level."[13] Reports that some corporations had been buying in their own

[12] The call loan rate was as high as 1½ per cent per day in the panic of 1873. It reached 3 per cent per day during the panic of 1884. In 1890 and 1899 the rate touched 180 per cent per annum, and in 1905 and 1907 it rose as high as 125 per cent. Margaret G. Myers, *The New York Money Market*, Vol. I (New York: Columbia University Press, 1931), p. 279.

[13] (October 5, 1929), p. 1.

stock at "bargain prices" were considered encouraging. One corporation was said to have acquired 100,000 of its shares with the intention of reselling them to its employees.

The strength of the rally that began on October 5 caused some brokerage firms to change the purport of their market letters from somber caution to renewed optimism. The rally was ascribed to both an "oversold" condition and the support of unnamed financial leaders and institutions that supposedly feared an adverse effect of falling stock prices on the generally prevailing high level of business activity. Some pool managers and other large traders were known to have taken advantage of the lower prices to "average down" the cost of their holdings, and this was considered reassuring. In spite of the decline that had occurred, the stock price averages at the end of the first week in October were still well above what they had been early in 1929.

In the period from October 5 through October 15 the market stabilized. The brisk rally that had begun on Saturday the fifth continued through most of the following Monday, with spectacular gains in a dozen or more leading stocks. On Tuesday, although some of the market leaders sold off, a large miscellany of other stocks moved upward. On Wednesday many stocks sold off, but some recovery appeared as the rate on call loans declined. In the remaining two trading days of that week, Saturday being a legal holiday, prices advanced—some quite markedly on Thursday, with strength in U. S. Steel and other steel stocks, as well as some of the railroad stocks, giving the appearance of "important buying." The continuation of the rise on Friday appeared to have been restrained by the announcement that the week's decline in brokers' loans had been $91 million, a much larger reduction having been expected. The general strength of the market late in the week was ascribed in part to the announcement that Secretary of the Treasury

Mellon "would remain with the Hoover administration to 1933, at least."[14]

On the following Monday, October 14, prices declined irregularly, with public utility stocks off from a few to several points. On Tuesday, "cross currents" of buying and selling caused a confusion of price changes and a generally downward appearance for the market as a whole. Steel and utility stocks were weak.

These were days of uncertainty mixed with renewed hope. Many who were still bullishly inclined thought that they saw in the market's action clear evidence that the long decline had spent itself. Some chartists expected an early recovery of at least 25 per cent of the decline. Others believed that stocks would regain about half their losses, after which further developments would indicate the direction of the major trend. There was talk of a "traders' market" and of the prospect of an "early winter upswing." Some brokerage houses, taking the optimistic point of view, listed in their market letters many stocks that they declared could be bought as bargains. Other, more pessimistic firms that advised their customers to "take profits" on any showing of strength nevertheless warned of the dangers in selling stocks short. Already, however, there was a substantial short interest, and the demand to borrow half a dozen or more important stocks for short-selling purposes was said to be very large.

Highly significant was the comment of one large operator who, noting the risk of obtaining a poor price if one sold stock "at the market," observed that stocks were "easy to buy" and "difficult to sell." Even more significant to experienced and objective traders during this period of comparative calm was the relatively small volume of transactions. After the quick, preliminary rebound in prices, trading had diminished to 2.8 million shares on October 14, the smallest volume of business

14 *Wall Street Journal* (October 12, 1929), p. 2.

for a full day on the New York Stock Exchange since July 30. At times the ticker simply halted while its operators waited for reports of transactions to be brought from the trading posts. This dullness was attributed to both the religious holiday being observed by many traders and the World Series baseball game that afternoon. On the following day, which was the last of this brief respite for the market and its bullish followers, volume was only moderately larger.

What may have seemed at first a comparatively small item of news soon had a markedly adverse influence on the public utility sector of the market. This was the announcement after the close on Friday, October 11, that the Massachusetts Departpartment of Public Utilities refused to permit the Edison Electric Illuminating Company of Boston, whose stock had risen from $280 to $440 during the year, to split its stock four shares for one, changing the par value of each share from $100 to $25.00. The five commissioners, who were unanimous in their decision, held that such a division of the stock would lead "many innocent people" to pay high prices for the new shares in expectation of higher dividends, but that fair rates charged the public for the company's services could not make higher dividends possible. Adding to the force of this blow was the initiation by the commissioners of a rate inquiry, their premise being that if a utility stock with a par value of $100 was selling well above $400 a share, the company was probably using its franchise monopoly situation to extract unreasonably high rates from its customers, most of whom had no alternative to the use of its services.

The more the stock-trading public considered this development, the more serious it appeared to be. The outcry of some public utility stockholders that this was "socialism" and that the commission's attitude was "Bolshevistic" probably reflected a disquieting realization that other utility commissions throughout the country would be emboldened or obliged to take much the same attitude, possibly reducing rates and generally limiting utility earnings more strictly. Consequently, on the following Monday Edison Electric shares fell to around 300 on the Boston Stock Exchange, where they were traded, and public utility stocks in the New York markets and elsewhere also declined. In the general break in the market that was to follow, public utility stocks were to suffer the most. Inasmuch as a marked rise in utilities, stimulated by many stock split-ups, had been one of the dramatic features of the year, the ruling by the Massachusetts Department of Public Utilities found that sector of the market especially vulnerable. And the adverse psychological effect seemed to be communicated to other sectors.

At this mid-October juncture, an analytical review of the market's action during the year and at certain times farther in the past was made by Colonel Leonard P. Ayers, a well-known economist, in the *Business Bulletin* of the Cleveland Trust Company. After calling attention to the very large amount of undistributed new securities issues that had been accumulating in much the same way as they had before the debacle of 1903, he undertook to show that during 1929 the apparent strength of the stock market had been deceptive in some important respects, and that the decline extending through the first week of October was, when viewed historically, of major significance:

> In a real sense there has been underway during most of this year a sort of creeping bear market that has been hidden by the fact that many of the utility stocks, and some of the rails, and certain other issues, have advanced so much as to carry the figures of most of the well-recognized stock averages upward to new high levels from month to month until the sharp decline of September began.
>
> This has been a highly selective market. It has made new high records for volume of trading, and most of the stock averages have moved up during considerable periods of time

with a rapidity never before equaled. Nevertheless a majority of the issues have been drifting down for a long time before the recent break began. Many of these have been the preferred stocks which have suffered along with bonds because the public did not prefer them.

Important declines in stock prices have occurred during the Autumn months in 28 of the past 30 years, usually in September and October. In those typical Autumn recessions the average decline in the Dow Jones industrial averages has been something more than nine percent. The decline from the first of September through the first week of October this year has amounted to 14 per cent. In the panic of 1903 the fall decline was 23 per cent, in that of 1907 it amounted to 28 per cent, and in the post-war reaction of 1919 it was 16 per cent. In all other years it has been less than this year.[15]

Throughout its long advance the bull market had been subject from time to time to major reactions, severe and sometimes abrupt, that corrected an "overbought" condition and prepared the way for a resumption of the upward trend. But every reversal had ended at a level well above the low point of the preceding one. The decline from early September to mid-October, however, was different from these. Each substantial price recession was succeeded by a rally that did not "follow through" to a level close to or above the peak of the preceding rally. At times, after a decline, prices did little more than stabilize before the decline was resumed. The very evident lack of sustained recuperative power in the market was a warning, but the multitude could not bear to acknowledge it. The shrewd and sophisticated, however, recognized it and acted to protect themselves.

Only long memories could recall the last major downturn, in the spring of 1920; once again the market by its action was

[15] The Cleveland Trust Company, Cleveland, Ohio, *Business Bulletin* (October 15, 1929).

saying that a great boom had ended. From mid-October onward the downward movement of prices accelerated in a sweeping decline that carried them to one depth after another.

On Wednesday the sixteenth the market turned quite weak. Prices quickly receded as buying orders were withdrawn and distress selling appeared. Leading the decline were such important issues as U. S. Steel, American and Foreign Power, General Electric, Consolidated Gas, and Western Union. Some commentators referred to this setback as a "secondary reaction," implying that it was to be expected in the usual course of events following the preceding marked decline and subsequent rally. Instead of being a mere reaction, however, it was the resumption of a trend that before long carried prices to a new low level. On October 17 the market broke further, but made a rapid recovery toward the close.

Despite the adverse weekly report on brokers' loans, which showed them to have increased by $88 million to within $3 million of their record high, the rally continued into the morning of Friday the eighteenth. It was soon halted, however, by heavy selling, some of which was coming, evidently, from large accounts. No substantial support appeared, and losses for the day in quite a number of stocks ranged from 3 to 12 points. As on many recent days, the final hour of the trading session was the worst. One grim trader remarked that the "creeping bear market" had changed to a "leaping bear market." This was more than borne out in the two-hour session on Saturday the nineteenth, as more selling engulfed the market, carrying leading stocks down by from 5 to 18 points in "a spasm of liquidation" that made front page news in many evening and Sunday newspapers. Toward the end of the session a small rally developed, due in large part to short covering by floor traders and other professional operators. The volume of trading was so large— 3.5 million shares—that the ticker ran on for nearly an hour and a half after the close.

Even before this severe extension of the decline many people had felt the pinch of lower prices and impaired margins, especially those with few funds in reserve and those who held stocks that had declined more than the averages. Here and there people began to draw on their savings accounts and rifle their safe deposit boxes for the wherewithal to hold on, at least until an upward reaction would let them sell to better advantage. The inevitable upturn that would rescue the beleaguered became a fond hope and a continual subject of conversation in the boardrooms. There was much expectant talk of "organized support" and "a period of consolidation," of "bargain buying," of covering when the bears were put to flight, and of a resumption of buying by the popular new financial titans, the investment trusts.

The powerful banking interests that sponsored many of the leading stocks were apparently reluctant to bid aggressively for them, as continuing weakness in these stocks attested. Such support was believed to have been attempted on the morning of October 19 and then abandoned because of the "avalanche" of selling. The buying power of bargain hunters who placed orders below prevailing prices was readily absorbed from day to day as prices dropped. Brief rallies failed to encourage aggressive bidding, for on each small upturn some discouraged shareholders seized the slight advantage to "unload." Presently, shares of stock that had been bought as bargains earlier in the decline fell back upon the market to augment the "distress selling." The bears, far from being inclined to take profits and retreat, became bolder, extending their lines of short sales; and some once-chronic bulls, including smaller traders, tried their hand at selling short. Whatever buying was done by the investment trusts was not much help to the market. Their managers suffered the same anxiety that assailed almost everyone else.

Further evidence of a decline in business activity had appeared, especially in steel and automobile production; and some third-quarter corporation reports showed a reduction in earnings. None of these developments, however, was of sufficient magnitude to account for the decline in stock prices. It was common knowledge that many new stock offerings were being postponed, and that there was a glut of "undigested" securities recently offered to the public. But these conditions were more the effects of the market's action than possible causes of it.

While the stock market was falling, two other important financial markets were on the rise. Bonds were in great demand, especially those of the government and the higher grade bonds of corporations and municipalities. The dollar exchange rates for various European currencies also had increased, the rate for British pounds reaching its highest level in more than a year. Some investors were switching their funds to the safest possible securities, and foreign capital that had been lured to New York by high interest rates was being called home.

During the boom the bulls had had their own way with the market most of the time. Now the bears were having their turn. A considerable short interest had developed, and individual bears and pools of bear operators were hammering away at stock prices wherever they believed them vulnerable. On each rally and also as prices receded they sold borrowed stock in increasingly large amounts. As the decline accelerated, many people believed that the privilege of selling stocks short was being abused. But by those who understood it, short selling was generally recognized as a useful and often appropriate kind of market operation. Those who borrowed shares of stock in order to sell them, putting up cash as security, eventually had to repurchase and return them to the lender, who meanwhile received interest on the funds deposited with him. Sometimes an extra charge or "premium" had to be paid for borrowing stock.

The most notorious bear operators as the panic developed were Jesse L. Livermore, once known as "the boy plunger," and William H. Danforth, a Bostonian. Other large operators on the short side of the market avoided publicity, for the public regarded bears as predatory and ruthless. Two and a half years later, when the Senate Banking and Currency Committee was investigating stock exchange practices, much more became known about the bears and their short-selling activities, both during the panic and during the subsequent long decline in stock prices.

During the panic, those who sold short were likened to such market marauders as Jim Fiske, Daniel Drew, and Jay Gould, who in the post-Civil War period had upset the market with their "raids." But this comparison was hardly apt. When the stock market was a much smaller affair a few strong bears probably could influence its course, at least briefly; but in the vast market of 1929, when their judgment was right, they merely hastened the decline that was inevitable in the issues they chose to attack.[16]

Dislike of the professional bears, which grew to hostility and venomous hatred, tended to conceal the fact that their operations, when they covered their short sales at lower prices, had a stabilizing effect on the market. Many of them were shrewd, and all were courageous. They had learned during the boom the danger of being "caught short" of stocks and "squeezed," perhaps ruinously, by an upturn in the market. Always the bears were aware that they had to buy back, no matter what the price might become, every share they sold short. An old-fashioned market ditty reminded them that:

> He who sells what isn't his'n
> Must buy it back or go to pris'n.

[16] Richard Whitney, president of the New York Stock Exchange, in a speech made in the autumn of 1930, defended short selling and insisted that its effect on the market had been very much exaggerated: "It is impossible for any individual or group of individuals to buy or sell securities in sufficient volume to affect the whole list." *Outlook and Independent* (October 29, 1930), p. 324.

Declining prices in the autumn of 1929 naturally attracted newcomers to the short side of the market. These "young bears" were discovering how highly profitable short selling could be. Also, this rather uncommon way of trading appealed to some temperaments. Perhaps a psychologist could perceive in their response to it elements of hostility and aggression, cynicism or pessimism; but being right when almost everyone else was wrong was an elating experience. In due time, many of those who sold short would learn that, as an old Wall Street saying has it, "A swelled head is what breaks the bear."

Two powerful Wall Street operators epitomized the bull and bear factions, personifying the forces of demand and supply. They were Arthur W. Cutten, enormously wealthy grain trader who had turned to stocks, believing, apparently, that the sky was the only limit to prices, and the daring Jesse L. Livermore, with his preference for the bear side of the market.

Ironically, Livermore, like many another long-time skeptic of the market place, had finally accumulated a substantial long position almost at the peak of the boom, and apparently he was on the bull side of the market in August and September when his bearish proclivity reasserted itself and saved him from disaster. As he turned to the selling side he undoubtedly perceived the market's underlying softness. This time his testing must have convinced him that prices were going lower, perhaps much lower, for he presssed large blocks of various stocks upon a yielding market, which Cutton and many others were frantically trying to support.

Cutten was as stubborn a bull as Livermore was a determined bear. As the panic developed he insisted repeatedly, in widely publicized statements, that stocks would sell at far higher prices. But from day to day the downward trend eroded his capital and weakened his position, and when in mid-October he was commenting on the "hysterical selling" and the market's bright future, Livermore was making a sensational comeback, boldly attacking the market with large short sales of various stocks that he believed were too high, some of them Cutten's favorites.[17]

The press played up the opposition of their interests, but the conflict, though deadly, was probably impersonal. Cutten, and all the unyielding bulls whom he typified, was on the defensive as the value of his holdings shrank, while Livermore and a comparatively few other bears, some of whom used their paper profits to pyramid their short positions, saw their resources rapidly augmented by every further recession in prices. On October 19 a severe break in the prices of wheat futures on the Board of Trade in Chicago hinted that Cutten and probably some other hard-pressed stock speculators were abandoning long positions in the grain market.

After October 15 the elements of panic were plainly discernible. The panic was, in fact, under way well before the first of the memorable days when it was at its worst. In the decline that followed the market's insubstantial rally early in the month, the deterioration of stock prices was progressive. As more and more margin calls went out, those who could not meet them, or who chose not to, let part or all of their holdings fall upon the market for the financially stronger or bolder to take up. Where accounts were impaired the customers' men telephoned or telegraphed for more margin. The stocks of those who did not respond promptly were sold at the market. This kind of selling, the voluntary sales of others, the bear "raids" on particular stocks, and mounting sales from abroad touched off stop-loss selling orders that had been placed below the market.

Already brokers' employees worked into the evening to keep

[17] In a public statement issued on October 21, Livermore denied that he was the leader of a "large bear pool" that was rumored to have caused the break in prices. He went on to say: "It is very foolish to think that any individual or combination of individuals could artificially bring about a decline in the Stock Market in a country so large and so prosperous as the United States." *Commercial and Financial Chronicle* (October 26, 1929), p. 2619.

up with the day's business, and during the day the Stock Exchange's facilities were sometimes strained beyond their capacity. Usually the volume of transactions was larger when the market was weak, and at such times the stock ticker ran far behind. When prompt reporting of prices was impossible, customers in the brokers' offices could not know what their individual situation was. Although occasional "flashes" from the floor of the Stock Exchange gave the latest prices of only a few leading stocks, at least their trend represented that of the rest of the market and so was something of a guide. When prices were falling, the hectic activity on the floor of the Exchange and the confusion in brokers' offices throughout the country, where bewilderment, apprehension, and sometimes hysteria prevailed, more than hinted of panic.

During these pre-panic days the higher priced stocks were hardest hit. There was marked weakness in the "blue chip" bank stocks and other prominent over-the-counter issues. This was ominous, for such securities were held mainly by those who were financially strongest—investors of large means and the bigger traders. Public utility stocks, many of which had been regarded as prime investment media in September, when they were priced at more than thirty-five times their annual earnings, were now selling, "ex-public imagination," at about twenty-four times earnings.

On Monday, October 21, the market was struck by successive waves of liquidation that carried prices downward until nearly three o'clock, when a strong rally, later ascribed to "organized banking support," set in. The larger losses for the day ranged from 5 to 14 points, except for two high-priced issues: Auburn Auto, which closed at 335, down 40 points, and Commercial Solvents, which closed at 520, down 145 points. These two were volatile issues in which the day's trading was, respectively, only 1,300 and 900 shares, but their losses dramatized the situation.

Again the market had made front-page news. The day's volume of transactions on the New York Stock Exchange—6.1 million shares—was the second largest of the year, having been exceeded only by the 8.2 million shares traded during the severe break on March 26. The 920 issues dealt in set a new daily record. On the New York Curb Exchange, trading exceeded 3.7 million shares, a new record. For an hour and forty minutes after the market had closed the New York Stock Exchange ticker continued to report transactions. That evening, while brokerage house employees were coping with the mass of accumulated paper work, Professor Irving Fisher was assuring the New York Credit Men's Association that stock prices were low and that a serious decline could hardly be expected.

The rally that began just before the close on Monday continued through most of Tuesday the twenty-second, leading stocks showing gains of from 1 to 16 points at the opening. Although it was not made clear which banks or bankers were attempting to stay the decline, or the extent of their operations, some sort of effort was being made, and quickly circulated reports of it brought in buying from the public. Nevertheless, during the last half-hour prices of many important issues fell back, some large gains quickly disappearing. At the close the price level was about where it had been at the beginning of the day. Although the rally had faltered, reports of the day's activity took on an optimistic tone, much stress being placed on the intervention of the unspecified banking interests.

Also helping to revive fading hopes of a substantial recovery were the public statements of various business and financial leaders, including that of Charles E. Mitchell, just returned from Europe, who said he believed that the "decline had gone too far" and that stocks were selling "below their true values." Aloof from the optimists, however, was Roger W. Babson, who telegraphed the United Press "that there was still a bear market and that new lows might be expected after a temporary rally." Many people remembered with dismay the dire prediction, already so well borne out, that Mr. Babson had made and been ridiculed for early in September.

On Wednesday trading began in an undramatic way, with some prices higher than at the preceding day's close. But during the morning a sudden weakness in automobile accessory shares was followed by a general recession in prices that quickly accelerated. By early afternoon a serious break was in process, and the last hour of trading became a debacle in which some 2.6 million shares changed hands. When the market closed most stocks were at or near their lowest prices for the day, as well as for the long period of decline. The over-burdened ticker continued to record transactions for almost an hour and three-quarters after trading had ceased. The largest losses were sustained by such high-priced and volatile issues as Adams Express, which was down 96 points, Auburn Auto, down 77, Commercial Solvents, down 70, J. I. Case, down 46, Otis Elevator, down 43, and Western Union, down 33. Losses of from several to many points in other issues were widespread throughout the list.

The selling came from many directions. A brokerage firm that dealt in more than 300,000 shares on this day noted that it had sold five times as many shares as it had bought for its out-of-town accounts. Various pools were rumored to have given up and thrown their accumulations of stock on the market. Also, rumors that many large operators were having to be "helped out" passed through the boardrooms. Undoubtedly many bears, encouraged by the softness of prices just before the close on Tuesday, had pummeled the market with their short sales, and whatever "covering" the professional short-term traders may have done toward Wednesday's close gave no lift to prices. In the last few minutes of trading large blocks of stock were sold at deep price concessions. The last sale in

Kennecott Copper, for example, was a block of 20,000 shares at 67, off 7 points from the previous sale and down more than 12 points from its high for the day.

This, at long last, was the trading session in which, according to adherents of the Dow Theory, a major bear market was conclusively established. The downward penetration of an important resistance point by the railroad average "confirmed" a similar breakthrough by the industrial average that had occurred on October 21. Of this the *Wall Street Journal* said:

> On the late Charles H. Dow's well known method of reading the stock market movement from the Dow-Jones averages, the twenty railroad stocks on Wednesday, October 23, confirmed a bearish indication given by the industrials two days before. Together the averages gave the signal for a bear market in stocks after a major bull market with the unprecedented duration of almost six years.[18]

Many earnest students of the market's action were deeply impressed by this development, and their reaction to it was probably a greater influence in the following day's decline than most commentators either realized or were willing to admit. These commentators probably were reluctant to dwell upon what it signified to the Dow theorists.

The market received front-page headlines in many evening and morning newspapers. A shocked public had expected at least a moderate rally. Professional explainers tried as best they could to find reasons why the worst must now surely be over: The investment trusts had been waiting for bargain levels and now were ready to buy heavily; leading bankers had conferred but did not believe that their reassuring words were needed; the market had been greatly "oversold" and would have to "snap back"; the Federal Reserve Board would undoubtedly

[18] (October 25, 1929), p. 1.

consider a reduction in the rediscount rate; since business generally was good, although not at quite the high level of a few months ago, a break in the stock market certainly could not go very far.

But the severe damage caused by the day's decline, and the fact that no rally had appeared toward the close to fortify the impaired margin accounts, were portents that could not be overlooked. Even perennial optimists conceded that there would be distress selling the next morning before the market could right itself. Although the decline was already of crisis proportions, this latest—and up to then the most devastating— episode was foreshadowing something far worse to come—the days of complete catastrophe when panic, in all its mad, blind terror, would sweep the exchanges and boardrooms. For most of the stock market professionals and the stock-minded public, though they could not know the future, the night of October 23 must surely have been one of apprehension.

6

The Panic Begins

ON THURSDAY, OCTOBER 24, few speculators and brokers were in a mood to enjoy the "fine fall day." Before ten o'clock that morning brokerage offices everywhere were packed to the doors with anxious or frightened people. Almost every Stock Exchange member was on the trading floor, even the elderly ones who seldom appeared there. Every available employee and extra telephone operators were on hand. A curious public thronged the New York financial district and crowded the galleries of the two major exchanges.

From the opening gong, the volume of trading was heavy. In the first few minutes some very large transactions were recorded on the ticker at prices that showed no particular pattern or trend. Kennecott Copper, which had struck an "air pocket" just before the close on Wednesday, was up 11 points on a 20,-000-share transaction, but this was obviously a readjustment. A 20,000-share block of General Motors showed a loss of seven-eighths of a point. Sinclair Oil was up one-half point on a block of 15,000 shares, and Standard Brands, on a block of 15,000 shares, was up three-eighths of a point.

During the night a vast quantity of both buying and selling orders had accumulated with the brokers, and on the books of the Stock Exchange specialists there were standing orders to buy stock at prices below—some far below—those at the preceding day's close. For the first half hour or so these open orders

119

and some new orders to buy absorbed the selling, and some stocks even made moderate gains. But the selling increased, and as prices dropped they touched off stop-loss orders.

By eleven o'clock the rush to sell had become a mad stampede. Large and small stockholders alike, whose margins were disappearing or were about wiped out, gave up any last frayed hope they may have had and tried either to salvage something from the debacle or avoid being put in debt to their brokers for more than they could pay. Many probably were already thus in debt, and many more would become so during the day. "Sell at the market!" was about all that the beleaguered customers' men could hear, over the telephones and from those who crowded around them. To "get out" regardless of price was the desperate resolve of thousands of these trapped speculators. Many whose accounts a week before had been in a strong condition, but since then had been eroded by the decline, saw them completely wrecked by the precipitous drop. They had to abandon their shrunken holdings for whatever they could get.

"Sell at the market!" was the only effective order that could be given. No one knew where he stood, for the stock ticker was far behind the market. It chattered away as rapidly as its operators on the floor of the Exchange could make it chatter, and the tape with its strictly abbreviated record of transactions glided swiftly through thousands of Translux projectors; but its symbols and numbers could tell only what had happened perhaps an hour before. Whenever prices of a few leading stocks were "flashed" over the bond ticker or the news service teletype, they were far below those being printed on the belated tape.

Late in the morning, as the flood of liquidation overwhelmed what little buying resistance was left, many stocks dropped steeply, with wide gaps between successively lower prices. No buyer was eager to step out into such a storm, and only great price concessions could tempt a bold few to take the stock that was being offered. The situation was worst when, at times, there were no buyers for various important stocks at any price. Confronted with such a vacuum, bewildered brokers, deluged with orders to sell, had to wait helplessly until a bid appeared. These "air pockets" in certain stocks were more terrifying than any other aspect of the panic. They were frightening enough to those who had to sell but could not; they were probably even more so to the bankers and brokers, who realized their effect on the value of the collateral pledged with the banks to secure a large amount of stock market credit. At this point, some banks and brokerage firms, had they been subjected to audit, would probably have been found insolvent.

On the floor of the Stock Exchange frantic brokers, some bedraggled and dazed, others nearing the point of exhaustion, kept grimly on, shouting their offerings and bids. Those who had to sell were doing the best they could to work off the sheaves of orders that breathless page boys rushed to them. On the annunciator boards high up on the north and south walls of the trading area, whereby brokers were called to the telephones, the numbered plates flapped back and forth. The floor was littered with scraps of paper. A steady roar from a thousand shouting brokers could be heard on the street outside. Clamorous spectators crowding the gallery added to the tumult below. That afternoon, and for some time thereafter, the gallery was closed to visitors.

Outside the Exchange a large crowd had gathered: anxious shareholders, curiosity seekers, tourists, riffraff, office workers, and gentry—some hoping for favorable news, others seeming to expect something dire to happen. Although they were orderly enough, the police for a time made it a point to keep them off the steps of the U.S. Subtreasury. Photographers for the newspapers and the newsreels were on the scene.

The whole financial district was a welter of excitement and confusion. Nothing could explain what was happening in the stock market; all that anyone knew was that it had "broken wide open." Thus emotional tension and hysteria favored the propagation of wild rumors that passed from boardroom to boardroom and out across the country with incredible speed: The stock exchanges in New York were about to close, and the Chicago Stock Exchange and others already had done so; brokerage houses and banks were failing; a wave of suicides was sweeping New York. Although such rumors as these were certainly false, no one could know that for certain. Probably many people, especially among the more credulous small speculators, upon hearing one or another of these fevered imaginings, gave up hope and threw their holdings on the market. The hysteria was contagious, and it blocked the critical faculties. To many on that woeful Thursday morning it must have seemed as though a gigantic beast, once amenable to their whims, had turned vicious and was about to destroy them.

Then something happened to change the whole dismal picture. It was well known that at least since October 15 a number of the large banks, acting individually, had attempted with little or no success to support various stocks as the decline proceeded. Probably well before this first day of outright panic banking leaders had discussed among themselves what they might do to ameliorate the situation. Each of them must have been keenly aware of what could happen to the whole financial system if the deluge of selling continued. Quite aside from their own personal concerns—whether they were themselves caught in the trap of speculation or waiting to buy bargains—they realized that immediate, vigorous, and substantial measures were urgently necessary, and that they and the institutions they represented had to take them.

At about noon on October 24 the five most important bankers in the city met at the office of J. P. Morgan & Company,[1] just opposite the Stock Exchange. They were Charles E. Mitchell, chairman of the National City Bank, Albert H. Wiggin, chair-

---

[1] Morgan himself was in London at this time, and coded messages to keep him informed were cabled to him.

man of the Chase National Bank, William C. Potter, president of the Guaranty Trust Company, Seward Prosser, chairman of the Bankers Trust Company, and Thomas W. Lamont, senior partner of J. P. Morgan & Company. This meeting was not meant to be secret, as were some that had been held during other panics, when the bankers had unfavorable facts to conceal from the public. Now there was no lack of confidence in the banks; the panic was still strictly a stock market affair. People knew the worst that had happened there and they feared still worse. Above all, these men of vast financial influence wanted to reassure them, and so as they arrived, one at a time, for their meeting they were glad to attract attention. They wanted the crowd to see them and to let the news go out that the nation's financial leaders were about to confer.

The bankers' dominating thought was to halt the panic. Unless they did so there could be a chain reaction of insolvencies that might topple the strongest financial institutions in New York and throughout the country. The billions of dollars that the banks had loaned to the brokers, and to their own customers also, were represented by paper certificates whose value depended on stock quotations. The brokers owed the banks, and customers owed the brokers. If the market should close that day at the fantastically low level to which it was rapidly descending, with no prices bid for some stocks, many brokers would be in debt to the banks beyond the value of their collateral, and many stockholders would be in the same situation with respect to their brokers. As the bankers knew from the past, the failure of one brokerage firm could cause other failures, and these could start a run of depositors on the banks. If, at the least, the market were stabilized long enough for those who were hardest pressed to find more funds or to liquidate their holdings for an amount sufficient to pay back their borrowings, catastrophe would be averted.[2]

---

[2] The severely cynical criticism voiced later that the bankers had acted only "to save their own skins" was unjust. If they could not save the stock

Even before the twenty-minute meeting had ended and the bankers' spokesman, Mr. Lamont, had made a short statement to the press, a rumor was spreading that they would support the market, and the selling pressure had begun to diminish. Rumor, this time, was correct, although Lamont's equivocal statement to the crowd of reporters that had gathered did not actually confirm it.

> The meeting of the bankers, he said, had been held largely to exchange information on the stock market situation and no plan of concerted action to support the stock market had been agreed upon.
>
> Despite this assertion, Wall Street was convinced that the bankers had agreed to bring to bear upon the market the immense support of their buying power.[3]

---

market and its myriad followers—and they must have hoped that they could—at least they might protect their depositors—their first concern. Beyond the immediately critical problem of the stock market was the fact that an important part of the country's money supply—the currency and checking account deposits that passed from hand to hand—had been derived from stocks pledged for loans at the banks. This helped to support the expansion of industrial and commercial activity that had taken place. By creating deposit credit to finance the purchase of securities the banks had monetized them, making them the basis of a significantly large part of the money-credit structure. That structure would necessarily contract as the shrinkage in stock values forced repayment to the banks.

[3] *New York Times* (October 25, 1929), p. 1. © 1929 by The New York Times Company. Reprinted by permission. The bankers were understandably reluctant to reveal their thoughts and actions to the public. They may have had qualms about using funds entrusted to their care in this way. The money each pledged was supposed to be that of his bank's investment affiliate rather than that of its depositors. Later, the bankers acknowledged that they had acted as a consortium in supporting the market on October 24, and in attempting to do so at certain times thereafter. The group's resources for the purpose were said to have exceeded $240 million; how much of this it actually used was not revealed. A considerable part of the stock the group acquired on October 24 apparently was sold during the rally the following day. At the time, and also later on, statements made for the banking group were evasive and subject to misinterpretation. In mid-January, 1930, when the banks' role in the panic was being reviewed in the press, one financial columnist wrote under the heading "Yarn," "A story printed yesterday purporting to give the 'inside facts' regarding the operations of the banking consortium was said by persons in a position to know to be inaccurate in all its important points." *New York Herald-Tribune* (January 17, 1930), p. 28.

At quarter-past one that afternoon, Richard Whitney, who was known on the floor of the Stock Exchange as a broker for the Morgan interests, walked to the United States Steel post and placed an order to buy 25,000 shares at 205. Not long before the stock had sold at 193½. From there he went to other parts of the floor placing orders with the specialists for large amounts of various other stocks. At the same time other brokers, acting for the bankers, began to bid for stocks. As soon as Whitney placed his order for U. S. Steel, news of this dramatic act was shouted by telephone clerks over their direct wires from the floor of the Exchange to the brokerage houses they served. Already the market had stabilized. A rapid recovery in prices now set in, especially for those stocks known to be favored by the bankers.

	LOW FOR THE DAY	CLOSE	LOSS AT LOW	CHANGE FOR THE DAY
American & Foreign Power	88	97½	24	−14½
American Telephone & Telegraph	245	269	27	− 3
Auburn Auto	190	235	70	−25
Baldwin Locomotive	15	33	20	− 2
Johns Manville	140	170	40	−10
Montgomery Ward	50	74	33¼	− 9¼
New York Central	197	208	13⅛	− 2⅛
Radio Corporation of America	44½	58¼	24	−10¼
U. S. Steel	193½	206	10½	+ 2
Westinghouse	160	185	30	− 5

The bankers' consortium had saved the day, but it was apparent at the close that their efforts had been much more effective in some parts of the market than in others. Accordingly, when the closing gong sounded on the floor of the Exchange, "a chorus of boos, hoots and Bronx cheers" rose from the weary brokers.[4] Though here and there this demonstration may have been due to revived hopes or to sheer relief from tension, these sophisticates of the market place may have sensed how ephemeral the dramatic intervention of the bankers would prove to be. Outside the Exchange, most of the crowd waited on for a while. The police had given up trying to keep people off the steps of the Subtreasury. As nothing exciting seemed likely to happen, the people gradually drifted away.

The Dow-Jones industrial average for October 24 showed a decline of 6.38 points, with the railroad average down 1.78 points. These changes in the averages minimized the extent of the whole market's decline, however, because many of the prices that made up the averages were those of stocks that had been favored by the banking group. The day's volume of trading on the New York Stock Exchange set a new record of 12,894,600 shares, which compared with the previous record of 8,246,700 on March 26. The stock ticker continued to record transactions until eight minutes after seven o'clock that evening. Throughout the day the call money rate was 5 per cent. The ease in the money market and the investment of funds received from the sale of stocks caused bond prices to rise. That afternoon the weekly report on brokers' loans showed a decrease of $167 million, the greatest decrease for one week since December, 1928.

For the cable department of the Western Union Telegraph Company this was the busiest day on record, as communications flashed between the New York financial district and almost every part of the world. Even far out on the Atlantic, on the *Berengaria*, the panic was brought to a multitude of distraught passengers who crowded into the ocean-going brokerage office of M. J. Meehan & Company. There in excited confusion they followed the course of the market as prices were received by radio and chalked on the quotation board.

[4] Jonathan N. Leonard, *Three Years Down* (New York: Carrick & Evans, Inc., 1939), p. 71.

The panicky selling had not been limited to the New York Stock Exchange. On the New York Curb Exchange and all the stock exchanges in the larger cities the blow had fallen with about the same force. Trading on the Curb Exchange set a new record of 6,337,415 shares, which compared with the previous record of 3,715,400 on October 21. The Curb ticker ran until fifty-four minutes past five o'clock. The recovery in the afternoon appears to have been greater on the New York Stock Exchange than elsewhere, owing undoubtedly to the fact that the bankers had centered their buying operations there. The over-the-counter market had been demoralized when the selling pressure was greatest by the impossibility of finding buyers for some stocks at any price, and trading was hampered by the decentralized nature of the market, in which practically all communication between brokers and dealers was by telephone. On the Chicago Stock Exchange, the next largest to the two major exchanges in New York, the break in prices and the recovery followed the same pattern, and the 1,220,000 shares traded set a new record there, too.

On the Curb Exchange, losses in various issues during the morning ranged from 10 to nearly 75 points. The value of some stocks was cut in half. Utilities declined farthest, but they rallied the most vigorously in the upturn during the afternoon. Electric Bond & Share, a favorite of Curb Exchange traders, dropped 21½ points to a low of 91 and then recovered 16½ points. Goldman Sachs Trading Corporation, after losing 19½ points, regained 15 to close at 80. In Cities Service, the volume of trading was enormous. The opening sale was off 3¼ points on a block of 150,000 shares, a record for a single transaction on any stock exchange in the United States, and the 1,151,900 shares of this one stock that were traded during the day also set a record. After declining 14 points from its previous close, it regained 6½ points.

The massive drive for liquidity in the stock market was quickly carried over to the great wholesale commodity markets in Chicago and New York, and from them to all the lesser markets where staple products were dealt in. On the Chicago Board of Trade, frantic selling of wheat futures forced the price down about 12 cents a bushel before a rally cut the loss for the day to about 5 cents. It was rumored that Arthur W. Cutten and other large speculators caught in the stock market crash were disposing of contracts for many millions of bushels in both the Chicago and Winnipeg markets. In the Chicago Wheat Pit confusion was so great that at times brokers attempting to buy and sell found it almost impossible to effect transactions. When news of the bankers' meeting in New York reached the Pit, however, prices turned upward, wheat futures regaining more than half of the morning's losses. Some corn futures showed a gain for the day of more than a cent a bushel. Commodity prices on other exchanges declined and rallied in sympathy with the decline and rally in stock prices, but only in wheat and coffee futures was the loss for the day substantial, the decline in the price of coffee being caused apparently by extensive selling in the Brazilian market. Cotton prices showed fair gains, and cocoa prices showed small gains for the day.

In Washington, the Federal Reserve Board met twice during the day. The first session lasted more than two hours, the Board keeping in close touch with the market situation while the decline in prices was at its worst. It met again from three-thirty to five o'clock, with Secretary of the Treasury Mellon presiding. A critical question was whether it should permit the Federal Reserve Bank of New York to reduce the rediscount rate, which had been raised to 6 per cent two months before. Although the decision against this had been made easier by the sharp recovery, it involved a certain hazard, since Mr. Lamont apparently had been misquoted over the news tickers to the effect that he expected the New York Federal Reserve Bank to reduce the rate, and the general belief that it would do so was presumed to account in part for the vigor of the upturn in stock prices.[5] When, after a long afternoon meeting, the New York bank's spokesman simply said, "No announcement," the banking group, greatly dismayed, met again at the offices of J. P. Morgan & Company.

Whatever reappraisal of the market situation may have been made at this second meeting, other developments apparently offset the public's disappointment at the Federal Reserve's refusal to lower the rediscount rate. While the assurance from the New York Stock Exchange that none of its members was in financial difficulty was helpful, the most important influence in sustaining the recovery, such as it was, for the next two days, was the general attitude of doggedly determined optimism that quickly crystallized. This was partly manufactured and partly a resurgence of the illusion that had fostered the greatest bull market in American history. There was a hopeful, well-intentioned conspiracy of many people to believe—and to make others believe—that dauntless faith and a certain capacity for what must be called rationalization were all that was needed to end the crisis.

Responsible bankers and brokers were not about to "talk the market down" at this critical juncture, with the smell of the morning's fright still in their nostrils. Most brokerage firms sought to reassure their customers, urging them not to sell when that seemed to be the inclination. In the afternoon, the Stock Exchange firm of Hornblower & Weeks took the initiative in calling a meeting of representatives of thirty-five of the most prominent brokerage firms, which together handled more than two-thirds of the Exchange's transactions. They agreed that the worst of the selling was over, and that the market would continue its recovery. They agreed also to make only optimistic statements to their branch offices and customers. Going still

[5] According to the "Broad Street Gossip" column, "At the close 90% of the Street believed that the worst was over and that stocks would not return to their low levels of yesterday." *Wall Street Journal* (October 25, 1929), p. 2.

further in promoting what seemed so good a cause, Hornblower & Weeks placed advertisements in eighty-five newspapers in which they repeated the same general recommendation to buy securities that they had published in June, 1926. It said, in part, "We believe that present conditions are favorable for advantageous investment in standard American securities."

In the newspapers, over the radio, and in the market letters and bulletins, optimism was the dominant note. Most commentators stressed the bankers' support of the market, their infallibility being sometimes strongly implied. A spokesman for the Treasury Department announced that business conditions were sound and that a substantial tax reduction was possible. While Senator Carter Glass blamed the panic largely on "Mitchellism," Charles Mitchell—who had opposed the Federal Reserve Board's tightening credit policy in the spring—said, "I still see nothing to worry about." Colonel Leonard P. Ayers, economist for the Cleveland Trust Company whose market opinions were much publicized, stated that "the stock market probably hit bottom today and a rally tomorrow is in order." Various other prominent people also sought to reassure the nation.

Letters sent out overnight by brokerage firms to their customers averred that "the worst is over," "the reaction was technical," "the market is oversold," "the panic was largely psychological," "now the better grade of stocks are on a sound investment basis," and so on.[6] The consensus now was that the market had been so long "overbulled" and "overbought" that the severe correction just experienced was inevitable. Where those who had retained at least a part of their position in the market congregated, it was in poor taste to be anything other than optimistic. Those who had been forced to sell their holdings were disposed, of course, to think that the decline would continue, but they were also simply confirming the old Wall

[6] Burton Rascoe, "The Grim Anniversary," *The New Republic* (October 29, 1930).

Street maxim: "There's no one so bearish as a sold-out bull."

Because of the tremendous volume of business done by every brokerage house, and because of the confusion, fatigue, "nerves," and errors, a mountain of paper work, some of it complex and exacting, had to be done. Customers wanted reports on their transactions, the stock clearinghouse deadline had to be met, and margin calls had to go out to those whose accounts were impaired. No brokerage firm dared carry its customers beyond the minimum margin point without risking its own solvency. By telegraph, telephone, and special delivery mail the demands were made for more money or collateral. Those who did not respond promptly would be sold out at the market.

Even before this, brokerage employees had been working into the evening; and from the night of the twenty-fourth onward for some time to come, lights would burn all night in many of the office buildings in the financial district as every available worker helped with the tangle of records and accounts in a marathon effort to bring some order out of chaos before the next trading session. Probably 50,000 employees remained at their desks long into the evening and many through the night. They were paid generously during the period of panic, many earning the better part of a month's salary in a week's time. But they worked too because it was expected of them and they recognized the obligation to do so in an emergency.

Some firms kept a nurse on duty for those workers who sickened or fainted. When a clerk succumbed, he or she was revived, allowed to rest a little, and put back to work. Those completely incapacitated were sent home. Food was brought in from nearby restaurants, many of which stayed open until midnight because of the emergency situation. Hotels across the East River and along the Brooklyn waterfront were filled, and extra beds were set up in corridors. In some hotels whole floors were rented by brokerage firms so that their employees could sleep for a few hours. One problem was to prevent those who frequented the local speakeasies from indulging in a drink or two too many when they escaped briefly from the confines of their offices. In the short periods of respite it was difficult to relax taut nerves and weary minds and bodies, but a little alcohol could quickly destroy whatever usefulness remained. According to one brokerage house employee:

> The telegraph operators handling our out-of-town business went without sleep for 30 and 35 hours, time and again. Trays with sandwiches and coffee were passed around every two hours. None of our clerks went home at all during the worst. My brother didn't sleep a wink in 27 hours. He had been working 18 hours a day for weeks, and he was only one of hundreds of clerks. Girls at the adding machines and typewriters fainted at their work. In one odd-lot house 34 keeled over in one afternoon from sheer exhaustion. In another, 19 had to be sent home. . . . Our worst trouble was answering customers who asked for reports on their orders. . . . Nobody knew where he stood. I know we didn't at times. Neither did the banks![7]

A Brief Interval

It was an anxious moment when the market opened on Friday, October 25. As the ticker recorded the first several transactions, however, anxiety changed to relief. The opening prices for many stocks were from one to several points higher than at Thursday's close. There was believed to be a considerable amount of short covering as prices moved higher, and distress selling due to unanswered margin calls was well absorbed. During the day, however, substantial advances in some stocks were offset by declines in others, and some increase in selling pressure toward the close marred the day's recovery. A gain of eleven points in American Bank Note was one extreme among

[7] Edwin Lefevre, "The Little Fellow in Wall Street," *The Saturday Evening Post* (January 4, 1930), p. 7.

the price changes, probably due to the tremendous increase in stock transfers, all of which required new certificates. At the other extreme was a loss of 18½ points in J. I. Case. For the day, the Dow-Jones industrial and railroad averages showed gains of 1.75 points and 1.01 points, respectively.

The hysteria that had pervaded boardrooms across the country on the twenty-fourth all but disappeared on the twenty-fifth. Although the volume of trading (5.9 million shares) was large compared with that of an ordinary day, it was less than half that of the day before. This was regarded as an encouraging sign by all who were looking for encouragement. That the amount of odd-lot purchases was greatly in excess of odd-lot sales seems not to have been considered an unfavorable indication. Many people believed that the market had entered a quiet and perhaps lengthy period of readjustment and slow recovery from the shock it had sustained during the week. And that shock was considerable. The "Detroit crowd," a group of large speculators associated with the fabulously profitable automobile industry, and the "Big Ten," who from various parts of the country operated in the market on an enormous scale, were said to have sustained large losses, some of them having had to seek financial assistance to maintain their market positions.

Thousands of accounts, some that had once been large and many that had always been small, had been closed out by the brokers. One broker, referring to this unpleasant duty, sadly commented: "I was obliged to sell out one of my best friends, for my protection and his. It was the toughest job I ever had to do."[8] Although here and there, on Friday and Saturday, one heard talk of a possible brief period of business contraction, some speculators were already thinking of regaining their losses, and some who had been sold out were finding money with which to re-enter the market. A considerable number of

[8] *New York Times* (October 26, 1929), p. 2. © 1929 by The New York Times Company. Reprinted by permission.

new accounts were being opened, some by newcomers to the market, some by speculators who were changing their brokerage connections.

The stock-trading public had been reassured by the action of the bankers. On Friday George F. Baker, Jr., chairman of the First National Bank of New York, became the sixth member of the consortium, and other bankers had expressed their intention of cooperating with it. By the end of the week it had disposed of a considerable part of the stock accumulated on Thursday. Probably most people understood that the banking group did not intend to maintain a long position in stocks, but that it would be ready to help the market if help were needed. The group met on Friday afternoon to appraise the situation, and then made known the considered opinion of its members that the crisis was over.

The spate of optimistic statements from those in high places continued. President Hoover declared that "the fundamental business of the country, that is production and distribution of commodities, is on a sound and prosperous basis," carefully avoiding any appearance of attempting to predict the future trend of stock prices. The president of the Equitable Trust Company, however, like many others, predicted it boldly and without qualification: "There will be no repetition of the break of yesterday. The market fell of its own weight without regard to fundamental business conditions, which are sound. I have no fear of another comparable decline." A prominent partner in a well-known brokerage firm declared for publication that "the lows made in Thursday's trading will stand for a long time to come." Unlike most of his contemporaries, E. H. H. Simmons, president of the New York Stock Exchange, who was vacationing in Honolulu, refused to comment.[9]

Although spokesmen for the executive branch of the federal government were careful to comment on the break in the stock

[9] *Ibid.*

market in ways that could only be construed as optimistic, some leading senators felt quite differently. The day's sensational developments immediately drew statements from those senators who had long been opposed to the inordinate use of credit for stock speculation. Senator King of Utah proposed an investigation of the Federal Reserve System. Senator Glass repeated his proposal of a 5 per cent tax on stock not held for over sixty days. Others wanted to levy a high tax on stock transfers and to restrict bank lending for stock purchases. Senator King was quoted as saying:

> Gambling in stock has become a national disease. This malady reaches all classes of people, from preachers to stable boys. . . . It was inevitable that a day of reckoning would come and that billions would be lost as the water and hot air were eliminated from hundreds of stock issues. In my opinion there will be further declines as the people begin to learn the facts and to use common sense. There has been not only an inflation in the value of stocks, but in various forms of property. This has resulted in a somewhat fictitious prosperity.[10]

Nevertheless, Senator Edge of New Jersey said resignedly:

> I do not see what the Senate can possibly do to help the situation. The main difficulty is overspeculation and the piling up of immense brokers' loans. It seems almost impossible to place the responsibility for this condition in any one quarter. Congress cannot pass laws to prevent people spending their money.[11]

On Thursday and Friday many members of the Stock Exchange sought to persuade the governing authorities to suspend trading on Saturday, October 26, because of the accumulating

[10] *Ibid.* (October 25, 1929), p. 3.
[11] *Ibid.*

clerical work and the near-exhaustion of their staffs. This was not done, however, for fear of disturbing public confidence just as the market seemed to be righting itself. On Saturday, during the two-hour trading period, transactions totaled 2.1 million shares. Although it was a calm session, prices in general were lower at the close, a considerable number of stocks showing losses of several points. The selling did not appear to be aggressive, but the brokers were still weeding out impaired accounts. The Dow-Jones industrial and railroad averages for the day showed a loss of 2.25 points and 0.19 points, respectively.

On Sunday, Broadway, Wall, Beaver, Broad, Pine, and Williams Streets, ordinarily deserted on this day of rest, were lined with parked cars. Sightseeing buses took in the financial district, their all-knowing guides awing the out-of-town visitors with tales of lost millions. Many restaurants were open for business, and special police details were assigned to the area. The brokers and their employees worked throughout the day, again many of them far into the night. The offices of stock registrars and transfer agents also were fully staffed, endeavoring to catch up on their duties. As the brokerage offices progressed with their work, more impaired margin accounts were revealed.

Sunday gave big traders and ten-share plungers alike time to think or merely to wonder about what the next day's market action would be. The great question in many minds was whether to buy or sell. But those who had received calls for more margin and could not supply it knew what they had to do.

7

The Panic Worsens

OCTOBER 28

THOSE WHO COULD VIEW the market's action in perspective must have realized that the slight gain on Friday and the somewhat larger loss on Saturday, which left the market below Thursday's closing level, might well mean that prices already had rallied as far as they possibly could under the dramatic stimulus of the bankers' intervention. Obscuring such an objective view of the situation, however, was the renewed spirit of confidence which infused the whole population of stockholders generally and speculators in particular. Even many of the very sophisticated probably believed that the predicted, almost promised, support would be evident at the opening on Monday the twenty-eighth, and that then the market would at the very least give some appearance of stability.

Again, in every boardroom in the country customers and staff waited tensely for the first dozen or so quotations to appear on the ticker tape. These would most likely tell what was in store. And they did. With shocked surprise observers saw how very weak the market was. U.S. Steel, which was regarded as the pivotal issue, opened at 202¼, off 1¼ points from its closing price on Saturday. International Telephone & Telegraph was off 3 points, and General Electric, 7½ points. Most other opening prices also were lower, including those of the blue chip stocks that the banking group had supported on Thursday. Some of the more experienced traders, waiting to see which direction the market would take and determined to go with it, already had both buying and selling orders written out and in the hands of the customers' men. One word was enough to place selling orders with the brokers on the floor of the Exchange. Some foresighted traders had placed stop-loss orders just a little above and below Saturday's closing prices so that whichever way the market went they would be "on board." Many others, because they could stand very little more of a decline or just because they had had enough of it, either had entered stop-loss orders below the previous close or had made up their minds to give up their holdings at the first sign of weakness. Thus a few minutes after the opening a tremendous wave of selling struck the market.

In the ensuing consternation, on the exchanges and in the boardrooms, one word, continually repeated, was clear and certain: "Sell!" "Sell at the market!" "Sell at any price!" "Sell!" The panic was on again in full fury. In the first half-hour of trading many stocks lost from 5 to 10 points. When U.S. Steel broke below 200, little hope remained that the bankers could stay the onslaught. At the end of the first hour the demoralization was almost as complete as it had been the preceding Thursday. Only lacking were the "air pockets" in which there were no bids at all for stock. It was believed that the bankers were at least seeing to this, as they later took credit for doing. All morning long incessant selling beat prices down to successively lower levels, where buying orders rested or where the new low prices attracted fresh buying orders. The stock ticker lagged far behind.

At a little after one o'clock the selling abated briefly and prices seemed to be stabilizing. Word had been sent over the news tickers that Charles E. Mitchell was seen entering the offices of J. P. Morgan & Company. And presently a Morgan broker began bidding for U.S. Steel, which quickly rose from 193½ to 198. Other leaders also moved upward briefly. Whatever belief there may have been that the same sort of tactics that had saved the market on the preceding Thursday would do so again was quickly dispelled, however. Within a few minutes after this try U.S. Steel had lost all of its gain, presently sinking to 190 and taking the rest of the market along with it. For the remainder of the day prices dropped, sometimes with losses of several points between sales. There was not even a hint of substantial buying resistance at the successively lower price levels—no sign whatever that even a feeble rally might be in the making.

Unlike the brokers, moving quickly from post to post, shouting themselves hoarse in frantic efforts to dispose of stocks for their customers, the customers themselves, crowding the boardrooms, could only watch and wait in an agony of anxiety. In almost any boardroom the scene was about the same. The place was packed with people from every walk of life. It was strangely quiet. Many faces were gray and lined with apprehension. Every so often a dozen or more quotations that had come over the news ticker from the floor of the Exchange were called out. Customers' men pushed their way back and forth through the crowd from the telephones to the order window. Occasionally someone cursed. Here and there a woman wept, probably from sheer tension as much as from loss and chagrin. Occasionally an older man suffered a heart attack and was carried out, or a usually sedate customer brandished a bottle and laughed or talked wildly. Those who sought to tell others near them how much they had lost received little attention.

"There goes my son's college education," said a gray-haired professional man to a stranger.

"And my life's savings," was the reply.

In one New York brokerage office, so the story goes, a youngish fellow, wild-eyed, confronted the managing partner. "I want my money back!" he shouted. "Ten thousand dollars!"

He dashed to the window and flung it open.

"Give me my money or I'll jump!"

The manager calmly called the cashier and told him to write the man a check. It was worth it to avoid the publicity.

Not all was solemn in the boardrooms, however. Sometimes the board boys, carefree, excited, and thoughtless of the distress surrounding them, laughed and joked among themselves as they chalked up prices that meant disaster to someone or other. And a few suddenly sophisticated, cynical bears were obnoxiously cheerful.

After a slight rally early in the afternoon, the decline continued without letup, the urgency of the selling becoming continually greater. Stocks, meeting little or no resistance, broke through their Thursday lows with ease, and continued downward. The final hour was the worst, prices sinking rapidly on an enormous volume of transactions. The 3 million shares that changed hands in that short period would have been a good day's business for the Exchange in ordinary times. In the five hours of trading the Dow-Jones industrial average declined 38.33 points, or 12.8 per cent, and the railroad average declined nearly 10.91 points, or 6.6 per cent. A week before, the possibility of this would have been almost beyond belief. This was the greatest drop in prices during a single day that had ever occurred on the New York Stock Exchange. The decline on the New York Curb Exchange also set a new record. Altogether, it was estimated that the loss in security values on October 28 was $14 billion. The *New York Times* said of the day's events:

> Yesterday's decline in the stock market . . . must be ascribed to a multitude of factors: lack of support, exhaustion of margins, selling by many frightened persons who had owned their stocks outright and a re-creation of the wave of fright which swept the speculative markets last week. It was the acute weakness of such issues as Steel Common, General Electric, Westinghouse, Anaconda Copper and others of the sort which spread terror through the ranks of holders of stock. . . . The slaughter of market values was a terrific one, even more im-

pressive than on last Thursday, and many persons who had congratulated themselves heartily after that break and the recovery on Friday and Saturday went quickly and definitely overboard yesterday when the market broke so badly.[1]

The most ominous aspect of this tremendous break in the market was that the lowest prices of most stocks were reached in the last few minutes of trading. Earlier in the day there had undoubtedly been a substantial amount of short selling by professional operators and floor traders, many of whom ordinarily would be covering their sales toward the close in order to take profits and also avoid the risk of holding their short positions overnight. Whatever the amount of stock absorbed by such purchases late in the day—and it probably was large—it was so overwhelmed by the tidal wave of selling that it had no visible effect. There was no "snap," "resilience," or "comeback" left in the market. This augured ill for the opening the next morning.

NEW YORK STOCK EXCHANGE	LOW FOR THE DAY	CLOSE	CHANGE FOR THE DAY
American Telephone & Telegraph	232	232	−34
Columbia Gas & Electric	70	70¾	−22
Eastman Kodak	181⅛	181⅛	−41⅞
General Electric	250	250	−47½
General Motors	47½	47½	− 6¾
International Business Machines	198	198	−22
Otis Elevator	290	290	−60
Radio Corporation of America	39¾	41¼	−18⅜
U. S. Steel	185	186	−17½
Western Union Telegraph	191	191	−39½

[1] (October 29, 1929), p. 42. © 1929 by The New York Times Company. Reprinted by permission.

NEW YORK CURB EXCHANGE	LOW FOR THE DAY	CLOSE	CHANGE FOR THE DAY
Aluminum Company of America	299¾	299¾	−50¼
Cities Service	27	27½	−18¾
Electric Bond & Share	83⅛	85	−22⅛
Goldman Sachs Trading Corporation	60	60	−16
Standard Power & Light	103	103	−27

On the New York Curb Exchange and the other smaller exchanges the decline was of the same extent and followed about the same pattern as that on the New York Stock Exchange. Over-the-counter trading was as confused and difficult as it had been during Thursday's break in prices. There were again the air pockets in which no bids could be found for some stocks. Those whose holdings were largely invested in unlisted stocks with thin markets found it difficult or impossible to liquidate them quickly, except at great sacrifice. Fortunately for many of them, most brokers required much higher margins for over-the-counter issues. Several New York City bank stocks were down 100 points or more for the day, and the bid price for First National Bank of New York was 500 points lower. The unlisted stocks of chain stores, which had been the vogue in some investment circles in the latter part of the boom, were especially hard hit. Now hardly anyone wanted them. Stock prices in the major European financial centers followed the same trend as in New York, but because of the time differential trading in these centers continued after regular closing time and on into the evening. Foreign brokers and traders could not close shop and go home when signs of further panic had appeared at the very start of the day's business across the Atlantic.

In the grain market, prices of wheat and corn rose, wheat being strengthened by a declaration of the Farm Board that prices were too low. There were severe breaks in the prices of rubber and coffee, the one in coffee being attributed to the closing of the coffee exchanges in Brazil because of a panic in those markets, apparently not connected with the panic in United States securities markets. The prices of most other commodities were off somewhat, but little urgent liquidation had appeared.

Although the break in prices was greater on October 28 than it had been at the extreme low on the twenty-fourth, the volume of trading was considerably lower, albeit still enormous by ordinary standards. On the New York Stock Exchange 9,212,800 shares were traded, and on the Curb Exchange 4,152,900. The number of shares traded in odd-lot transactions came close to equaling the 4 million traded on Thursday. Although on Friday and Saturday the public had bought much more stock in odd lots that it had sold, on Monday odd-lot selling exceeded buying, and a large number of small traders boldly sold short. As on the preceding Thursday, reports of transactions were long delayed, and confusion and error sometimes compounded. One trader who was said to have sold "at the market" 150 shares of an especially volatile stock received confirmation slips two days later showing that he had gotten 106 for the hundred-share lot and 87 for the fifty-share odd lot.

Many of the events that occurred and the conditions that developed as a result of the panic situation on October 24 reappeared on the twenty-eighth, and would be seen again during the succeeding days of panic. The lateness of the stock ticker, which ran on until forty-seven minutes past five, and the inconvenience and frustration that it caused the many whose stocks were not among those that were quoted frequently over the news tickers, on the twenty-eighth, were now taken for granted. Again, telephone, telegraph, and cable facilities in New York were used to capacity as orders poured in from every part of the country and the world, and as brokers' calls for more margin were sent forth. Again, Stock Exchange authorities rejected suggestions that they suspend trading for a time to help bring order out of chaos. And again began the grueling, night-and-day effort on the part of brokers' employees to reduce the new mountain of paper work that had accumulated.

Making the many thousands of margin calls was a continual problem for the brokerage staffs. Keeping track of the condition of the accounts, their values deteriorating rapidly as prices fell, was a formidable task in itself. If at all possible the customer was given a moderate amount of time to raise the required funds if he appeared to want to do so. This seemed only fair play, and often it was necessary to retain a good customer relationship. During these times many people transferred what remained of their accounts to other brokerage firms because of bad feelings or embarrassment.

Brokers, however, ran a serious risk when they did not insist upon prompt deposit of more funds or additional collateral when an account became impaired. Wiser brokers knew that it was better to lose a large and profitable trading account than to be caught in the position of having to carry it when the value of its securities became less than the amount it owed. Moreover, if a comparatively small brokerage firm carried an account that held a large amount of one particular stock, the firm could become insolvent. If the account's holdings were sold at a time of weakness in the market—just when selling them would be most necessary—they might bring a fantastically low price. By this time many big traders were in serious financial trouble, and many of their brokers were close to being in serious trouble, too, because of them.

The bankers' consortium met again late on Monday afternoon, with several Morgan partners as well as Thomas Lamont in attendance. Afterward, Lamont and George Whitney talked informally with reporters, again voicing the group's concern with the market situation and stating their aim to preserve an orderly market and to prevent demoralization. In the next morning's accounts of this interview one reporter observed: "Following the bankers' meeting the spokesmen showed no disposition to predict an immediate rally in stocks. It was indicated that an irregular opening might be expected this morning, with some further liquidation carrying prices lower than at yesterday's close."[2] Other bankers with whom reporters talked were less cautious in their statements. Some emphatically asserted that massive buying support was now about to enter the market, not only from the investment trusts but from the banking consortium itself.

Nevertheless, by now it was starkly apparent how futile had been the widespread "conspiracy" to "talk the market up" after Thursday's debacle. Efforts at optimism now seemed false, almost inappropriate. Further talk and published predictions of effective support from the bankers, investment trusts, life insurance companies, wealthy bargain-hunters, and thousands of thrifty small buyers who were now ready to seize the opportunity to acquire sound stock values at low prices were no longer reassuring. Here and there, no doubt, hope was stirred by such wishful thinking, but the false prophets were now widely recognized as such. The cold and bitter facts had proved them wrong. Certainly one of the coldest and bitterest of those facts was the action of the stock market on October 28. After the most drastic decline in the market's long history, it had closed at the day's lowest level. Few knowledgeable observers of market activity would be disposed under such circumstances to believe that the decline would go no further.

OCTOBER 29

October 28 and 29 seemed to run together in one long wave of liquidation. Tuesday the twenty-ninth was the worst of all the panic days. According to the record, 16,410,030 shares

[2] *Ibid.* (October 29, 1929), p. 2.

were traded on the New York Stock Exchange, and 7,096,300 on the Curb Exchange. The actual number of shares involved may have been much larger, however, for in the turmoil and frantic confusion at the trading posts a considerable number of transactions probably were not noted for the official reporters. The volume of trading was by far the greatest on record for both of the large New York exchanges, and on smaller stock exchanges it also set new records.

At ten o'clock, when the reflection of the ticker tape began to move across the Translux screen, even those who expected prices to be lower at the opening were astounded by the declines from the preceding close, and by the enormous blocks of stock recorded as single transactions. There were opening sales of 10,000 shares or more for fifty-eight different issues, and several of these were 50,000-share blocks.

	SHARES	OPENING PRICE	OFF
General Motors	50,000	45¼	2¼
United Corporation	50,000	26	7½
Standard Oil of New Jersey	50,000	57	7¾
International Telephone & Telegraph	50,000	71	17
Radio Corporation of America	30,000	30	10¼
Westinghouse	25,000	130½	14½
Timken Rollerbearing	25,000	70¼	19¾

The break in some less well-known stocks was even more drastic than in these. The most dramatic price change was that of Transamerica Corporation on the Curb Exchange, which opened at 20¼, being down 42½ points from the preceding close. Another startling loss was in Electric Bond & Share, which opened at 50¼, off 34¾ points from the preceding close and nearly 23 points below its previous low for the year. Al-

Above: Wall Street looking west, on a quiet day in the 1920's.
Below: The same scene, during the height of the panic.

Brown Brothers

Richard Whitney, five times president of the New York Stock Exchange before disaster overtook him, with his wife and

Wide World Photos

Jesse L. Livermore, renowned bear trader whose losses and gains were sometimes the sensation of Wall Street.

Above: A small boardroom in the early 1920's.

At Right: William C. Durant, the biggest of the plungers.

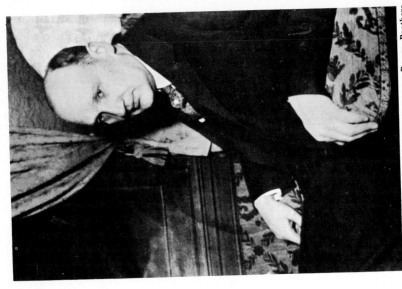

At Left: The tape shows prices rising during a trading session in 1928.

At Right: Ivar Kreuger, "Match King of the World," whose suicide demoralized the stock exchanges of Europe and America.

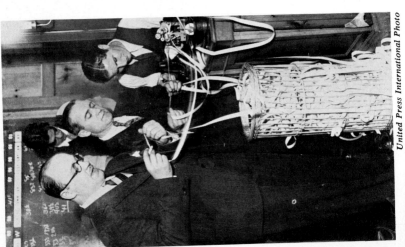

"*Up three points? My Gawd, I jumped too soon!*"

"On Margin"

By James Montgomery Flagg.

"Where's that nine cents you was keepin' for the gang?"

"Maybe I done wrong, but I bought two thousand shares of stock wit' part of it."

Above: Employees of a brokerage house phoning for more margin at 1:00 A.M., October 25, 1929.

Below: Brokers' messengers sharing a scarce newspaper at the height of the panic.

Discontent and hardship followed in the wake of panic.

Apple sellers in New York City.

Part of the "Bonus Army" takes over the
Pennsylvania Railroad yards in Cleveland—June, 1932.

Above: A bread line—early 1930's.
Below: Charles E. Mitchell, banker and securities super-salesman, is flanked by his attorney, Max Steuer, and a somewhat embarrassed U. S. Marshal.

Life

Finis.

most in an instant, thousands of speculative accounts that had survived the severe pressure of the day before were wiped out. Holdings of those who had not yet responded to brokers' calls for more margin sent out the preceding afternoon or evening had to be sold at once. How to get funds from those who had just been made vulnerable by the opening plunge in prices was an extremely difficult problem for the brokerage firms. The announcement during the morning of the failure of a small Curb Exchange firm added to the gloom in the boardrooms. It was feared that this was to be just the first of a series.

The extension of the panic to much lower price levels caught many of the more conservative traders, some of them once very wealthy, who two days before could hardly have imagined themselves overcommitted. Their holdings, unlike those of the small traders, were extremely damaging when thrown upon the market. These holdings accounted for many of the large transactions at the opening on the twenty-ninth and throughout the day.

Within the first half-hour over 3 million shares changed hands. While apparently there was a considerable amount of buying by banks, investment trusts, insurance companies, and other institutions, it was not sufficient to absorb the necessary selling. Prices sank lower and lower throughout the morning and well into the afternoon. The scenes and happenings on the stock exchanges and in the boardrooms were similar to those of the preceding days of panic. Perhaps greater than before was the awe with which many observed the rapid erosion of values. The mere change of a figure on the ticker tape meant that some people throughout the country were poorer by millions of dollars. Those who wondered where this wealth went might well have wondered also where it had come from, and what kind of conjuring had created and destroyed it. What sort of wealth was this?

Apparently the bankers' consortium and the financially

powerful sponsors of various better known stocks were doing their best to keep at least the semblance of a market in leading as well as other stocks, but in lesser issues the change in price from one quotation to the next was sometimes as much as 5 points or more. The story is told of a Wall Street messenger who half facetiously had placed an order to buy 100 shares of White Sewing Machine at $1.00 a share. The stock had sold as high as 48 earlier in the year, but had closed at 11⅛ on the day before. His order was quickly filled on the twenty-ninth, and the next day the stock rebounded to 11 before closing at 8½.

During a panic and, conversely, during a boom, it is easy to forget that every transaction is both a purchase and a sale. Even at the worst of the panic it was not all selling and no buying, as some newspaper headlines led one to suppose. Before two o'clock on the twenty-ninth the influence of the buying factor began to appear, at first just perceptibly in a leading stock here and there, when its price seemed reluctant to recede further, then appeared to be stabilized, and then perhaps gained a fraction of a point. As those who have watched price changes at critical moments know, signs such as this are sometimes quickly followed by a reversal of the prevailing trend. So great was the downward momentum on this particular day, however, that the upturn took a little time to develop, making its appearance quite dramatically in the last fifteen minutes of trading.

In this late rally many stocks made substantial recoveries, although for almost all of them the net change for the day placed them far below the previous closing. The vigorousness of the reversal, and the fact that it was the first one of any significance in nearly two whole days of trading, did much to modify the general despondency that had developed. Though it might prove to be only a rally in a bear market, it could go much farther because of the extent of the decline. At the close, the Dow-Jones industrial average was down 30.57 points, and the railroad average was down 8.35 points from the preceding day's close.

	LOW FOR THE DAY	CLOSE	CHANGE FOR THE DAY
American Telephone & Telegraph	204	204	−28
American Can	110	120	−16
General Electric	210	222	−28
General Motors	33½	40	− 7½
New York Central	175	189½	+ 3½
U. S. Steel	166½	174	−12
Westinghouse	100	126	−19

Despite the enormous volume of trading, the New York Stock Exchange ticker was not as far behind as on other panic days. It completed recording the day's business at thirty-two minutes past five, but the Curb Exchange ticker was recording transactions until seventeen minutes past six. Two contrasting features of the day's business were the enormous blocks of stock that changed hands and the very large proportion of odd-lot transactions, estimated at approximately 6 million shares. During the worst of the selling in the stock market, bond prices also declined markedly, recovering most of their losses before the end of the session. In the commodity markets, only grains and cotton seemed to be affected by the panic, and the decline in their prices was small. Practically all over-the-counter stocks were badly affected. Prices of New York City bank stocks experienced severe declines: National City Bank lost 115 points to close at 325 bid, Guaranty Trust lost 150 points to close at 625 bid, and First National Bank of New York lost 1,600 points to close on a bid of 5,200. Evidently, during the panic, the very marked shrinkage in the value of bank stocks was not regarded by the public as indicating doubt as to the banks' solvency.

Again, the financial centers of Europe felt the impact of panic in Wall Street, and shares were thrown on the markets for what they would bring. As the London *Daily Chronicle* of October 30 reported the reaction in London on the preceding day:

> The Wall Street avalanche left some of its debris in Throg-morton-Street, and long after the [London] stock exchange had closed last night there were excited Street dealings in Trans-Atlantic stocks.
>
> Dozens of dealers stood about in knots under the archway and in Shorters' Court, buying and selling—but chiefly selling —as the echoes of the avalanche came over the wires from New York.

The popular press abroad played up the dramatic, human-interest aspects of the panic. The London *Daily News and Westminster Gazette* of October 30 reported that

> Americans on holiday in Europe whose fortunes have been shattered in the great crash on Wall Street are frantically seek-ing passage to the U.S. to attempt to retrieve their fortunes. . . . Most of the Americans caught flat-footed are on the Continent. . . . A good many of those at sea will be facing disaster on land-ing.

This same periodical, on November 1, commented on the use of the transatlantic telephone that linked London and New York:

> It has had to be rationed. All day, and especially between 2 and 6 P.M., there have been more people to pay £3 a minute for it than could possibly be accommodated, even when all three circuits were in operation. . . . One big operator has spent £300.

In the same issue it was reported that "a considerable number of Catholics are concerned over rumors that the Vatican has lost most of its ready money on Wall Street." Later information indicated that this was probably not true.

Quite a number of the stock-trading public had deserted the

long side of the market to sell short. Their quick gains and their hopeful pessimism stirred resentment. One Wall Street speculator commented:

> But some traders are now so bearish they would sell America, the Sub Treasury, Bank of England, Europe, Brooklyn Bridge and the Federal Reserve Board short if they could borrow them.[3]

How very bad the market situation had become began to be revealed. A headline in the New York *Herald-Tribune* read: "Street Puzzled when 37 Active Issues Vanish."

> One of the most peculiar circumstances surrounding yesterday's trading was the absolute disappearance of the market in thirty-seven of the list's active issues. Wall Street was at somewhat of a loss to explain this anomaly, but, in a few cases, it was learned that the specialists in the issues in question received large selling orders and could find no bids.
>
> Rather than offer the shares "for a bid," which would have meant sacrificing them at outrageously low prices, the specialists refused to open the market. While the thirty-seven stocks have been among the active issues for some months, they were not traded in at all yesterday.
>
> In the case of these stocks the offers as well as the bids were withdrawn at the close, so that there was no market in them that could be quoted.
>
> It is understood sponsors of the stocks will have bids in the market when trading starts today.[4]

Among these mystery stocks were such well-known issues as Anaconda Wire & Cable, Endicott Johnson, Freeport Texas, Pacific Lighting, Seaboard Airline, and Wabash Railway.

[3] *Wall Street Journal* (October 30, 1929), p. 2.
[4] (October 30, 1929), p. 35.

Before the opening on October 29, the New York Stock Exchange had announced the lowering of the call money rate from 6 to 5 per cent. This announcement was an unprecedented action that seemed to indicate an overpowering desire to devise some piece of good news. And early in the day two members of the banking consortium, speaking for themselves, offered their opinion that stocks were "cheap and near a turn." Efforts such as these hardly rang true, and probably had little effect. By the end of the day, however, several developments were eagerly accepted as favorable to the market.

Most important of all, the market itself was at last showing signs of recuperative power. Also, unexpected favorable dividend actions by the American Can Company and the United States Steel Corporation were considered highly reassuring as to the outlook for general business activity. The American Can Company not only declared an extra dividend of $1.00 a share, repeating a similar declaration made a year before, but it inceased its regular quarterly dividend from $0.75 to $1.00. The United States Steel Corporation declared an extra dividend of $1.00 a share, in addition to the regular quarterly dividend of $1.75. In announcing this, the directors stated:

> Earnings for the first nine months of 1929 show $15.82 a share on the common stock outstanding; compared with $8.17 a share for the like period of 1928. . . . The corporation's plants are operating at 82% of ingot capacity at the present time.[5]

Of much greater significance than the dividend actions was the action of the New York City banks, led by those whose heads were members of the consortium, in reducing their margin requirements for loans to brokers from 40 per cent to 25 per cent. A similar reduction was made by banks in other cities. Brokers who required more than a 25 per cent margin also reduced their requirement to this lower percentage for

[5] *Wall Street Journal* (October 30, 1929), p. 1.

their customers. This bank action may have saved some brokerage houses from insolvency, and it probably reduced the
number of margin calls that the brokers themselves had to make
because of the day's extensive decline.

The Federal Reserve Board, with Secretary of the Treasury
Mellon present, was in continuous session on the twenty-ninth
from ten o'clock in the morning until four o'clock in the afternoon, but it made no announcement after its meeting, though
Board members were said to be optimistic. Although the hoped-
for reduction in the discount rate of the New York Federal Reserve Bank was not forthcoming on this day, it was not the
day of the week when such an announcement ordinarily would
be made anyway. The bankers' consortium also met in the
morning, and again late in the afternoon. After the second meeting its spokesman reaffirmed the bankers' intention of helping
to maintain "a free market for securities in good order." He
flatly denied a current rumor that the group had been selling
stocks.

Again, statements poured forth from many different sources,
averring true faith in the New Era and urging the public to buy
stocks at prevailing bargain prices. Those who still held a position in the market began to take hope. Many thousands of
others on the evening of October 29, however, found themselves suddenly impoverished or destitute. And some were also
deeply in debt to their brokers.

ANOTHER BRIEF INTERVAL

The upturn in prices that occurred just before the close on
Tuesday, October 29, was the beginning of probably the greatest short-lived rally that the Stock Exchange had ever experienced. On Wednesday and Thursday, the days on which the
rally occurred, the Dow-Jones industrial average gained more
than 43 points, and the railroad average gained nearly 13
points.

At the opening on Wednesday, prices of many leading stocks were up several points or more. Typical initial gains on the New York Stock Exchange were American Telephone & Telegraph, up 6⅛; North American, up 10; U.S. Steel, up 3; and Westinghouse, up 4 points. On the Curb Exchange, American Superpower was up 1½, Cities Service, up 1⅞, and Electric Bond & Share, up 10⅝ points.

The long-awaited reversal thus seemed to be announcing itself, and thousands of speculators and investors hastened to take advantage of it. Many selling orders above the market were cancelled, and "buy at the market" was the common directive of those fearful of missing the opportunity to "get aboard" early in the movement. Sizable blocks of stock were taken by the more affluent traders, some of whom had recently "cashed" large profits on the bear side of the market. U.S. Steel led the rise, which continued throughout the session.

About an hour before the close on the thirtieth, a report came over the news ticker that John D. Rockefeller, Sr., had announced that for several days he and his sons had been buying "sound common stocks." This news gave further strength to the market. Already a cheerful atmosphere had replaced the gloom of the preceding two days. Twice, loud cheering broke out on the floor of the Stock Exchange: at the opening, as prices moved dramatically upward, and later in the day when Richard Whitney, acting president of the Exchange, announced that the governors had decided to limit trading on Thursday to three hours in the afternoon and to close the market for Friday and Saturday. This holiday was urgently needed by brokers and the members of their staffs, many of whom were close to the point of complete exhaustion.

During October 30, 10,727,320 shares were traded on the New York Stock Exchange, and on the Curb Exchange 3,809,-200 shares changed hands. The stock tickers for both exchanges continued to record transactions until about half-past five. Odd-lot transactions on the Stock Exchange were believed to approximate 6 million shares, about the same amount as on the preceding day; but this time buying orders predominated. The revival in the stock market appeared to influence the wheat market, where prices rose several cents a bushel. In many stocks, gains for the day on both the New York exchanges were 10 points or more, and some exceeded 20 points.

Again, at the opening of the three-hour afternoon session on Thursday, initial prices were markedly higher than at the preceding close. On the Stock Exchange, American Telephone & Telegraph gained 9, Radio Corporation of America, 5⅜, Anaconda Copper, 9, U.S. Steel, 5, and the volatile Auburn Auto, 70 points. On the Curb Exchange, Cities Service gained 12, Goldman Sachs, 5, and Electric Bond & Share, 20 points. Prices rose somewhat from their high opening level, and then receded, to close, nevertheless, with large advances for the day. Some observers said this recession indicated that the market was "stabilizing."

Two items of good news appeared after the close. The Federal Reserve Bank of New York announced a reduction in its discount rate from 6 to 5 per cent. Earlier in the day a reduction in the Bank of England's discount rate from 6½ to 6 per cent had led most traders to expect the New York bank's action, although many had supposed it would cut the rate by only ½ of 1 per cent. Even more impressive, however, was the announcement of a record decline of $1,096,000,000 in brokers' loans. A decrease of only two-thirds of this amount had been expected. Thus, after the market had closed for the three-day weekend, all those who were bullish had very good reasons for expecting the advance in prices to continue and perhaps even accelerate on the following Monday.

NOVEMBER 4–13

Over the weekend, expectations of a strong, perhaps violently strong, market on Monday ran high. These expectations were more firmly grounded than at similar junctures earlier in the panic. Important items of favorable news, not fully discounted in the market's show of strength on Wednesday and Thursday, gave reasons, rather than rationalized, biased opinion and ballyhoo, to support those expectations.

In New York and perhaps elsewhere those who could not wait until Monday morning to buy stocks found ways of doing so. Informal markets sprang up in the financial district—in barber shops, on street corners, in restaurants, and in the lobbies and corridors of office buildings. Stock Exchange members were forbidden to take any part in this "gray" or "gutter" market, as it was called, although such transactions were entirely legitimate. Banks were deluged with inquiries from small depositors, some of whom wanted to buy only one or two shares. A phenomenon that had developed early in the panic, when margin calls had put pressure on people for funds, now was caused by the impetuous desire to obtain bargains in the stock market. Where people had no savings to draw upon, they borrowed on life insurance policies, furniture, jewelry, and even on shares in unsettled estates, often at exorbitant rates of interest. Some pawnbrokers ran out of cash and had to stop lending, and finance companies did a record-breaking business.

A large segment of the general public was convinced that bargain day was at hand. Most of the buying that these people would do at the opening on Monday would be in odd lots and for cash. From Friday to Sunday, a flood of small orders poured into brokers' offices, and the odd-lot brokerage houses were swamped. On Sunday, the *Herald-Tribune* commented: "Never before in the annals of Wall Street have security orders collected in such vast quantity, according to brokers"; and in its Monday morning edition a headline read, "Wall St. Expects Record Revival of Bull Market Today."[6]

But on Monday morning, November 4, prices opened "sharply off," and they continued to decline throughout most of the session. The surprise and disillusionment was tremendous,

[6] *New York Herald-Tribune* (November 3 and 4, 1929), p. 1.

among the brokers at the exchanges and on down to the one-share buyers. Evidently the amount of stock that had to be sold far exceeded the amount that the eager public wanted to acquire. The good news after the close on Thursday and the enormous volume of small buying orders that had accumulated could not support stock prices in the day's initial transactions—not even momentarily. The psychological impact of this setback must have been extreme. It seemed as though the market would go its own way—downward—regardless of every circumstance. The public's reaction to this unpleasant surprise probably helps to account for the long, gueling, inexorable decline that continued, almost without interruption, until the lowest depth of the panic was reached on November 13.

The daily changes in the Dow-Jones averages in this period most simply outline the decline.

NOVEMBER	INDUSTRIAL AVERAGE	RAILROAD AVERAGE
4	−15.83	−3.60
5	market closed	
6	−25.55	−10.73
7	+6.06	+1.56
8	−1.66	+0.47
9	market closed	
10	market closed	
11	−16.14	−4.64
12	−10.65	−8.54
13	−11.05	−6.27

In many respects, these days of decline resembled earlier days in the panic, when prices were falling rapidly. The reactions on the part of the people involved were about the same. Many who had entered the market as bargain-buyers a week or so before, now became just as vulnerable as those from whom they had bought stock had been then. The three-hour trading sessions and the closing of the market on Election Day and on Saturday reduced the confusion. Every day, hopeful, prominent people allowed themselves to be quoted to the effect that the worst was over. Most of the business news during this time was unfavorable, but even on the eleventh, when the United States Steel Corporation announced a substantial increase in unfilled orders, its stock, instead of rising in response to the unexpectedly good news, dropped 11½ points. It was characteristic of the panic, and later of the long depression decline, that very often the most encouraging kind of news item, to which the market formerly would have responded with vigor, seemed to have no effect. The market's reaction to good news became, in a way, a measure of how bad the underlying situation was.

During this phase of the panic the bears renewed their attack on stock prices wherever particular issues seemed to be vulnerable. Whereas there once had been complaints that lack of a large short interest (which would be covering short sales on declines) made possible sudden severe breaks in various stocks, as the panic developed, hostility toward the bears intensified, becoming widespread. Talk of a powerful bear pool, never clearly identified, which raided the market and resorted to unscrupulous tactics, found willing listeners everywhere. If the bears could be intimidated or forced to buy in their short commitments, the decline would probably stop and prices would go upward, at least temporarily. In an article explaining how the bear pool operated, the *Herald-Tribune* said:

> One of the ruses of this pool, it is reported, is to offer blocks [of stock] a fraction above the closing price every day in certain stocks so that bidding would be discouraged and any chance of a rise would be throttled.
>
> The pool is also understood to be one of the sources of disquieting rumors, such as the one about the emergency closing of the Stock Exchange.[7]

On November 13 the governors of the New York Stock Ex-

[7] (November 14, 1929), p. 1.

change announced that brokers would be required to report all sources of short selling. They did not forbid such activity, but this was a form of suasion that would at least discomfort the bears, many of whom preferred anonymity. The order was expected to help the market.

The panic reached its lowest point on November 13. Although the closing prices showed large losses, a rally had set in late that day. A technical upward reaction was long overdue. Three encouraging influences, all coming into play at nearly the same time, seemed to do most to reverse the downward trend. These were the official attention being directed at short selling, the proposal by the President and the Secretary of the Treasury that Congress substantially reduce the income tax, and the announcement early in the afternoon of the thirteenth that John D. Rockefeller, Sr., had placed with his brokers an order to buy a million shares of Standard Oil of New Jersey at 50. Although not yet known, on the following day the Federal Reserve Bank of New York would announce a second reduction in its rediscount rate, from 5 to 4½ per cent.

Record of Leading Stocks
During the Panic

NEW YORK STOCK EXCHANGE	1929 HIGH	PANIC LOW*	DECLINE FROM HIGH
American Can	184½	86	98½
American Telephone & Telegraph	310¼	197¼	113
Anaconda Copper	140	70	70
General Electric	403	168⅛	234⅞
General Motors	91¾	33½	58¼
Kennecott Copper	104⅞	49⅜	55½
New York Central	256½	160	96½
Radio Corporation of America	114¾	26	88¾
United Aircraft	162	31	131
U.S. Steel	261¾	150	111¾

NEW YORK CURB EXCHANGE	1929 HIGH	PANIC LOW*	DECLINE FROM HIGH
Aluminum Company of America	539½	180	359½
Cities Service	68⅛	20	48⅛
Electric Bond & Share	189	50	139
Goldman Sachs Trading Corporation	121¼	32	89¼

* These lows were reached on different days, principally November 13 and October 29.

8

Human Aspects of the Panic

THROUGHOUT THE PANIC, as throughout the boom, the human factor dominated all others. Hope and fear were both causes and effects of panic developments. But the panic stimulated other emotions besides these, and revealed traits of character that in some cases must have surprised even their possessors. Notwithstanding the herd psychology that surely played a part both in the boom and in the crisis that followed, not all those in apparently similar circumstances reacted in the same degree, or even always in the same way.

There were, of course, the weepers and the wailers, and those who blamed their misfortune on others; the shocked and numb, who had yet to comprehend the reality of their losses; the despondent, for whom the financial reversal was simply too much to bear; and the shamed and disgusted, who realized their folly and the folly of those around them. One chagrined speculator said to a financial journalist: "Write a piece about the biggest fool in the world. I'll give you my photograph."[1] Some believed the panic to be a scourging by Divine Providence of themselves or of others for selfishness and greed. One thoughtful observer saw in the panic's ravages retribution for particular character traits: "The Street has the peculiar faculty of finding the Achilles heel of each who enters the lists. . . . Ignorance,

[1] Edwin Lefevre, "The Little Fellow in Wall Street," *Saturday Evening Post* (January 4, 1930), p. 102.

161

timidity and bravado receive their due reward. The grasping, the wastrel, the suspicious, the obstinate, write their own characters on the ledgers of their brokers."[2]

There were all degrees of good and bad sportsmanship among the losers. Fortitude was a common trait. Some seemed, or pretended, to bear their losses lightly, shrugging off the painful experience with a devil-may-care attitude, or looking back on the boom as "fun, while it lasted." One good sport, a woman whose account was sold out because her equity in it of nearly a million dollars had vanished, said to her broker: " 'But let me tell you first that I had a perfectly stunning time while it lasted. I never knew before what fun it was to make money. No wonder you men want to monopolize the business. . . . Of course, I wish I had the money in cash now, so I could—' She caught herself."[3]

The women, like the men, ranged the gamut of possible reactions, from stoicism to complete collapse.[4] Many, rich and poor, young, middle-aged, and older lost all or most of what they had. The pattern of family life that had been distorted in various ways during the boom, when husband, wife, or both—and sometimes the children, too—were enthralled by the stock market, was affected again in various different ways when the panic struck. In some households there was recrimination and

2 Barnie F. Winkelman, *Ten Years of Wall Street* (Philadelphia: The John C. Winston Company, 1932), p. 31.

3 Edwin Lefevre, "A Trip on the Magic Carpet," *Saturday Evening Post* (February 1, 1930), p. 19.

4 While the panic was still in progress, an astonishing description of the women speculators' reaction to it appeared in a London newspaper. It was so far from the truth that the reader must wonder what conceivable purpose such reportorial mendacity could serve: "These women are much too hard for tears, and they took their apparent ruin with stoicism. . . . Haggard and unshaven brokers may be collapsing under an intolerable strain on the nerves, messenger boys may drop in the streets from sheer fatigue and valuable securities roll from their hands into the gutter, but these Madame Defarges of New York have never turned a glossy hair during the crisis." "The Women Gamblers of Wall Street," *The Daily News and Westminster Gazette* (November 1, 1929), p. 9.

bickering, in others consolation and determination to put up a brave front. Some hard-hit families spoke humorously of "keeping down with the Joneses," and some referred to themselves as the "*nouveaux pauvres*."

It was natural for those who had been hurt by the panic to seek a scapegoat. Someone was certainly to blame, reasoned many burnt speculators, but they could not agree on who it was. Some blamed the bears, and some denounced the bankers and the Federal Reserve Board. Others thought the whole thing was a "foreign plot." Still others found an explanation in astrology, and blamed the course of the planets. Some ascribed the panic to a too rapid technological advance in industry. The customers' men took more than a fair share of abuse. Occasionally, disgruntled losers threatened them with violence. At least one large brokerage firm for a time kept a plainclothes detective on guard in each of its boardrooms.

Many who had not ridden the bull market through its upward surges, as well as some who had, delighted in other people's losses, especially their friends'. Edwin Lefevre, a prolific and sophisticated writer of the period whose favorite theme was stock speculation, told of having asked a delicatessen proprietor whether any of his friends had lost in the panic. "His face brightened up instantly, so that I knew several of them must have lost everything, after months of telling him all about their profits. . . . 'I don't know how so many smart people lose so much money after they made it so easy,' he said."[5]

Some who watched the prices of their holdings sink from day to day worried frantically from the time the market closed until it reopened, while others tried or pretended to forget the market between the trading sessions. Some seemed under a compulsion to talk about their losses, as though they acquired a certain prestige from them. They were even inclined to exaggerate. A

[5] "A Trip on the Magic Carpet," *Saturday Evening Post* (February 1, 1930), p. 19.

fashionable New York restaurant ran an advertisement requesting its patrons not to discuss Wall Street while dining. And New
York's fun-loving mayor, Jimmy Walker, asked the city's mo-
tion picture exhibitors to show only cheerful movies. Probably
most of those who were able to exorcise the evil demon of panic
by ignoring it were not caught up in it. Most of those who were,
however, had to talk about it.

Various stories, some perhaps apocryphal, were told. There
was the one about the New England spinster who, although of
very limited means when the market first attracted her, had
prospered greatly in it. Just before starting on a long-anticipated
cruise in September, 1929, she had told her customers' man to
sell all her holdings. He, however, being an apostle of the New
Era and wanting to do her a favor, delayed the sales, and while
prices were falling he kept waiting for the rally that came much
too late to save his client. Another sad tale was that of the
garment manufacturer who had made his million dollars or so
during the boom, and who at almost the top of the market had
liquidated his holdings and sold short. Just before the days of
panic late in October, 1929, his smart son, on the pretense of
giving orders for the father, covered the short sales and bought
stocks to the limit of the account.

There was the chronic inebriate who, as he sat in the boardroom depressed by the erosion of stock prices, increased his
alcoholic intake and continued to shout selling orders to the
customers' man long after he had sold out his holdings. A few
days later he learned, to his astonishment, that he was short a
substantial amount of stock at prices far above the market. For
at least one simple and conservative couple, life was made
pleasanter by the panic. Their mounting fortune during the
years of the boom had swept them into an endless, tiring round
of social activities and civic responsibilities. Well before the
decline set in the prudent husband had quietly sold their stocks
and invested the proceeds in high-quality bonds. After the crash

they reduced their style of living and let their many acquaint-
ances suppose that they too had lost most of their wealth.

For many, far more was lost than money. Respect, prestige,
reputation, and sometimes honor passed from them. Especially
were the brokers, bankers, and professional investment analysts
and economists downgraded in the eyes of those who had relied
on and been influenced by them. Surely, the thought was, these
men of background, training, technical knowledge, and supposed financial wisdom should have foreseen at least the possibility of a crash and tempered their overconfidence and often
blatant optimism with prudent restraint. The amateur analysts
and advisors came in for their share of opprobrium too, from
their relatives and friends who, being less directly in touch with
the market, had relied on them for investment guidance and,
while the boom lasted, had thought them endowed with remarkable acumen. Many a businessman, astute and successful in his
own line, learned that he was not also a master of stock speculation, as did his relatives and friends, to their regret.

The metamorphoses wrought by the panic were many and
varied, but practically all were tragic:

> Accountants, architects, engineers, lawyers; all who served
> industry directly and indirectly, merchant and manufacturer
> who supplied its needs, went down in the general debacle. Men
> of character and standing, who from youth had been pillars
> of the social structure, found themselves derelict. Their posts
> of trust and service were gone; their savings of a lifetime were
> lost; their investments were worthless. Craftsmen whose skilled
> hands had ever assured them a livelihood, wandered aimlessly
> in futile quest for work.
>
> Past wealth or past glory meant nothing: men inured to
> leadership for generations found themselves without means
> and without prospects. Thousands who had given generously
> to others in the past became recipients of charity.[6]

[6] Winkelman, *op. cit.*, p. 353.

While disclosures of defalcation and embezzlement were to become commonplace during the depression, the panic itself yielded a crop of them. Trusted officers and underlings in financial institutions and business firms, tempted by the get-rich-quick possibilities of the rising market and by the opportunities their positions offered for misappropriating funds, yielded to the temptation and "borrowed" the means to finance their speculations. Thousands of them, fully intending to repay, were trapped by the market's violent decline. But not all instances came to light immediately, and probably some never did.

The most spectacular of the embezzlements revealed during the panic, in both the amount of money and the number of people involved, was that of a large part of the resources of the Union Industrial Bank in Flint, Michigan. During the later years of the bull market, about a dozen of the bank's officers and clerical employees, at first independently and later together, misappropriated more than $3.5 million, the greater part of which they lost in the stock market. Because almost all of the bank's officers were involved, there was scarcely anyone to check on anyone else. Lax management and skillful manipulation enabled them to outwit the bank examiners and even to consummate a merger with another bank. Having sustained losses in the later part of the boom by selling short, they reversed their position by purchasing a large amount of stock just in time to be caught in the panic. Their awful predicament when the market crashed late in October caused some of the conspirators to confess their crime to the bank's directors.

Almost as fantastic as the cooperation and the adeptness of this embezzlement was the heroic action of one of the bank's directors, Mr. Charles S. Mott, who covered the entire shortage with his own funds. Thus the depositors were protected from loss and the bank was enabled to continue its banking operations pending the payment of insurance claims and some restitution—with new officers and staff members. Mr. Mott became the bank's new president, and a statement was issued explaining what had occurred:

> Encouraged to get into the market, and seeing the profits that were being made, the use of the bank's funds for speculative purposes was carried on in a small way as early as 1926. These were individual manipulations, the largest single transaction running seven to eight thousand dollars. Stocks were bought but not paid for, until they appreciated in value. They were held as cash items or in the collection department. There apparently was no thought of theft, the bank and its funds being used in what was believed to be a sure proposition.
>
> It was not long before the men gradually began to know about the operations of one another, and it was adversity that brought them together. [They forged notes and manipulated securities held as collateral for genuine notes; and tellers failed to turn in funds received at their windows.]
>
> This procedure was followed throughout 1928, and this year was quite successful. Christensen said that by the spring of 1929 he had accumulated profits of about $100,000 without actually having stolen any of the bank's funds.
>
> There was a big volume of buying and selling, as they were "scalping the market," more of their time and thought, perhaps, being devoted to these transactions than to the bank's business.[7]

No doubt this statement threw many another bank director and bank examiner into a cold sweat.

It was obvious long before the boom had ended that whatever might be said for security speculation as a skill or an art of the shrewd and perceptive few, for many others it had become scarcely more than betting from day to day on the changing quotations. What most of the crop of boom-nurtured specu-

[7] *The Literary Digest* (December 7, 1929), p. 82.

lators wanted was easy, unearned money, the thrill that came with getting it, the enhancement of the ego, and the proof of Fortune's favor.

This proclivity to gamble, seen so generally in every great boom, was not so much wickedness as it was an elemental inclination of human beings, expressed in various degrees in such things as church raffles, bingo games, horse races, and poker games. Perhaps, in man's past, risk-taking has had a high survival and developmental value. Perhaps too, as some psychologists suggest, it is used by the morbid subconscious mind for purposes of self-punishment in order to allay inhibited guilt feelings. Whatever may be the explanation, most of those who took their chances in the stock market in 1929 paid dearly.

The blindness and delusion of a self-sure generation at a time of such great scientific and technological advance, seen in retrospect, must have seemed a cosmic paradox. Perhaps the great majority of people always is blind or deluded in important areas of contemporary life, with reality partly concealed, distorted, and out of perspective at the time.

Leaving this kind of speculation to others, we might take note of a few observations that have been made of human expectations and market actions. Panics, by their very nature, are unexpected. If panics were generally anticipated they would not occur, because preparation for them would remove their cause. That panics have occurred many times before, far back into the past, and that they recur indicates an insufficient grasp of history's lesson on the part of the great majority of human beings. Unchanging, elemental human nature has been the one great constant throughout the history of booms and panics. When conditions are right it exaggerates its hopes and grasps for too much, and so creates the conditions that presently thwart the hoping and the grasping.

Some especially cogent thoughts about speculation as it involves both the individual and the group were expressed by

Edward D. Jones, an economist writing before the turn of the century:

We do not see things as they are, but as they appear through the media of our education and interests. . . . [The] distortion of recollection [through the effect of a powerful desire] . . . tends to destroy the basis of sound judgment. In falsifying memory it renders nugatory the results of experience. . . . The effect of a strong desire upon expectation is equally remarkable. In an act of anticipation the judgment is to a certain extent freed from the correctives and checks which restrain us from error in realizing the present and recalling the past. There is thus range for a greater degree of error due to prejudice. And these errors may everywhere be observed in acts of anticipation. . . . In so far as the course of the future is uncertain, our beliefs regarding it are likely to be formed according to our desires. . . . What we may logically expect in the future, from analogy with the past, is not what we do actually expect.

.   .   .   .

[As Lester F. Ward said:] "Even in man those individuals are rare whose judgments are of any value against their interests. Prediction of results is in most cases nothing better than betrayal of preferences. Men as a rule believe that that will happen which they wish to happen."

.   .   .   .

The active and energetic and self-reliant, who naturally became the leaders in industrial society, are of the intellectual type most prone to optimistic exaggeration. Experience proves that, to the optimistic, gambling is particularly easy. . . . The coercive power of a generally accepted view is very great, and only the most independent minds can hold out against it. . . . States of mind, hopes and beliefs, are communicated from one to another by means of what is best described as sympathy. . . . An undue concentration of interest resulting in intense emotion is always prejudicial to sound reasoning. The general tendency of emotion is to paralyze thought, and particularly to withhold the mind from those considerations which are out of harmony with itself. . . . The sympathetic influence we are considering is doubtless allied to hypnotic influence.[8]

Jones also quoted two British students of speculative cycles. Walter Bagehot: "All people are most credulous when they are most happy. . . . Almost everything will be believed for a little while." Lord Overstone: "So long as human nature remains what it is, and hope springs eternal in the human breast, speculations will occasionally occur, and bring with them their attendant train of alternate periods of excitement and depression."

Throughout the panic of 1929, the continually recurring thought in many minds was that "bargain day" had come. For those who were already overcommitted in depreciated securities, the thought was tinged with bitterness and the regret that their stock purchases had not been deferred, or a liquid reserve set aside for just such an opportunity. Others, who had substantial funds available, watched the precipitous decline with mixed feelings if they also held stocks, and with a certain relish if the liquid portion of their resources was large. Many an old man, and others not so old, recalled that great fortunes had grown from opportunities seized upon when prices had collapsed. It was said that the Rothschilds had established the basis of their great wealth by buying French *rentes* when blood drenched the streets of Paris; and from every American panic, it was known, some new millionaires had emerged.

George F. Baker, enormously wealthy president of the First National Bank of New York, was one of those who thought he knew that "bargain day" had come and who had funds at his command with which to welcome it. It was said that while seriously ill he learned of the late October break in stock prices.

[8] Edward D. Jones, *Economic Crises* (New York: The Macmillan Company, 1900), pp. 186, 188, 189, 190–91, 192, 203–4, 206, 206n.

While he was preparing to set out for his office his physician objected.

"Why the great hurry this morning?" he was asked.

"There is a panic in Wall Street," he replied. "I have made money in every panic in the last sixty years, and I do not intend to miss this one."[9]

Baker died soon afterward. Whether he would have sold out during the post-panic rally or held on to his "bargains" through the utter depths of the market in 1932 cannot be known. The stock of his bank, of which he was a very large holder, declined from about $8,300 per share just before the panic to about $865 in the summer of 1932.

Wall Street, the focal point of the panic, is sometimes sinisterly described as a short street with a river at one end and a graveyard at the other. The graveyard, which is a part of the Trinity Church property, is very old, and many who rest there knew nothing of stock speculation or high finance. The beautiful old church and its yard continually attract the historically minded who come to New York from every part of the country. But on the business days of the week it is in a special way Wall Street's church. Often during the day a few people from the financial district can be seen in the nave, kneeling in prayer. And during panics it is thronged with the anxious, the frightened, and the desperate. According to the verger, during the collapse of stock prices in 1929 many crowded into the church to pray that they would not be wiped out.

To the strictly religious it may have seemed shockingly crass for anyone to pray about money matters, and perhaps there was something strange in this mixture of the mundane and the spiritual. But to those troubled people who bore the brunt of the panic's violence had come the realization that they were not losing mere money but all that money—the great intermediary for all other things—could be exchanged for. These things included not just food, clothing, and shelter, but the great in-

[9] Winkelman, *op. cit.*, p. 331.

tangible values of security, peace of mind, and some measure of freedom, prestige and self-esteem—even health and integrity. They had perceived that money, in its various ways, had a very real connection with "the higher things of life."

The emotional strain of the panic could not be fully comprehended, for much of it was concealed. What one could see of it indicated much more, however. A sympathetic observer in one of the boardrooms wrote:

> I saw them sold out, dozens of them, scores of them. I watched their faces when the customers' men gave them the news. I saw men's hair literally turn white. I saw a woman faint dead away; they carried her out cold. I heard a middle aged doctor say: "There goes my son's college education."
>
> Terrible sights. Terrible sounds. Sitting there hour after hour, watching my own "investments" shrink and shrivel, my heart ached for the poor people around me. . . .[10]

Heart attacks and strokes were the commonest signs that breaking points had been reached. These occurred with some frequency in brokerage offices as the tension increased; and no doubt many more that were due in part to the panic occurred elsewhere. In some, when events became unendurable the mind gave way. Late in 1929, a physician at one of the New York hospitals stated: "There were thousands of cases of nervous collapse among men and women who lost everything in the stock market—not only well-to-do people, but school teachers, bookkeepers, wage earners of all degrees."[11]

Fevered minds were easy prey to tales of horror. Rumor had it that a wave of suicides was sweeping New York. One enterprising London correspondent was said to have cabled his paper that the canyons of the financial district were filled with the bodies of those who had jumped from the tall buildings. Near

---

[10] "Now I've Gone Back to Work," *American Magazine* (February 1930), p. 92.

[11] Edwin Lefevre, "The Little Fellow in Wall Street," *Saturday Evening Post* (January 4, 1930), p. 7.

the Stock Exchange a crowd gathered to watch a painter at work high up on a scaffold. Someone had said that he had been caught in the crash and was about to jump. Reactions such as these were ludicrous in a macabre way; but as the panic progressed, the daily newspapers carried an increasing number of stories of suicides, and of so-called "accidents" that probably were acts of self-destruction. Shootings, drownings, and other ways of "ending it all" were reported, but jumping from a high building was supposed to be the favored method.

More or less typical of these stories was that of the violent demise of the prominent sixty-year-old president of one of the country's largest cigar manufacturing concerns. As reported in the newspapers, on October 29 he "either fell or jumped" (a phrase that became common) from the window of his luxurious sixth-floor apartment. His death was officially recorded as "accidental," but a fact that could not be overlooked was the decline in his company's stock from 113⅜ to 4.

The morbid interest in suicides probably led to an exaggeration of the number of them during the panic. Later, however, when people more fully realized the havoc that the panic had created in personal affairs and faced the reality of a depression-ridden world, and when defalcations and embezzlements could no longer be concealed, the number of suicides throughout the country increased considerably.[12]

The panic had its bright side too. Here and there one noted acts of kindness and deeds of financial valor. Julius Rosenwald, philanthropist and multimillionaire Sears Roebuck executive, unconditionally guaranteed the brokerage accounts of all his company's employees. Samuel Insull supplied collateral to prevent any employees in his vast utility empire from being wiped out by margin calls. Lord & Taylor announced that it would

[12] From 13.5 acts of self-destruction per 100,000 of population in 1928, the proportion increased to 17.4 per 100,000 in 1932, apparently the highest rate on record for the United States. U.S. Bureau of the Census, *Historical Statistics of the United States, Colonial Times to 1957* (Washington, D.C.: Government Printing Office, 1960), p. 26.

use all its resources to protect the margin accounts of its employees. Several of the Standard Oil Companies made loans to protect their workers' stock holdings. Henry Ford tried to give business a stimulant by reducing the price of his automobiles. John D. Rockefeller, Sr., entered an open order to buy a million shares of Standard Oil of New Jersey.

Bits of humor helped to leaven the lump of misery, fright, and ruin. One evening during the panic, at the corner of Fifth Avenue and Eighty-first Street, a green and yellow parrot of unknown origin strode about, cawing raucously, "More margin! More margin!" The patrolman who caught it took it to the police station, where he and his comrades fed it a sandwich. After pecking away at the sandwich the parrot again cawed hoarsely, "More margin!"

A cartoon in *Life* pictured two hoboes riding in a boxcar, one of them saying, "It seems like only yesterday that I had stock in this company." Brokers were said to be advising their clients to buy stock in gas companies and companies that manufactured red ink. As for suicides, it was reported that every morning a fleet of top hats could be seen floating down the East River.

It had become customary, one heard, for the hotel clerk to ask a guest when he registered whether he wanted the room for sleeping or jumping. And there was the story of the two speculators who jumped hand in hand from the top of the Woolworth Building because they had had a joint account. A thrifty German-American was said to have declared that he would never again save any more than he could afford to lose.

For a while the remark that "gentlemen prefer bonds" was good for a laugh, but it got tiresome. So did the following quip, in the various forms it took:

"Why do you look so glum today?"

"You'd look glum too if you had arteriosclerosis at forty-five."

"That's nothing. I had Internal Combustion at 103."

9

The Post-panic Rally

ON THURSDAY, November 14, the long-dreamed-of upturn began, and speculative optimism quickly revived. On the fourteenth and fifteenth a vigorous and well-sustained buying movement raised the Dow-Jones industrial and railroad averages by 30 and 13 points, respectively, somewhat less than half of this advance taking place on the fifteenth. This was just before the weekend, when the market would be closed. Although most speculators were overjoyed that stocks had turned upward, many of them fearfully remembered the much more extensive rally on October 30 and 31, immediately before a three-day market holiday, which had been succeeded on the following two market days by a decline of more than 41 points in the industrial average and more than 14 points in the railroad average.

Apprehension during the weekend changed to tentative relief on Monday the eighteenth when at the close each of the averages showed a decline of only about a point. In the next three days the industrial average gained more than 20 points and the railroad average, 8. This was a critical juncture in the course of what became a small-scale bull market that extended into the spring of 1930. During the earlier part of this rise, for all that anyone could tell, it might have been no more than another moderate upturn before a renewal of panic selling. But with further indications that the massive force of liquidation had

spent itself, prices continued to advance until the second week
of December.

As the conviction grew that the panic was over, much the
same pattern of events and circumstances that had characterized the old bull market developed. Further gains confirmed
the initial advance, and the speculating public became jubilant.
Again the boardrooms were pleasant, gossipy places to drop
into and chat about the market, to talk of this stock and that,
and of what this or that big operator was doing or saying. Some
pools had become active again, and the old boardroom sport
of trying to guess their tactics and "go with them" revived.

It was astonishing how many traders who had gone broke
during the panic were back in the market, some of them doing
very well for themselves. In many cases those who had once
traded thousand-share blocks of stock now traded hundred-
share lots, and former hundred-share traders "swung a line"
consisting of a few small odd lots. Apparently, once adjusted
to their new, more humble status, they experienced just about
as much fun, excitement, worry, and fear as they had in what
many of them already probably thought of as "the good old
days." With many, the dominating intention was to regain, as
quickly as possible, the losses that they had sustained during
the panic. The primary question was not whether this could
be done, but how soon. In tempered form, the doctrine of the
New Era was again promulgated. Panics could happen, of
course, but another one was surely a long way off.

Again, there was the unconscious conspiracy to talk the market up. For the most part, the conspirators were also the victims.
Most of those who served, professionally or otherwise, as con-
sultants to others, who wrote market letters or reported the
news, as well as most of those who prepared formal articles
or made speeches, let a wishful bias give overtones of optimism
to what they wrote or said. Some were apparently unable even
to conceive of any possibility other than a rising market and

renewed prosperity. From the most prominent businessmen, bankers, and securities dealers on down to the average man who merely discussed the market with his friends, the generally accepted opinion was that the great bull market had been resumed, having all the farther to go because of its setback.

Here and there a respected voice questioned and warned, but most did not care for the questionings and warnings. They knew what they wanted to be told, and the greater part of the popular press catered to that preference, perhaps because most publishers, editors, and writers had the same preference themselves. Professional economists, much as they had before, affirmed the favorable outlook. Even as conservative a one as Benjamin M. Anderson, Jr., of the Chase National Bank, who had severely criticized the Federal Reserve authorities for their expansive credit policy, spoke optimistically. In an address on November 21 he said:

> . . . we find ourselves bruised and scratched, and with our nerves unstrung. But no bones are broken, and there are no internal injuries. We are perfectly able to get up and walk. It is just as well, however, that we should not try to run very fast immediately. There are those who would like us to start running immediately, by applying great doses of the same false stimulant that set us on our head-long, break-neck, heedless race that culminated in the fall over the hill. . . .

> That demand will fall off, and [is] falling off in luxury lines, and in certain other lines, is obvious, and that business will have a slower pace in coming months than in the past twelve months is reasonably to be expected. . . .

> Stock market prices have had an immense slaughter. Whether the next move will be up or down, I do not know. But the market has a bottom. There are cushions, and even powerful springs at the bottom, in the buying by investors who are

waiting for the turn, and in the covering purchases by short sellers.

... It is a fighting market, and a two-sided market, and it is an immeasurably safer market than it was a month ago.[1]

Colonel Leonard P. Ayers, prominent economist and vice-president of the Cleveland Trust Company, wrote on November 15:

General business has slowed down somewhat, and will probably slow down still more, but the losses in the stock market, gigantic as they are, have not impaired the soundness of our banking system, or decreased the efficiency of our industry, our commerce, or our agriculture. In the main the stock losses are not business losses, and their effect will probably not be nearly so serious for business as their size would lead us to expect.

.   .   .   .

The great fall in stock prices has once more made good stocks cheap as investments, even when judged by the old standards that prevailed before the great bull market got under way.[2]

Nearly everyone conceded that a decline in business activity, already apparent, had to occur; but it was expected to be mild and of short duration. They remembered the brief recessions in 1924 and 1927, and considered them more or less representative of what was to come. Many assumed that the stock market had already discounted the slackening of business and was beginning to forecast a wave of prosperity even greater than before. Some substance had been given this belief by the widely publicized intention of President Hoover and other government leaders, as well as leaders in the business world, to increase the flow of purchasing power throughout the nation.

[1] *The Commercial and Financial Chronicle* (November 30, 1929), p. 3408.
[2] *Ibid.* (November 23, 1929), p. 3255.

The President's determination to prevent the country from slipping into a depression was an important sustaining influence during the post-panic rally. After conferring with various business leaders and government officials, Hoover announced on November 15 that he would call a preliminary conference of representatives of industry, agriculture, and labor "to develop certain definite steps" toward "the coordination of business and governmental agencies in concerted action for continued business progress. . . . My own experience has been . . . that words are not of any great importance in times of economic disturbance. It is action that counts." Citing the Federal Reserve's "establishment of credit stability" and the proposed tax reduction as first steps in the program, he went on to say: "The next practical step is the organizing and co-ordinating of a forward movement of business through the revival of construction activities, the stimulation of exports and of other legitimate business expansion, especially to take such action in concert with the use of our new powers to assist agriculture."[3]

The President and appropriate members of his cabinet held meetings with railroad executives, officers of the United States Chamber of Commerce, bankers, representatives of manufacturing industries, public utilities, and various commercial activities, as well as with representatives of farm organizations. Conferences called by the President were held on November 19 with railroad officials, and with members of the Federal Reserve Board and the Federal Advisory Council; on the twenty-first, with business and labor leaders; and on the twenty-second, with representatives of the building, construction, road-building, and construction-financing industries. Regional meetings of public utility representatives were planned.

[3] President Hoover's plans at this time for sustaining business activity and the conferences that were held at his behest are described in the *Commercial and Financial Chronicle* for November 23, 1929, pp. 3261–65, and for December 7, 1929, p. 3576.

The purpose of these conferences, according to the President's statement, was to survey the general situation and to encourage the expansion of construction work "in every prudent direction, both public and private, so as to cover any slack of employment. . . . It was found that a preliminary examination of a number of industries indicated that construction activities can, in 1930, be expanded even over 1929." As a result, large expenditures on various projects in 1930 were more or less pledged by the railroads, the electric power companies, the Bell Telephone System, by those concerned with building and highway construction, and by others whose cooperation was enlisted or attracted.

Perhaps the most remarkable outcome of the conferences was that the representatives of industry authorized the President to state "that they will not initiate any movement for wage reduction," and that labor leaders authorized him to state that it was "in their individual views and as their strong recommendation to the country as a whole, that no movements beyond those already in negotiation should be initiated for increase of wages. . . ." Henry Ford, after the conference in which he participated, announced that a general wage increase would soon be put into effect for all his employees.

The lists of the conferees, which included the names of the top leaders in business and finance, were thoroughly impressive. And the apparently unanimous determination of the participants to cooperate with the government in sustaining a high level of business activity, employment, and income flow was almost everywhere acclaimed as highly encouraging.

To follow up these conferences, at the instigation of the President a large meeting of business leaders was held by the United States Chamber of Commerce in Washington on December 5. In addressing the meeting, the President urged "expansion of the construction and maintenance work of the country. . . . It has long been agreed by both businessmen and economists that this great field of expenditure could by its acceleration in time of need, be made into a great balance wheel of stability."

The President's vigorous leadership seemed appropriate, and the favorable response to it from every segment of the economy in all parts of the country seemed to augur well for the period ahead. Nevertheless, a few thoughtful critics questioned whether an attempt at forced stimulation of business was wise, and whether it could succeed. And many an industrialist who avowed that his firm would maintain a high level of expenditure may have held unvoiced reservations as to what lengths to go in doing this. Many more were probably agreeable to the general idea, hoping that others would carry the load.

An editorial in the *Annalist,* while conceding that seeking to avoid an "excess of pessimism" was sound policy, said:

> It is probably expecting too much, however, to hope that a marked downward drift in business, the product of a great complex of influences . . . can be wholly checked even by a cooperative effort to avoid so far as possible curtailment of business activity. For while a group of executives may assent to the idea that such a cooperative policy is desirable, each individual nevertheless finds himself confronted with very definite and urgent money considerations; and in most cases his position compels him to be governed by these conditions rather than by a consideration of the policy that might be socially desirable if it were practicable in each particular case.[4]

The editor of the *Commercial and Financial Chronicle* believed that a slackening of business activity was inevitable and necessary to a wholesome readjustment of the economy:

> The President has continued his laudable efforts to minimize the effects of the collapse of values on the Stock Exchange. . . .

[4] *The Annalist* (November 29, 1929), pp. 1049–50. © 1929 by The New York Times Company. Reprinted by permission.

[But] slowing down of trade and business is already in evidence in many quarters, and there is no way in which this can be avoided. . . . The gigantic inflation of the stock market, so long continued, and attended, as it was, by the flotation of security issues of most astounding magnitude, acted as an inordinate stimulus to trade, raising it to unnatural and fictitious proportions, and now that that stimulus is gone, trade must be expected to settle down to normal proportions, which means nothing more or less than a lessened state of activity.[5]

In commenting on the supposedly temporary shutdowns of Ford assembly plants in various parts of the country for production "readjustments," this editor added:

There is only too much reason for fearing that "readjustments," as they will be called, will necessitate extensive shutdowns elsewhere from time to time, notwithstanding the unqualified assurances now so freely given that employment is to be maintained without diminution.[6]

At this time businesses were, in general, in a financially strong position. The sale of stock issues on a large scale during the boom and the redemption of debt in the form of bonds and bank credit, as well as the substantial accumulations of cash in many instances, were favorable aspects of the situation. But otherwise there were serious weaknesses in the credit structure of the economy, especially within the banking system. Many banks were vulnerable because of large holdings of illiquid securities, large and poorly diversified loans to businesses, and loans on various kinds of property that was either overvalued or that could not easily be marketed. Real estate mortgage holdings that represented speculatively inflated prices were an especially weak element in the assets of many banks. Although

[5] *The Commercial and Financial Chronicle* (November 30, 1929), p. 3361.
[6] *Ibid.*, p. 3363.

the President and the many who rallied to the support of his plan to step up private and public spending stressed the idea of an enlarged program of building construction, speculative real estate ventures during the boom had provided most cities with more building space than they needed. Already, in November, 1929, the real estate maladjustment was so great in Philadelphia that the city's leading trust companies had agreed to the Philadelphia Real Estate Board's proposal of a six-month moratorium on the payment of first mortgages and first mortgage instalments.[7]

Undoubtedly the President's zeal and energy in "doing something," and his firm confidence—shared by many—that the measures proposed would succeed, contributed to the strength in the stock market that lasted into December and was renewed later in that month. In the second and third weeks of December, however, a substantial selloff, which impaired some margin accounts and forced further selling, revived old fears. But after prices had fallen less than halfway to their lows of November 13, they resumed the upward movement.

Helping the rally along was the abundance and cheapness of credit for speculative purposes. By the spring of 1930 the rate on call loans had dropped to 3 per cent, and successive reductions by the Federal Reserve banks had lowered the rediscount rate to 3 per cent also.[8] Interest rates would go even lower thereafter, but then the stock market, affected by adverse forces

[7] *Ibid.*, p. 3362.

[8] "Early 1930 saw a renewal of artificially cheap money. Talking with a small group of leading Federal Reserve officials in the last week of December, 1929, one came away with the conviction that Federal Reserve policies, if left free from political interference, would be conservative, and that the disposition was to let the money market 'sweat it out' and reach monetary ease by the wholesome process of liquidation. The opinion was expressed by a particularly well-informed Federal Reserve official that easy money was not in sight on the basis of any natural forces, and a good deal of time must pass before easy money could be looked for." Benjamin M. Anderson, *Economics and the Public Welfare* (New York: D. Van Nostrand Company, Inc., 1949), pp. 222–23.

that far exceeded the influence of cheap money, would disregard them. A consequence of this credit policy in the first half of 1930 was a marked increase in the amount of new domestic and foreign corporate securities sold to the public. In the second quarter of that year the total of these exceeded that of any preceding quarter.[9]

The *Annalist*'s combined index of business activity, which had been 108.5 in July and 94.2 in November, 1929, was 93.1 in April, 1930. The severe depression decline was yet to come. Under the policy of stepped-up spending by business and government, however, the economy had scarcely held its own. Probably the most ominous development during the five months of the post-panic rally in the stock market was the almost unremitting decline in the prices of wholesale commodities. These prices, now regarded by economists as one of the more reliable indicators of future business activity, had been declining continually since July, 1929. The *Annalist*'s weekly index of wholesale commodity prices, which had been as high as 150.4 in July and 141.0 late in November, 1929, was 132.3 late in April, 1930.

The peak of the secondary boom was reached in the spring of 1930. The highest point for the Dow-Jones industrial average was 294.07, on April 17; for the railroad average it was 157.94, on March 29. Stocks had recovered just about 50 per cent of their decline.

Record of Leading Stocks
During the Post-Panic Rally

NEW YORK STOCK EXCHANGE	PANIC LOW	RALLY HIGH	ADVANCE FROM LOW
American Can	86	156½	70½
American Telephone & Telegraph	197¼	274¼	77
Anaconda Copper	70	81½	11½

[9] *Ibid.*, pp. 223–24.

NEW YORK STOCK EXCHANGE	PANIC LOW	RALLY HIGH	ADVANCE FROM LOW
General Electric	168⅛	381½ *	213⅜ *
General Motors	33½	54¼	20¾
Kennecott Copper	49⅜	62¾	13⅜
New York Central	160	192¾	32¾
Radio Corporation of America	26	69⅜	43⅜
United Aircraft	31	77¾	46¾
U. S. Steel	150	198¾	48¾

NEW YORK CURB EXCHANGE

Aluminum Company of America	180	356	176
Cities Service	20	44¼	24¼
Electric Bond & Share	50	117⅞	67⅞
Goldman Sachs Trading Corporation	32	46¾	14¾

* These figures represent an adjustment to take account of a 4-for-1 stock split.

10

The Descent to the Depths

ALTHOUGH A DISCUSSION of the long, deep depression of the 1930's carries us beyond our story of the boom that preceded the depression and the panic that ushered it in, some description of the events and conditions in those sad years fills out the larger picture. The depression was a consequence of the boom, and the panic was an early part of the transition from a period of great business activity, widespread prosperity, inordinate speculation, and marked inflation to one of deflation, business stagnation and bankruptcies, massive unemployment, and widespread poverty.

In retrospect it is possible to date the depression from August, 1929, when the business cycle reached its peak.[1] At that time

[1] Whether one sets the termination of the depression at the cyclical trough reached in March, 1933, the subsequent trough in June, 1938, or at some other date before the wartime expansion of industrial activity began may depend upon his political persuasion or economic philosophy. To Mr. Roosevelt and his New Deal followers the depression ended in March, 1933. To Mr. Hoover and many others it did not end until some time in 1941. A severe decline in the prices of securities and commodities that lasted from the spring of 1937 through the spring of 1938 was accompanied by a marked decline in business activity that seemed to many people a resumption of the depression, from which only a temporary recovery had been made. In this later period industrial stocks lost almost 50 per cent of their value and railroad stocks lost about 70 per cent. Unemployment, which had represented 24.9 per cent of the labor force in 1933, was still very high (19.0 per cent) in 1939. For dates of cyclical peaks and troughs, see Geoffrey H. Moore, "Measuring Recessions," *Business Cycle Indicators,* Vol. I, a study by the National Bureau of Economic Research (Princeton: Princeton University Press, 1961), p. 121. For unemployment data, see U. S. Department of Commerce, Bureau of the Census, *Historical Statistics of the United States, Colonial Times to 1957* (Washington, D.C., U. S. Government Printing Office, 1960), p. 73.

no one could have known with any certainty what the future course of business activity was to be. For several months the decline in the various indexes that reflected the condition of the economy was gradual, and prevailing opinion held that this was a salutary slackening of pace—a "breathing spell"—that soon would be followed by a resumption of the general upward trend. The post-panic rise in the stock market seemed to confirm the general optimism about business conditions. But what was believed to be the renaissance of the great bull market proved to be only an extended rally that was not at all out of proportion to the extent of the decline during the panic. By April, 1930, stock prices again had turned downward.

For a while, however, almost everyone was willing to believe that prosperity was "just around the corner." Political, industrial, and financial leaders made innumerable optimistic statements to the press; and from the same ivied towers whence had come academic reassurances that a New Era was at hand, with the trend of stock prices ever upward, now came sage declarations that the boom was sure to revive. But as the depression worsened the nation became skeptical of its wishful prophets. A little book by Edward Angly ridiculed the banalities of those who sought to talk the economy into revival. It juxtaposed their words against events that marked the deepening of the depression, and it bore the cynical title *Oh Yeah?*[2]

Although the stock market panic marked the transition from prosperity to the long period of depression in the United States, depression had already set in elsewhere in the world. Business activity, or stock prices, or both, had already receded in such countries as Great Britain, France, Germany, Canada, Holland, Sweden, and Japan, even before the panic began in the United States.

After the stock market rally had ended in the spring of 1930, the depression went through three major phases, during each of which securities prices continued downward. The first phase

[2] (New York: The Viking Press, 1931).

extended to mid-December, 1930, after which, for a short time, signs of possible recovery appeared. The second lasted until the summer of 1932, when a short but vigorous revival occurred. The third phase of the depression went from autumn, 1932, to early March, 1933.

During 1930 the market continued on its downward course, from April almost to the end of the year. Although the Dow-Jones railroad average broke through its panic low late in June, the industrial average did not enter new low ground—thus giving a Dow theory confirmation that the major trend was downward—until the second week of October. Thereafter, the decline continued until a selling climax in mid-December brought it temporarily to a halt.

In this phase of the long decline there were several adverse developments of great magnitude which, by further impairing confidence, deepened the depression and facilitated the downward movement of stock prices. The first of these was the enactment, in June, of the Hawley-Smoot Tariff Bill, of which one prominent economist wrote:

> But there came another folly of government intervention in 1930 transcending all the rest in its significance and in its baleful consequences. In a world staggering under a load of international debt which could be carried only if countries under pressure could produce goods and export them to their creditors, we, the great creditor nation of the world, with tariffs already far too high, raised our tariffs again. The Hawley-Smoot Tariff Bill of June, 1930, was the crowning financial folly of the whole period from 1920 to 1933.

> .   .   .   .

> But once we raised our tariffs, an irresistible movement all over the world to raise tariffs and to erect other trade barriers, including quotas, began. Protectionism ran wild over the world. Markets were cut off. Trade lines were narrowed. Unemploy-

ment in the export countries all over the world grew with great rapidity, and the prices of export commodities, notably farm commodities in the United States, dropped with ominous rapidity.[3]

While the bill was being debated in Congress, more than a thousand members of the American Economic Association signed a protest against it that was presented to the President, Senator Smoot, and Representative Hawley, to no avail.[4] After the announcement that the President would sign the bill, stock prices broke badly. The country most severely affected by the trade restraints imposed by the bill was Germany, with her enormous foreign obligations arising from war reparations and large postwar borrowings. The increasing unemployment and growing discontent in Germany led to the rapid political advancement of Adolf Hitler; and when, in the German election of September 14, 1930, the Nazi party made startling gains, there was an immediate acceleration in the decline of stock prices in New York.

The market had not yet been stabilized when, in December, doubt arose as to the financial condition of a large New York bank, the Bank of United States. This institution was heavily committed on real estate mortgages, including many second and third mortgages that had fallen into default and whose market had all but vanished. Increasing withdrawals by depositors indicated the imminence of a run on the bank. The state superintendent of banking and the other banks of the city sought ways to save it, but its condition made this impossible. The closing of the Bank of United States on December 11 was a severe shock to public confidence; stock prices sank to new low levels.

The selling climax on December 17 brought an end to the first phase of the 1930–33 decline. From then until late Febru-

[3] Anderson, *op. cit.*, pp. 224–25.
[4] The full text of the protest appears in the *Annalist* (May 9, 1930), p. 1003.

ary, 1931, a vigorous rally developed. During the first quarter of 1931 there were signs of business recovery, such as substantial increases in employment, industrial production, and commodity prices, as well as in securities prices. Possibly at this time the trend of economic activity could have continued the upward course and the depression would have ended, had it not been for the increasingly grave financial situation in Europe.

The market declined gradually from late February, 1931, until the latter part of April when, from the twenty-first to the twenty-ninth, waves of urgent selling carried prices down by more than 13 per cent. This break in the market was variously attributed to the realization that the federal government was operating at a large and increasing deficit, and to successive reports of renewed declines in business activity, employment, and commodity prices. A more fundamental cause of this retreat from incipient recovery, however, was the foreshadowing of a succession of national financial crises in Europe that were to make 1931 a grim and tragic year for most of the world. These crises were the delayed results of an all but universal wartime and postwar inflation, international political rivalries, and many unsound economic and financial measures. The approaching financial collapse of most of Europe and the resulting disturbance to trade and to international financial relationships, as well as the urgent liquidation of securities and other forms of property in world markets, would drag the American economy far deeper into depression.

The first of these European crises occurred in Austria, precipitated, apparently, by French hostility to the customs union that had been agreed upon by Germany and Austria in March, 1931. France, which at this time was financially the strongest country in Europe, began to make large withdrawals of funds from Austria, especially from the great but none too strong Austrian bank, the Oesterreichische-Credit-Anstalt. By late

May, confidence in this bank and in the credit of the Austrian government was so impaired that the limited efforts of other banking institutions throughout the world to save the situation failed.

Almost at once, a foreign run on German banks began; and Germany, heavily indebted abroad on short-term accounts, was especially vulnerable. The German people, taking fright, also began withdrawing their deposits. On July 15, German banks were obliged to acknowledge that they could no longer meet demands for payment. Again, attempts by foreign banking institutions to prevent collapse were too limited, and came too late. On June 20, President Hoover made the bold proposal of a year's moratorium on the debt payments of European governments to the United States, conditioned upon a suspension of Germany's reparations payments to the European governments. Its announcement temporarily halted the run on Germany, but as France delayed acceding to the proposal, fearful that she might be giving up reparations forever, the panic in Germany was renewed, and even France's acceptance on July 6 failed to halt it.

From February into June, 1931, the stock market had declined severely. In June, however, it rallied, and in July it seemed to be stabilizing. The resumption of the decline in August was ascribed to the generally worsening domestic economic situation. The low level of industrial production (steel output, for example, was at about 28 per cent of capacity), declining business earnings, dividend reductions and omissions, a staggering amount of unemployment, and a large number of business and bank failures created a bleak picture. The adverse psychological effect of the domestic situation was augmented by fear of further unfavorable developments abroad.

The financial collapse of Austria and Germany, and the attendant depreciation of their currencies in foreign exchange markets, had brought under suspicion the financial status and the future value of currencies of other countries. By mid-July, even the supposedly invincible British pound sterling had become suspect, and during the next two months there was severe pressure upon the exchange rate of sterling as foreigners sought to reduce their holdings of it and as speculators, perceiving the weakness in England's situation, sold it short. In consequence, the Bank of England was obliged to ship large amounts of gold abroad to those who exercised their claims upon it, thus substantially reducing the gold reserve that was the base of England's money-credit structure and that, in conjunction with the long tradition of British financial integrity, made sterling "as good as gold" everywhere in the world.

Late in August, the resignation of the British Labor party cabinet and the formation of a cabinet made up of members of the three major parties was followed by intensive planning to balance the government's budget through a reduction of expenditures and increased taxation. Confidence in the pound began to revive. The unpopularity of such measures, however, was dramatically emphasized by the mutiny of British sailors whose wages had been reduced.

Perhaps the political pressure on the new cabinet was more than it could resist; perhaps other influences as well undermined the resolution to give strong support to the pound. A strange timidity seemed to guide the policies of the Bank of England, which throughout the crisis set its discount rate at no more than 4½ per cent. Although a substantially higher rate would have caused a temporary demoralization of the securities markets in London, it would almost certainly have assured the world of the bank's determination to save the pound. A high enough bank rate would have held foreign funds in London and probably attracted more, thereby halting the outflow of gold and perhaps even reversing it.

Until practically the last moment before the Bank of England suspended gold payments, the governor of the bank,

Montagu Norman, had declared that this would not be done; but on Sunday, September 20, the suspension was announced. England thus defaulted on her commitment to redeem British pounds with gold at a fixed amount per pound. The news that she had abandoned the gold standard astonished the world and deepened the fear of similar defaults in still other countries. The *Commercial and Financial Chronicle* referred to this suspension as "one of the catastrophic events of the century."

An immediate consequence of the suspension was a decline in the dollar price of the pound, the gold parity of which had been $4.86⅝. On September 21 the exchange rate of the pound dropped to a low of $3.70, but by the end of the day it was quoted at about $4.20. All who held pounds in the form of currency or credits lost accordingly. The Bank of France, which was a large holder, lost seven times the amount of its capital, and was saved only by a large gift of non-interest-bearing securities from the French government, which would serve at least as a bookkeeping asset. A week after England abandoned the gold standard, Sweden and Norway did likewise. An oddity of the situation was that immediately following its suspension of gold payments, the Bank of England increased its discount rate to 6 per cent. This was surely like trying to lock the barn door after the horse was out. England of course gained some temporary advantages from this *de facto* devaluation, but she was no longer the monetary bulwark of the world.

Following the announcement, a foreign run on the gold stock of the United States began, and within six weeks about 15 per cent of it was drawn away by foreign claimants. But as the country's gold position was strong, and there was practically no inclination on the part of Americans to convert currency into gold, the run subsided. Nevertheless, the domestic liquidation of credit continued, putting severe pressure on the weaker banks as their reserves shrank. To ease this situation the National Credit Corporation was formed by the larger and stronger banks in the autumn of 1931, at the instigation of President Hoover. Banks in need could borrow from the corporation by pledging collateral that was sound but ineligible for rediscounting at the Federal Reserve banks. The functions of this useful but limited banking intermediary were taken over by the newly formed Reconstruction Finance Corporation early in 1932.

The London Stock Exchange and most of the other stock exchanges in Europe did not open on September 21. The officials of the New York Stock Exchange, after some deliberation, decided to keep it open for trading, although they forbade short selling. After declining in the early dealings, stock prices made a good recovery; and throughout the week they fluctuated irregularly, sometimes moving sharply upward and sometimes sharply downward. Although September was a month of severe decline, the worst of the drop had occurred before England's default was announced.

In December, 1931, stock prices moved into new low ground. Then, for about three months, there was no marked trend in either direction. From mid-March into July, 1932, however, an almost unbroken decline reduced stock prices by almost 60 per cent. Bond prices, which had declined almost continuously since the summer of 1931, were at such low levels in May of 1932 that many bonds of moderate quality rating sold to yield a return of 12 per cent or more.

Two significant legislative developments early in 1932 were the creation of the Reconstruction Finance Corporation, which was to supply financial aid to banks, other financial institutions, and railroads; and the passage of the emergency Glass-Steagall Act, which permitted the Federal Reserve banks to use government securities, as well as commercial paper, as collateral for Federal Reserve notes for a limited period of time. These measures greatly eased the banking situation by preventing further contraction of bank reserves. They were especially timely because of the second foreign run on the U. S. gold stock that began late in March and continued into June, during which time about $450 million of gold was withdrawn. When the run ended, the gold stock was still far in excess of domestic monetary requirements.

As stock prices reached their extreme lows of the depression, a combination of several favorable influences in June and July, 1932, brought the decline to a halt and caused a reversal of the trend. Although the market would be subject to severe setbacks later on, it would not again reach the incredibly low level of the summer of 1932. Opinions differ as to the nature and relative importance of the causes underlying the revival.

It seemed at the time, however, as though the long and painful deflation had finally run its course, and that businessmen, investors, and the general public were ready to respond to a modicum of encouragement in a constructive way. After all, the banking system had easily withstood the second run on the gold stock, a demonstration of how very strong the money-credit system was in this respect. The defeat on June 17 of the veterans' bonus bill, which would have put more than $2 billion of new currency into circulation, was regarded as a victory for sound money and the gold standard. It had been feared that the inflation the bill was intended to produce would impair international confidence in the dollar and perhaps require countermeasures unfavorable to industry and commerce.[5] In July, a provisional agreement of the European powers to cancel Germany's reparations obligations brought hope of an eventual settlement of all international debts resulting from the war. At about the same time, what had been a serious banking situation in Chicago was remedied by a large loan from the Reconstruction Finance Corporation.

[5] Many readers may be surprised to learn that in this period the stock market reacted bearishly to inflationary proposals of a kind that later on would be likely to cause a rise in prices. Departure from established principles of monetary and fiscal policy were looked upon by the financial community as harmful, and the market reacted to them accordingly.

Perhaps the strongest influence of all arose out of the two political conventions. On June 16, 1932, the Republicans renominated President Hoover, and on July 1 the Democrats nominated Governor Roosevelt. The platforms of both parties were conservative; neither party sought to cater to those who wanted to try inflation or some other panacea for the nation's economic ills. Especially notable was the fact that the platform of the Democratic party proposed strict economy in government, a "competitive tariff for revenue," and "a sound currency to be maintained at all hazards."[6]

Perhaps other influences, less clearly defined or having less bearing on the immediate domestic situation, were also at work to bring the depression to an end, for the revival that began in the summer of 1932 was worldwide. In the United States the recovery, while it lasted, was swift and dramatic. Industrial activity expanded into September, employment increased, the rate at which banks were failing decreased markedly, and stock prices surged upward. In a period of less than three months industrial stock prices practically doubled and railroad stock prices more than tripled. In September, however, stock prices turned downward, and through the autumn and winter business activity, after leveling off, again declined.[7]

The approaching presidential election brought uncertainties and doubts, even though both candidates had declared themselves emphatically in favor of sound monetary and fiscal policies, and of strict adherence to the gold standard. Following the election, hints and rumors, never strongly denied by the President-elect, circulated that the new administration would tamper in some way with the monetary unit and make some sort of radical change in the nation's money supply. In January,

---

[6] For a fuller discussion of the various developments in June and July that appeared to be conducive to the recovery, see Anderson, *op. cit.*, pp. 273–76.

[7] For a full-scale study of the 1932 revival and the subsequent collapse, see Lawrence Sullivan, *Prelude to Panic* (Washington: Statesman Press, 1936).

1933, it was widely known that Roosevelt was consulting with advocates of various forms of inflation and devaluation. By this time, runs on banks had developed to a calamitous extent in various parts of the country, and in mid-February the panic of bank depositors in Michigan was so great that all banks in the state were closed by the governor.

By Inauguration Day, March 4, banking operations had been suspended in a majority of the states. On the preceding day the banking situation had become so critical, apparently due to a large demand for gold at the New York City banks,[8] that Governor Lehman declared a state-wide "banking holiday" in New York for Saturday and Monday, March 4 and 6. Just after midnight on the sixth, the President proclaimed that all banks of the country would remain closed until March 10.

Subsequently, the gold standard was abandoned domestically, the currency no longer being redeemable in gold. The dollar was devalued by about 40 per cent. This devaluation reduced the amount of pure gold in a standard U. S. dollar from 23.22 grains to 13.714 grains. The dollar thus became 1/35 of an ounce of gold instead of approximately 1/21 of an ounce.

The extreme change that took place in the American economy between 1929 and 1932–33 is highlighted by the following figures:

	1929	1932–33
National income	$88 billion	$40 billion (1933)
Wholesale price indexes (1926=100):		
Farm products	105	48 (1932)
Food	100	61 (1932)
All other commodities	92	70 (1932)
Wages: average weekly earnings in		
manufacturing	$25.03	$16.73 (1933)

[8] *The Annalist* (March 10, 1933), p. 361.

	1929	1932-33
Number of unemployed	1,550,000	12,830,000 (1933)
Percentage of the labor force unemployed	3.2	24.9 (1933)

Source: U. S. Department of Commerce, Bureau of the Census, *Historical Statistics of the United States, Colonial Times to 1957* (Washington, D.C.: U.S. Government Printing Office, 1960).

Whereas in 1929 it had seemed as though almost everyone owned shares of stock and was in the market, by 1932 stocks were entirely out of fashion.[9] Few people talked about them or paid any attention to the market.

High and Low Points in the Dow–Jones Stock Averages
(Rounded figures)

	1921 LOW	1929 HIGH	1929 PANIC LOW	1930 POST-PANIC HIGH*	1932 LOW
Industrials	64	381	199	294	41
Railroads	66	189	128	158	13
Utilities	†	145	65	109	17

* The rally.
† Not computed.
Source: *The Dow-Jones Stock Averages, 1914–1963; Monthly High and Low of Closing Averages*. Compiled by Dow-Jones & Company, Inc.

While stock prices were sliding toward their depression lows, Congress initiated its famous, long-extended inquiry into stock exchange and banking activities. The hearings, begun in April, 1932, by the Senate Committee on Banking and Currency, extended with some interruptions into May, 1934, and yielded more than 12,000 pages of testimony.[10] At first the hearings

[9] For a comparison of the highest prices of various prominent stocks in 1929 with their lowest prices in 1932, see p. xiii.

[10] For the rather elaborate citation of the published record of these hearings, see Bibliography.

were directed only to the investigation of "practices of stock exchanges with respect to the buying and selling and the borrowing and lending of listed securities, the value of such securities and the effects of such practices." Later this scope was broadened to include "the matter of banking operations and practices, the issuance and sale of securities, and the trading therein . . . with a view to recommending necessary legislation, under the taxing power, or other Federal powers."

In the first stages of the hearings, those prominently associated either with the New York Stock Exchange itself or with the buying and selling of securities on that and other exchanges were asked to testify. Richard Whitney, acting president of the Exchange during the panic and its president the following year, was the first witness. His attempt to convince the committee that stock trading activities conformed with a generally high level of business ethics was unsuccessful; and most of the witnesses who followed him also made a poor showing. It was obvious that market-rigging and price manipulation had been common practices. Among the large operators from whom the committee sought to elicit information were Michael J. Meehan, the specialist in Radio Corporation of America; Harry F. Sinclair, oil operator and market plunger; Arthur W. Cutten, whose obdurate bullishness had cost him many millions; and such bearishly inclined persons as Bernard E. Smith, Matthew C. Brush, and Percy A. Rockefeller. Many of the witnesses were evasive and obstructive. The committee's counsel, who did most of the interrogating, was often so sharp-tongued and sarcastic that at least once in the earlier phase of the hearings Senator Glass, who was far from friendly to Wall Street, protested against the "bullyragging" of a witness.

One of the many aspects of stock market trading that the committee sought to investigate was short selling. This procedure, explained in Chapter 5, had mystified many laymen and often had been criticized or condemned by those hurt by declining prices; the investigators wanted to know more about it and about the big traders who had engaged in it. Three men from whom they obtained considerable information were Smith, Brush, and Rockefeller, all of whom had been heavily long in stocks at the time of the panic, but who had played the bear side of the market to great advantage for some years thereafter.

"Sell-'em Ben" Smith had begun his career as a clerk in a brokerage office, and while only in his teens had been an active and aggressive speculator. Sometimes he was highly successful, but he also took many "trips to the cleaners," as he put it. In 1927 and 1928 he sold short, bucking the trend, but when the panic came he was carrying a large line of stocks with his brokers. He soon changed his position, however, selling short with the strong conviction that prices would drop further. Often he would say to others, "Sell-'em—they aren't worth anything," hence his nickname. During the depression, as stock prices sank lower and lower, his fortune increased by millions of dollars.

Matthew C. Brush, one of the most prominent operators in the market during the depression, had been long in stocks to the extent of about $15 million when the panic began; and, like Smith, he was converted to the bear side of the market. At one time, his line of short sales involved as many as 125,000 shares, and his profits, apparently, were enormous. In discussing speculation he said, "It's pathetic the basis on which the average traders buy stock."[11] In testifying before the committee, he averred that short selling was a proper and necessary part of dealings in the market; without it, he said, prices would fluctuate much more widely, with changes of 20 points or so on a single trading day.

Percy A. Rockefeller, nephew of John D. Rockefeller, Sr., also had turned to the bear side of the market. Although he

---

[11] "The Great Senate Bear Hunt," *Literary Digest* (May 7, 1932), p. 8.

did well with his short sales, his gains were much less spectacular than those of Smith and Brush. While short in certain stocks, he probably held many others on a long-term investment basis, including shares of various Standard Oil companies. He testified that, altogether, the profits from his short sales were small indeed compared with his losses, which were "a great many, many millions."[12]

The hearings continued after Franklin D. Roosevelt took office, following the landslide election of November, 1932. The new Congress was even more hostile to "the vested interests," especially those in the securities business and in banking, and the desire to fix the blame for the nation's financial ills was stronger than ever. Major legislation resulting from the hearings was the Securities Act of 1933, the Securities and Exchange Act of 1934, and, to some extent, the Banking Acts of 1933 and 1935.

The Banking and Currency Committee's investigation had revealed, through the inquisitorial efforts and brilliant strategies of Ferdinand Pecora, far more that was unsavory about U. S. banking, especially the investment side of it, than the public could have suspected. Most of the witnesses were treated as miscreants—as some in fact proved to be—and often were questioned as though they were being prosecuted. Those who once had been regarded as the heroic titans of finance now became the whipping-boys and scapegoats on whom much of the blame for the disastrous developments of 1929–1933 was being placed.

Some of these witnesses querulously observed that they had not transgressed the laws and customs of the times, and perhaps they had not; but by 1932 the times and customs had changed, and new laws would soon be written. The buoyant, rosy optimism and the unassailable belief in "perpetual prosperity and progress"—as the boosters and the Babbitts might have ex-

[12] *Ibid.*

pressed it—were all but forgotten. In their stead a pall of dark pessimism overhung the nation: it seemed as though the depression could never end. And out of the depression was developing a new set of mores, which favored government control and regulation, frowned on speculation and the derring-do of big operators and promoters, and at its extreme caused many individuals to look askance at all profit-seeking, even when the profit accrued from productive enterprise.

11

Human Aspects of the Depression

THE FALL OF THE MIGHTY

TO THE GREAT and near great of the New Era, on whom the floodlights of exposure were turned by congressional investigation, lawsuits, prosecutions, receiverships, and bankruptcies, as well as to those who escaped the public revelation of their misfortunes or misdeeds, the new morality must have seemed to add insult and shame to the burden of loss or ruin that so many of them had endured. Nemesis had indeed laid a cruel, uncaring hand upon them. Some of the great and near great had been quickly impoverished by the panic; others, who managed to hold on to a part of their wealth, saw it subjected to a relentless attrition. Not only personal wealth but also high status and positions of power were jeopardized or lost. Some of those, however, who were less hard hit or whose financial strength ebbed less rapidly, held on and preserved or recovered at least a part of their fortunes and prestige.

William C. Durant, eternally the optimist and perhaps the greatest of the bull market operators, rode the market down as he had ridden it up. The panic and its aftermath wiped him out, and in time he declared himself bankrupt. His only remaining assets, which he valued at $250, were the clothes he was wearing. But even at the nadir of his fortunes he did not give up. After unsuccessful tries at the lunchroom business and at operating a supermarket, he attempted for a time to distribute a dandruff cure. And in 1947, not long before he died at the age of eighty-five, Durant still talked of making a comeback.

Jesse L. Livermore's career did not end with the dramatic recouping of his fortune during the panic, when as an aggressive bear he pounded the vulnerable market with his short sales and made millions of dollars. Whatever further success he may have had in the market, however, was presently overshadowed by failures and misfortune; and family troubles added to his misery. In 1934 he went through bankrupcty for the fourth time, his liabilities being well over $2 million. He might have made another comeback, but the rules of the game as he had played it were changing. Late one afternoon in 1940, he stepped from the bar of the Sherry-Netherland Hotel to a washroom off the lobby and shot himself through the head.

Arthur W. Cutten, the great bull speculator who obdurately insisted while the panic was raging that stock prices would go to far higher levels, may well have been what a government lawyer once called him, "the greatest speculator this country has ever seen." His losses during the panic may have been as much as $40 or $50 million, though he was said to have recouped them by well-timed short sales in the grain markets. Despite his obdurate bullishness during the panic, he was still a rich man when he died in 1936, at the age of sixty. Apparently Cutten, better than most of the great speculators of the period, realized the pitfalls and hazards of speculation. He is quoted as having once said: "Yes, I have taken my bit out of the market. Oh, quite a bit. But I would advise other men to stay away from it. If I had a son I wouldn't let him touch it with a ten-foot pole."[1] Although he was then referring to the grain markets, he doubtless also had the stock market in mind.

However badly the Fisher brothers may have been set back

[1] Earl Sparling, *Mystery Men of Wall Street* (New York: Greenberg Publisher, 1930), p. 96.

financially by the panic, and to whatever extent their fortune shrank during the long attrition of values in the early years of the 1930's, they remained men of substantial wealth, and they continued to be a powerful influence in the automobile world.

Louis W. Zimmerman, the West Coast trader who, to his brokers, was little more than a voice on the telephone, had taken his profits of millions of dollars out of the market in good time. It was said that his aversion to short selling was so great that when the panic came he simply stood aside, preferring not to try to profit from it. We find no record of how he fared during the depression.

As for Harry F. Sinclair, the oil magnate, stock plunger, and gambler, though the panic and depression probably cut severely into his fortune, he was still a wealthy man long afterward. In 1950, six years before he died at the age of eighty, he was reported to have incurred gambling losses of $800,000 in two nights at a Miami Beach club.

The two Van Sweringen brothers, who had built a $3 billion railroad empire by selling securities on a vast scale, saw the earnings of the properties in their system change to deficits while debt services continued and the market prices of their securities fell to extremely low levels. Though the brothers sacrificed practically all of their fortunes in trying to help their empire ride out the depression, it was to no avail. When Mantis died in 1935, his estate was valued at slightly more than $3,000; and Oris' estate, following his death in 1936, was valued at $700,000.

Samuel Insull, the Chicago utility magnate, weathered the panic of 1929, and during the earlier part of the depression he continued to expand his empire. Believing that prosperity would soon return, he increased the debt burden of various companies within his system. As the prices of the stocks that he had sold to the public declined, he spent large sums in trying to support them; he believed this to be "absolutely necessary" in order to aid the many investors who were involved. To secure the means to save the situation he transferred funds from one company to another—to no avail. When his system finally collapsed, he assigned what remained of his personal fortune to receivers. Insull's efforts to save the system and to retain control, rather than his earlier financial dealings, brought him into serious trouble. Accused of defrauding the public of around $100 million, he fled abroad, hoping that the almost universal outcry raised against him by the press and by politicians would abate. Apprehended, he was returned to the United States and brought to trial, along with his son and others. Their exoneration was sensational news at the time, for Samuel Insull had become a depression-ridden nation's number one whipping-boy.

Howard C. Hopson, mogul of the Associated Gas & Electric System, whose securities had been sold to half a million buyers, held on to his empire much longer than had Insull. During the depression he maneuvered with more cleverness than honesty, making his weakening holding-company system ever more complex and less comprehensible. But finally the system collapsed and the law closed in. Hopson was sentenced to a prison term, after which, broken mentally, he spent his last days in a sanatorium, supported by a modest annuity. When, after years of litigation, a federal court confirmed a plan of reorganization for Hopson's two top holding companies, the common and preferred stockholders and the holders of subordinated indebtedness got nothing, and the holders of senior indebtedness received only from 8 to 40 cents on the dollar. *Fortune* described the long and difficult process of unravelling the corporate knots that Hopson had tied as "one of the longest and most delirious hangovers from the business moonshine of the twenties."[2]

In Paris, in March, 1932, Ivar Kreuger, "Match King of the World," committed suicide. Demoralization thereupon swept

[2] "Through the Wringer with A.G.&E.," *Fortune* (December, 1945), p. 165.

the Paris Bourse, and stock exchanges in other financial centers reacted severely; the Swedish government closed the Stockholm Stock Exchange. That Kreuger was in trouble had hardly been suspected. The panic had not seemed to harm his companies, although the prices of their shares had declined along with the rest of the market. Far into the depression he and his companies seemed to be withstanding the worldwide adversity. But the long decline in security prices and the ravages of the depression had impaired the solvency of Kreuger's great empire. He concealed the true situation by issuing securities and using the proceeds to pay dividends. Soon after his death it was revealed that for years the accounts he presented to the investment bankers who marketed his companies' securities had been falsified and that he had forged many millions of dollars worth of securities, including some $80 million of Italian treasury bills. The investment bankers had taken Kreuger's word for the condition of his companies without investigating, and through them many thousands of investors had been duped. In Sweden, where his companies' securities were widely held, many individuals faced financial ruin, and numerous suicides followed upon Kreuger's.

John J. Raskob, whose true love throughout the boom was the stock of General Motors, no doubt "stayed with it" during the panic and the depression. We find no record of how he felt about the stock when it reached its low of 7⅝ in 1932 (compared with its 1929 high of 91¾), but in the following decades it regained its prestige; and Raskob, who died in 1950 at the age of seventy-one, was still thought of as one of the financial tycoons of the age.

To "Mike" Meehan, the Stock Exchange specialist who had helped to push Radio Corporation of America upward by 500 points or so, the panic was a severe blow. No doubt his own and his firm's holdings of the stock were very large, and when Radio's long descent brought it to 2½ in 1932, he must have wondered at his former great faith in it. That he was apparently a good loser was illustrated one day during the worst of the panic, when he was reported to have said cheerfully to one of his partners, "Well, I understand I'm broke. Guess we'd better give all the boys in the office a two weeks' bonus to prove it."[3] Perhaps this remark was in response to uninformed gossip, for neither he nor his firm was ruined, although they were undoubtedly hard-hit. In 1935, on his son's twenty-first birthday, he presented him with a membership on the New York Stock Exchange, which had cost him about $130,000. But the panic and depression wore Meehan down. He suffered a personality change, becoming distrait, morose, and hostile, and he was beset by trouble with the Securities and Exchange Commission. His confinement in a sanatorium could not be avoided, but the firm that bore his name continued and prospered. To this day one of its partners keeps the specialist's "book" for Radio Corporation, and the firm is reputed to be "the most heavily capitalized" of the Stock Exchange's specialist houses.

The panic and depression wreaked havoc with the personal affairs of Charles E. Mitchell, the great banker and super-salesman of the boom. His losses were even greater than those of most of the people to whom he had sold some $15 billion of bonds and stocks when stock prices were high and the public was willing to buy, on bankers' recommendations, bonds with such poor prospects that they should never have been underwritten. Mitchell's $30 million fortune went by the board, he lost his positions with the National City Bank and the National City Company, a federal court tried him for tax evasion, and by 1933 he was, reportedly, $12 million in debt. Mitchell's story, however, has a happier ending than that of most of the stock-market great who flourished in the 1920's. Even though overwhelmed with debt and pursued by adversity, he refused to take refuge in bankruptcy. Instead, he started over again in the

[3] *Time* (December 7, 1936), p. 73.

investment underwriting business, becoming chairman of the respected firm of Blythe & Company. He prospered, paid off his huge debts, and lived until 1955, when he died at the age of seventy-eight.

The Nation in Adversity

Statistics cannot tell the story of the losing struggle for financial survival of the many who were in business and the professions; of the impoverishment of those who depended upon investment income that diminished or disappeared; of the demoralizing idleness of the unemployed; of the widespread destitution and sometimes unallayed hunger; of the wretchedness, misery, and despair that were common phenomena of the depression. As the depression continued, fewer babies were born and fewer students entered college. For many people, the simple physical amenities of life and the small cultural enjoyments to which they had been accustomed became luxuries beyond their reach. As factories closed and stores were emptied, the country seemed to quiet down. Fewer trains sped between cities, and there was less automobile traffic on the roads.

One of the earliest adaptations to the depression, especially in New York and other large cities, was made by the unemployed people who became apple-sellers, setting up little stands at busy street corners and subway entrances. For a short time there seemed to be the illusion that if only everyone would buy apples from everyone selling them, economic conditions would right themselves.

In most large cities, long lines of somber individuals became a common sight. There were employment lines, where even one small job opening had attracted hundreds of applicants; there were bread lines, where the penniless waited for the rude fare that private charity or local government provided.

Missions in the cities' blighted areas saw a change in the kind of derelicts who sought relief—more of them victims of economic circumstance rather than of alcoholism, vice, or mental deterioration. Many other economic outcasts, who had detached themselves from their families or had none, took to the road to follow the harvests or to pursue rumors of work opportunities around the country. They walked, hitched rides on the highways, and rode in empty freight cars. These transients swelled the population of the hobo "jungles" covertly established on the outskirts of many cities. On urban waste land or near the cities' refuse heaps so-called "Hoovervilles" sprang up —squalid little communities where shacks of tin, tar paper, paperboard, and discarded pieces of wood sheltered the uprooted and the dispossessed.

Looking back on those years, it may seem remarkable that the country did not come close to violent revolution. As the depression wore on and unrest deepened, threats of violence were heard here and there, especially in the Middle West when farm mortgage holders sought to foreclose. The Bonus March on Washington was the biggest organized demonstration of protest. While violence was not the intention of the majority of the veterans demanding bonus payments from Congress, a communist-inspired left wing appears to have agitated for rioting and bloodshed in the hope that these would set off a revolution. In one mass foray with the District of Columbia police, two of the marchers were killed.

Protest, however, usually took the form of schemes and proposals that ranged from the advocation of equal redistribution of all wealth, limitless currency inflation, and universal brotherly love to the agitation for the five-day week and the abolishment of prohibition. Not all the panaceas for ending the depression were proposed by crackpots, money cranks, and their ilk. Some were urged by prominent and influential people. Many of the proposals required government spending on a vast scale. Some of these favored special groups, such as war veterans, regardless of individual needs, the intention being to pump newly created money into circulation. Others were directed toward the relief of suffering and prevention of hunger generally. Although many of the plans disregarded the deficits they would cause, others included measures for increasing the government's revenue. The latter particularly favored higher tax rates for the higher income brackets. The labor leaders who urged a five-day week with no cut in pay failed to show convincingly how beleaguered employers could meet the extra cost. And putting an end to prohibition, thereby letting the government obtain through taxation of alcoholic beverages what was being taken instead by bootleggers and racketeers, would have been at most a small part of any solution for so vast a problem.

Several large organized movements of a more or less utopian nature arose. The first of these, and the shortest-lived, was Upton Sinclair's E.P.I.C. (End Poverty in California). In essence, it proposed a $50 monthly old age pension, to be financed by increased income and inheritance taxes, as well as by a tax on unused land, and it advocated the widespread establishment of cooperatives. Even before Sinclair's program withered on the vine, Dr. Francis E. Townsend, also in California, was organizing a movement to provide a $200-a-month pension for unemployed people over sixty years old, all of which had to be spent within a month. Such pensions were to be financed by a 2 per cent tax on all transactions. Another movement, also originating in California, supported the "Ham and Eggs" or "Thirty Dollars Every Thursday" pension proposal for every resident of the state who was over fifty years old.

Less naïve than these was the "Share-Our-Wealth" plan of Huey Long, senator and demogogue from Louisiana, who was aiming for the White House and dictatorship when he was assassinated in 1935. Another demagogue who gathered a large following was Father Charles E. Coughlin, who established the National Union for Social Justice, a movement that embodied various aspects of socialism and Nazism. In one way or another during the depression, millions of people's hopes were raised but never fulfilled by these and other movements and leaders that appealed to both human kindness and cupidity, to utopian idealism and a craving for political power, and, perhaps most of all, to a desire to "do something" about the depression.[4]

What is apt to be overlooked in reviewing the tragedy of the depression is that to a large part of the population the depression was a long-lasting inconvenience that thwarted personal plans, rather than a cause of degradation or ruin. Although those who were not impoverished bewailed the lack of opportunity for advancement, feared the loss of employment, or felt quite painfully the pinch of hard times, three-fourths of the population kept its jobs, its businesses, and professional occupations. A minority, whose salary or other income was not impaired, was better off than before because of lower prices. But many changes in individual lives were unhappily dramatic. Once-wealthy families eked out a subsistence from small vestiges of their former incomes, and some had to manage on tiny remittances from relatives or friends little better off than themselves. Sacrifice and humiliation were a daily part of many people's lives.

Men and women adapted themselves to adverse circumstances as best they could, however, sometimes cheerfully but more often bitterly. Most changes of occupation were downward. Men of high training and exceptional skill were forced to take clerical jobs, when they could get them, or they worked as common laborers. Debutantes became store clerks and waitresses. Women of culture and fashion sold things from door to door or solicited magazine subscriptions over the telephone.

---

[4] For an extended account of these movements and of many other social and political developments of the depression, see Dixon Wecter, *The Age of the Great Depression, 1929–1941* (New York: The Macmillan Company, 1948).

Here and there people discovered unexpected satisfactions that made up for loss of status, but they were few compared with the many to whom the loss was at best something to be endured.

Because of financial retrenchment, family life suffered in some respects and benefited in others. Where there was enforced idleness some spouses saw too much of each other, the demeaned ex-breadwinner often was touchy and felt blame for his family's plight, and some husbands and wives took out their frustrations on each other and on the children. But in many families the need to economize brought the members together in pleasurable ways. Games once thought old-fashioned were revived. Parlor stunts and charades saw a renaissance; and checkers, dominoes, jigsaw puzzles, and similar diversions became popular. A new game—"Monopoly," ironically enough—gave one the opportunity to play at high finance, and Contract Bridge acquired millions of devotees.

Inexpensive hobbies flourished. There was a revival of bicycling, and for a short time early in the depression miniature golf enjoyed a tremendous vogue. Reading also was a pastime and a way of forgetting one's troubles. Books like Margaret Mitchell's *Gone With the Wind* and Hervey Allen's *Anthony Adverse*, bargains because of their great length, provided enjoyable entertainment and became tremendous best-sellers. Those who could afford the movies found in them an anodyne for their worries. Some movie houses sought to stimulate attendance by instituting double features, Bingo or Keno games played for prizes, and a lottery-like attraction called Bank Night, while others gave pieces of chinaware to their patrons. For a time a chain-letter craze seized upon a large part of the population, whose frenzied efforts to get a large return from a tiny outlay were for the most part frustrated. One such device presumed that whoever complied with its rules would eventually receive, in return for a dime mailed to the name at the top of a list, dimes from nearly 50,000 others who were expected to follow in the chain.

One cannot say that the American people endured the depression with good humor, for in general they did not. Much of what humor there was had a tincture of cynicism. While most humorous magazines lost many of their readers and fell upon hard times, one newcomer to the newsstands, *Ballyhoo*, made a great success of ridiculing advertising, advertisers, and high-pressure salesmanship. The "cup-of-coffee" joke, a phenomenon of the period, arose from the customary plea of panhandlers, a growing legion of more or less professional beggars, for "a nickel for a cup of coffee." When one such derelict asked for a dime for a cup of coffee and the response was, "Why a dime?" he was supposed to have said, "I want you to have one with me." Another, when asked to explain why he wanted a dollar for a cup of coffee, was said to have replied, "I just got a margin call from my broker."

Quite a number of the songs that became popular, most of which were lighthearted and cheerful, had themes relating to the depression: "Now's the Time to Fall in Love (Potatoes Are Cheaper)," "Let's Have Another Cup of Coffee," "Shanty Town," "I Found a Million Dollar Baby," "Brother Can You Spare a Dime?" and, ironically, "Happy Days Are Here Again."

In these stark years of depression most state and local governments did what they could to relieve the extremes of hardship within their boundaries, but as their expenditures generally exceeded their revenues, and borrowing became more and more difficult, the tradition of non-intervention by the federal government came to an end. The Hoover administration stepped up spending for public works, provided subsidies for agriculture, and established the Reconstruction Finance Corporation. And the New Deal administration, free of concern for large deficits, a rapidly increasing debt, and inflationary (or "reflationary") monetary policy, entered upon a vast program of "pump-priming," which brought on the four-year upswing in business activity that culminated in the severe recession of 1937–38.

12

Causes

THE CAUSES OF THE PANIC, and of the depression that it heralded, were complex and deep rooted. They were spread out over the world, and they could be ascribed in some degree to the great war that had begun fifteen years before. Many of them seemed remote and hardly related to the phenomena of American prosperity and of the stock market boom that led up to the panic. Even today economists differ in the emphasis they give to the various influences that were at work. Most of those influences, however, were associated with the dominant one, namely, *inflation*; that is, an unwarranted increase in currency and bank credit.

Among the immediate or precipitating causes were the unjustifiably high prices of common stocks; the vulnerability of stockholders who had bought beyond their means and carried their securities on thin margins; declining prices in foreign securities markets; the precedent-setting refusal of the Massachusetts Department of Public Utilities to permit recapitalization for stock market purposes; the traumatic effect on the London markets of the revelation of the Hatry defalcations; the delayed but inevitable reaction to the change in Federal Reserve policy that began with cautionings and warnings early in the year and that culminated with the Federal Reserve Bank of New York raising its rediscount rate to 6 per cent in August; and the increase in the Bank of England's discount rate to 6½ per cent in September, 1929. If stock prices had been less inflated, and if ideas as to future corporation earnings and the extent to which stock buyers anticipated them had been more temperate, the panic would have been less severe. It is a bromide, but nevertheless true, that the higher stock prices rose, the further they had to fall.

More fundamental forces, however, were at work to end the stock market boom and the era of widespread prosperity. In the United States the inflationary extension of credit, not only for stock speculation but for business, real estate, and consumer purchases, had led to an unwholesome, illiquid debt condition on an enormous scale. Internationally, too, the credit situation was bad. The day of reckoning for war debts, reparations, reconstruction, unbalanced national budgets, insecure currencies, international trade restrictions, and deep mutual distrust among nations merely had been put off by the temporary zeal of American investors to buy foreign bonds.

Although the great inflation in the United States was made possible by policies of a quasi-governmental institution, the Federal Reserve Board, which by law was intended to act independently of other government agencies, the inflation was aggravated by private rather than governmental abuse of the credit that was made so readily available through the Federal Reserve System. Usually, when a bank made a loan it merely added the amount to the borrower's checking account, thus creating new deposit money that the borrower could put into circulation by drawing checks. Checking account deposits and currency were, of course, interchangeable. While the nation's credit mechanism was complex, and much borrowing and lending did not directly involve the banks themselves, it was, nevertheless, the commercial banks and the Federal Reserve banks behind them that were accountable for the unwarranted increase in the credit supply. And much of the increase was used for speculative ventures that did not create material things of

value, the sale of which would have liquidated the increased
amount of credit created for their production.

The Money-Credit Supply, 1921, 1929, 1933
(in billions of dollars)

JUNE 30	CURRENCY OUTSIDE BANKS	DEMAND DEPOSITS ADJUSTED	TIME DEPOSITS*	TOTAL DEPOSITS ADJUSTED AND CURRENCY OUTSIDE BANKS
1921	3.68	17.11	16.58	37.37
1929	3.64	22.54	28.61	54.79
1933	4.76	14.41	21.66	40.83

* In commercial banks, mutual savings banks, and the Postal Savings
System.

Source: U.S. Department of Commerce, Bureau of the Census, *Historical
Statistics of the United States, Colonial Times to 1957* (Washington, D.C.:
Government Printing Office, 1960), p. 646.

The overly liberal credit policy of the central banking authorities was readily acquiesced in by most commercial bankers,
partly because of the resultant increase in banking profits and
partly because of the general optimism that conditioned the
thinking of even the most astute of them. To avoid inflating the
money supply they would have had to limit their securities
loans and other non-commercial loans to the amount of their
banking capital and the savings deposited with them, restricting their extensions of credit in the form of demand deposits
to short-term, self-liquidating commercial and industrial loans.
Instead, many of them permitted or even invited an inordinate
amount of borrowing of various kinds that under older, tradi-
tional principles of commercial banking would not have been
countenanced.

As the stock market boom progressed, brokers borrowed
immense sums to lend to customers who bought on margin. A
significant tightening of credit at any point in the course of the

stock market boom might quickly have brought the boom to a halt. But the Federal Reserve Board and the twelve regional Federal Reserve banks, of which the Federal Reserve Bank of New York was the leader, followed an easy money policy throughout most of the 1920's, thus making it possible for the member banks to expand their lending, regardless of the purpose of the loans. Brokers' borrowings, reported monthly by the New York Stock Exchange, increased from $1.1 billion at the end of 1920 to $8.6 billion on October 1, 1929. By the end of 1932 these had decreased to a mere $0.4 billion. The table shows the volume of lending to brokers and securities dealers, in millions of dollars, by the New York City banks that were members of the Federal Reserve System.

1921:	June 29	735
	Dec. 28	899
1922:	June 28	1,328
	Dec. 27	1,489
1923:	June 27	1,440
	Dec. 26	1,217
1924:	June 25	1,478
	Dec. 31	1,932
1925:	June 24	2,237
	Dec. 30	2,908
1926:	June 30	2,565
	Dec. 29	2,788
1927:	June 29	3,118
	Dec. 28	3,718
1928:	June 27	4,178
	Dec. 26	5,091
1929:	June 26	5,542
	Oct. 2	6,804*
	Dec. 31	3,424
1930:	June 25	3,416
	Dec. 31	1,926

1931:	June 24	1,406
	Dec. 30	591
1932:	June 29	342
	July 27	331†
	Dec. 28	394

Source: *Federal Reserve Bulletin.* Data were reported for the week ending on the day indicated. Prior to 1926, data are available only for the 43 banks reporting daily to the Federal Reserve Bank of New York. Succeeding data are from the 61 member banks in New York City.

* Largest weekly total.
† Smallest weekly total.

The excessive money-credit supply in the United States spilled over into Europe and Latin America as American investors bought large amounts of publicly and privately issued foreign securities, many of which eventually lost most of their original stated value. The flow of funds from both the United States and Britain to Germany and France in the latter half of the decade was enormous. The United States and Britain were both on the gold standard, and as the key currencies of the world the dollar and pound were universally respected. But France and Germany, and many other countries not as well off, had established their monetary systems on what is called the gold *exchange* standard. The reserves that backed their currencies, unlike the reserves of the United States and British monetary systems, consisted only partly of gold, the rest being dollars and pounds sterling. Although the money-credit systems of the United States and Great Britain were based on gold, a part of that same gold base helped to support the currencies of many other countries. Thus the large flow of funds from the gold standard countries to those that were limited to the gold exchange standard made possible an enormous expansion of credit in the gold exchange standard countries, which followed much the same easy money policies as those pursued in the two principal gold standard countries. As a result, what passed as "money" throughout much of the world was largely paper currency and bank deposits that to a large extent represented a combination of illiquid and fictitious assets.

The United States was not solely responsible for this worldwide inflation; but the inflation would have been much less, and the subsequent deflation accordingly less severe, if U.S. monetary authorities had followed less inflationary or non-inflationary policies.

The earlier part of the 1920's had witnessed a sound business recovery in the United States, with comparatively little speculative excess. Much-needed construction, put off by the war, strengthened the recovery. Later in the decade speculative building induced by liberal credit and grandiose thinking was an adjunct of speculation in the stock market. By 1925, the optimism fostered by increasing prosperity was growing into the notion that a New Era of perpetual boom was at hand.

The rise in stock prices in its earlier stages seemed justified by the business expansion and the attendant increase in corporation earnings. While some stock owners pyramided their paper profits as the boom progressed, others spent them for many kinds of consumer goods and services, thus diverting to the channels of commerce funds that had originated in bank credit created to finance speculation and investment.

Because of a recession in business activity in 1924, the Federal Reserve banks expanded credit and lowered interest rates. They continued this policy during 1925 at the urging of the heads of the Bank of England, the Reichsbank, and the Bank of France. Benjamin Strong, the influential governor of the Federal Reserve Bank of New York, concurred with the proposals of these central bankers that an easy money policy should be adopted in the United States, so that funds would flow to Europe to strengthen the British pound and the major currencies of continental Europe. Throughout Europe, unbalanced government budgets due to vast expenditures for postwar rehabilitation and other public works, for military establishments, and for politically inspired extravagance had led various governments into serious financial difficulties; and rather than balance their budgets and spur their people to more hard work, thrift, and greater productivity, they sought American dollars to help them along the path they preferred to follow.

For a time, because of protests from influential senators and others in the government, the credit expansion was halted, but in 1927 Governor Strong's views again prevailed. The Federal Reserve Board went even further in its effort to ease credit in order to aid the European governments. And as the reaffirmation of the Board's inflationary policy gave renewed encouragement to speculators to use the easily available credit in the stock market, the rise in prices was accelerated. Between September, 1927, and October, 1929, as brokers' borrowings to carry their customers increased from $3.7 billion to $8.6 billion, common stock prices just about doubled. The table shows changes in the rediscount rate of the Federal Reserve Bank of New York between 1921 and 1930.

DATE EFFECTIVE		RATE
1921:	May 5	6½ %
	June 16	6
	July 21	5½
	September 22	5
	November 3	4½
1922:	June 22	4
1923:	February 23	4½
1924:	May 1	4
	June 12	3½
	August 8	3
1925:	February 27	3½
1926:	January 8	4
	April 23	3½
	August 13	4
1927:	August 5	3½

1928:	February 3	4
	May 18	4½
	July 13	5
1929:	August 9	6
	November 1	5
	November 15	4½
1930:	February 7	4
	March 14	3½
	May 2	3
	June 20	2½
	December 24	2

Source: Board of Governors of the Federal Reserve System, *Banking Studies,* by members of the staff (Baltimore: 1941), pp. 454–56.

Thus much of the responsibility for the credit excesses of the boom, hence for the severity of the panic and the depression, must be placed on the members of the Federal Reserve Board and other high officers in the Federal Reserve System who encouraged the unwarranted credit expansion. Their excuses were that easy money helped the western farmers, that it reduced the flow of gold from Europe and so aided in rehabilitating the European currencies, and that in 1927, when the easy money policy was most actively undertaken, the country was experiencing a business recession, albeit a very mild one.

Perhaps those who determined the Federal Reserve's policies did not comprehend how dangerous they were; but if they— the nation's top monetary authorities—did not, how could those caught up in the great speculative frenzy have been expected to foresee and understand the dangers? One might say, of course, that easy money and credit should not have tempted those who made use of it to speculate in the stock market and in other ways, that it was they who induced the inflation by using the funds that the bankers were so willing to create for them. But this reaction of people seems commonly to have been a part of the inflation syndrome.

The inflation that developed in the United States in the 1920's was not the result of unsound government finance, as major inflations often are. The government was not pumping newly printed currency into circulation or monetizing deficits through the banking system. In every fiscal year from 1920 through 1930 revenues exceeded expenditures; and the federal debt, which had been more than $25 billion in 1919, was reduced to less than $17 billion in 1930. Although the government sometimes sold short-term securities to the banks rather than directly to the public, this seems to have been of comparatively small significance over the whole decade.

High government officials did, however, acquiesce in the boom, apparently regarding the rise in the stock market as merely a reflection of general prosperity. "Coolidge prosperity" and "Hoover boom" had become common expressions. President Coolidge, who declared in 1927 that he did not "choose to run" again for office, may have sensed with Yankee shrewdness that the good times could not last forever. But he seemed to see no cause for concern in the great expansion of credit that was taking place. Early in 1928, when brokers' loans were increasing rapidly, he ascribed the increase to "a natural expansion of business" that was "not large enough to cause any unfavorable comment."

President Hoover, a man of sound business judgment, did not encourage speculation or look with favor upon it, but he too revealed that he shared the national optimism when he declared in accepting the nomination for the presidency that, with God's help, the time was in sight when "poverty will be banished from the nation." Nevertheless, as early as 1925 he was aware of the rising tide of speculation, and as it continued he repeatedly protested against the inflationary policies of the Federal Reserve Board. While President, he sought in various ways to induce financial leaders to cooperate in ending the speculative orgy. At his request, Secretary of the Treasury Andrew Mellon, who had served also under President Coolidge, tried to warn the country of the dangers inherent in the situation.[1]

Looking back on the great stock market boom from the perspective of the panic and the long depression, it is hard to realize clearly how pervasive was the illusion that never again would the nation experience panic and depression. It was generally believed that the Federal Reserve System, through its various instruments of currency and credit control, would keep a boom from getting out of hand and would stimulate business activity when that was called for. Thus, it was reasoned, a New Era was at hand from which the business cycle, with its phases of contraction and expansion, had been eliminated. Even most of the nation's bankers seemed to believe this. The widespread faith in the immunity of the economy from adverse developments was variously expressed:

> We shall have no more financial panics. . . . Panics are impossible. . . . Business men can now proceed in perfect confidence that they will no longer put their property in peril . . . . Now the business man may work out his destiny without living in terror of panic and hard times. . . . Panics in the future are unthinkable. . . . Never again can panic come to the American people.[2]

It seems that no matter how irrational a widely held belief may appear in retrospect, only a mind of remarkable independence can resist its compelling force when it is flourishing. The general confidence in ever-rising stock prices, with its supporting rationalizations that justified speculation, was symptomatic of the phenomenon that Bernard Baruch and others have referred to as "the madness of crowds." Although still largely unexplained by behavioral scientists, this so-called "madness"

[1] *The Memoirs of Herbert Hoover; The Great Depression, 1929–1941* (New York: The Macmillan Company, 1952), pp. 5–20.

[2] *Ibid.,* p. 7.

must be taken into account in any attempt to explain major booms and panics.

Other influences, although of secondary significance compared with inflation and the speculative use of the funds it provided, distorted economic processes and increased the need for readjustments. In the first place, the remarkable increase in productivity during the 1920's did little to lower prices. Also, while wages of industrial workers increased and business profits grew substantially, the farm and white-collar workers benefited very little. This maladjustment of income distribution, and the greatly increased industrial output that had arisen in response to the production losses during the war, reduced demand in some areas of the economy late in the 1920's, most notably in building construction and capital goods. Elements of monopoly, special privilege, and exploitation were also adverse influences. And the complexity of international political, economic, and financial maladjustments loomed in the background. The unsolved problems of war reparations and debts, and the ever-higher level of import duties in the United States, were especially unwholesome elements in the situation.

Nevertheless, it seems probable that the prosperity of the United States in the 1920's—which developed first from war-created scarcities and then from the tremendous amount of innovation and the great gains in productivity that lowered costs—could have been sustained on a comparatively sound basis, given gradually declining prices and without the increase in the money supply that resulted from bank-financed speculation in real estate, in unwisely conceived business projects, and especially in the stock market. At some point, doubtless, the era of prosperity would have been brought to an end by distorting influences other than the monetary one, with the usual sequence of developments so well known to students of the business cycle. But then, it seems certain, the extent of the boom and the ensuing crisis and depression would not have been such that it placed them among the most dramatic episodes of economic and financial history.

It would seem that the money-credit inflation and the mass psychology or "madness of crowds" responsive to it were the primary causes of the extended boom and of the compensatory and corrective panic and depression that followed. Although attention here has been focused on the boom and panic developments in the United States, inflation and the human response to it were present in many other countries also; and the resulting worldwide maladjustment apparently accounts for the length, extent, and depth of the depression that followed. The boom could not have gone to the extreme that it did, either in the United States or elsewhere in the world, without the implementation of overextended and misused credit.

There have been many causal interpretations of the boom and panic of the 1920's. Some follow essentially the same line of thought presented here. Others give little or no attention to the inflation factor. Practically all of them recognize the causal relationship between both the boom and the panic and the panic and the depression. Many of them differ principally in the emphasis that they place on various circumstances and developments. In some the ideological overtones—the echoes, at least, of particular socio-economic philosophies—can be distinguished. In some, too, the "insight" of the authors seems to be much more in the nature of revelation, or reasoning from a favored premise, than an objective consideration of facts.

Since it would be virtually impossible to bring together and do justice to all of the interpretations that have appeared, the following summary statements relating to the causes of the boom and panic, and often those of the depression as well, are offered as examples of the diversity of views and emphases that has existed ever since the events. They show, furthermore, that the "inflation" hypothesis has respectable support and that the "mass psychology" factor is frequently recognized. In reading

these excerpts one must of course bear in mind that their authors, in most cases, had much more to say on the subject, and
that for our limited purposes the quotations have been taken
out of context.

Many of the explanations of the panic that found wide acceptance at the time it occurred or soon afterward were, as
might be expected, superficial or predominantly concerned
with short-run developments and market technicalities. The
comparatively few voices, however, that had long decried the
boom and warned of its consequences also were heard again.

E. H. H. Simmons, president of the New York Stock Exchange when the panic occurred, took occasion to express his
views in January, 1930, when the strong post-panic rally was
still taking place:

> The primary cause of the panic was undoubtedly the high level
> of prices which so many leading American share issues had
> attained. . . . It became evident that there had been industrial
> overproduction, particularly in automobiles and steel. . . . For
> various reasons, some of which I will mention later, we have
> had in the stock market an extraordinary willingness to buy
> and an equally extraordinary unwillingness to sell. It was this
> lack of equilibrium which really made trouble . . . the colossal
> output of new stock issues thrust on the market during Sep-
> tember and October. . . . [Aggravating factors were] income
> taxes on capital gains . . . [and] the mechanical inadequacy of
> the present stock ticker quotation system. . . . In the last
> analysis, however, I do not believe that it was due to credit
> conditions that the stock market collapse occurred. . . . Any
> attempt to make the Federal Reserve system a scapegoat for
> the securities panic last fall would be both unjust and un-
> desirable.[3]

[3] *The Principal Causes of the Stock Market Crisis of Nineteen Twenty-
nine*, address delivered at the Thirty-First Annual Dinner of the Transportation Club of the Pennsylvania Railroad, at Philadelphia, Pennsylvania,
January 25, 1930.

The communist press reacted according to doctrine:

> This business boom was erected on the increased production resulting from the rationalization drive against the American working class and the past few years of tremendous expansion abroad of American imperialist export of capital and commodities.
>
> The increasing difficulties of American capitalism to secure an unobstructed growth of markets both at home and abroad, are deepening the general crisis of American capitalism (as part of the world crisis) and the development of the economic crisis. Over-production of automobiles (the strong point in recent "prosperity"), oil, coal, textiles, shoes, building construction, agricultural products, etc. are some of the evidences of this economic crisis. The crisis is now asserting itself on the stock Exchange.[4]

Theologian Reinhold Niebuhr wrote:

> The bull market was created by phenomenal profits in a few leading shares. Even in these shares there were not sufficient profits to justify the prices which prevailed before October 28. These prices were purely speculative, based partly upon the appropriation by the owners of all the wealth which the modern machine is producing (the skilled workers sharing a little and the unskilled workers sharing not at all in the increase of wealth), and partly created by owners and buyers anticipating future profits.
>
> .   .   .   .
>
> The fact is that the whole problem of speculation is merely a vivid revelation of the unethical character of our entire civilization. It reveals the artificiality of an age which hides human and social factors behind the abstractions of money; it portrays the anti-social character of a profit-mad civilization which

[4] "The Wall Street Crash and the Working Class," *Daily Worker* (October 28, 1929), p. 1.

looks upon industry purely from the perspective of human greed.

.   .   .   .

The speculation mania is merely the symptom of a civilization which does not deal ethically or humanely with its complex relationships, which has abstracted all human and social meaning from business relationships until only the economic implication remains, and greed becomes the sole motive to which an appeal can be made.[5]

Gustav Cassel, a Swedish economist whose writings were translated and widely read throughout the world, stated:

If we want to go farther in our inquiry and find out the deeper psychological causes behind the forces which have brought down prices in the gold-receiving countries, we shall have no difficulty in ascertaining the main influences responsible for this development. Among these influences American puritanism stands out as perhaps the most important. From this side the stock exchange speculation of 1928–9 was regarded as particularly sinful behavior which had to get its punishment. To that end credit had to be restricted and prices to be forced down. The great danger of such a proceeding for American production and trade and generally for the world's well being was put aside as unimportant in comparison with a punishment regarded as a commandment of the highest justice. People of this mind are inclined to believe in deflation just as they believe in suffering as a means of education.[6]

One British point of view was expressed by the prominent economist Lionel Robbins:

But why did inflation take place?

[5] Reinhold Niebuhr, "The Speculation Mania," *The World Tomorrow* (January, 1930), pp. 25, 27.
[6] Gustav Cassel, *The Crisis in the World's Monetary System*, 2nd ed. (Oxford: The Clarendon Press, 1932), p. 76.

. . . .

The answer seems to be that it was the direct outcome of misdirected management on the part of the Federal Reserve authorities—an error of management, however, which Englishmen at any rate have no right to speak of with reproach, for it seems almost certain that it was carried out very largely with the intent to ease our position.

. . . .

By 1927 the [British] position was one of great danger. International assistance was sought. And in the summer of that year, partly in order to help us, partly in order to ease the domestic position, the authorities of the Federal Reserve System took the momentous step of forcing a regime of cheap money. A vigorous policy of purchasing securities was initiated.

. . . .

The policy succeeded. The impending recession was averted. The London position was eased. The reflation succeeded. Production and the Stock Exchange took on a new lease of life. But from that date, according to all evidence, the situation got completely out of control. By 1928 the authorities were thoroughly frightened. But now the forces they had released were too strong for them. . . . Velocity of circulation, the frenzied anticipation of speculators and company promoters, had now taken control. With resignation the best men in the system looked forward to the inevitable smash.[7]

The London *Economist* observed in December, 1929:

Looking back over this period, one may describe Reserve Bank policy as both vacillating and ineffective. The three increases of ½ percent in the New York rediscount rate made during 1928 were none of them sufficient to check speculation, and their cumulative effect was just as negligible. Open market

[7] Lionel Robbins, *The Great Depression* (London: Macmillan and Co., Ltd., 1934), pp. 51–54.

policy was clearly lacking in consistency of purpose, and . . . had little effect on the growth in brokers' loans. It is difficult to refrain from ascribing the course of events on Wall Street, in part at least to the absence of any continuous policy on the part of the Reserve Banks and to their preference for the use of the inadequate weapon of open market policy instead of the stronger weapon of substantial increases in the rediscount rate.

The truth is that the banks, whether Reserve Banks or member banks, were only in partial control of the situation, simply because Wall Street derived a substantial portion of its funds from "others," and each attempt by the Reserve Banks to exert pressure on the member banks, and each reduction the latter made in their call loans, was more than offset by loans made by "others." . . . So long as there was the demand for call loans, whatever the call rate might be, it was difficult for the banks actually to prevent "others" from meeting the demand. Only a policy of drastic credit deflation would have dried up the home supply of money, and the adoption of such a policy might well have precipitated a general business collapse.[8]

The Swiss economist Wilhelm Roepke stated:

Although the economic tendencies in the individual countries sometimes ran counter to each other, there can be no doubt that during the time from 1925 to 1929 the productive powers of the world had grown to an extraordinary extent. That this growth was not organic, but was accomplished amidst tremendous economic and, particularly, political tensions, was one of the main causes of the collapse at the end of 1929. World production and world trade increased from year to year and finally surpassed the pre-war level. An ever broadening stream of credits poured from the countries with a surplus of capital . . . to the parts of the world where capital was scarce. . . . The advance of technical knowledge with its tendency to

[8] *The Economist* (December 7, 1929), p. 1070.

reduce production costs put everything that had gone before in the shade. The increase in investment activity, which on this occasion also was the chief characteristic and chief stimulus of the boom, was due principally to the new industries connected with the production of durable consumption goods . . .: and to the activity in building. This growth was matched by a widespread, intense optimism which in the end deteriorated into lack of perspective and discipline. This optimism went so far in places that people began to believe that there was such a thing as "permanent prosperity," and that economic crises could be eliminated.[9]

Dr. Murray N. Rothbard has offered the following analysis:

[The American] economy was, in fact, a mixture of two very different, and basically conflicting, forces. On the one hand, America experienced a genuine prosperity, based on heavy savings and investment in highly productive capital. This great advance raised American living standards. On the other hand, we also suffered a credit-expansion, with resulting accumulation of *malinvested* capital, leading finally and *inevitably* to economic crisis. Here are two great economic forces—one that most people would agree to call "good," and the other "bad"—each separate, but interacting to form the final historical result. Price, production, and trade indices are the composite effects. We may well remember the errors of smugness and complacency that our economists, as well as financial and political leaders, committed during the great boom. Study of these errors might even chasten our current crop of economic soothsayers, who presume to foretell the future within a small, precise margin of error. And yet, we should not scoff unduly at the eulogists who composed paeans to our economic system as late as 1929. For, insofar as they had in mind the *first* strand —the genuine prosperity brought about by high saving and in-

[9] Wilhelm Roepke, *Crises and Cycles* (London: William Hodge & Company, Ltd., 1936), pp. 51–52.

vestment—they were correct. Where they erred gravely was in overlooking the second, sinister strand of credit expansion.[10]

According to Professor Milton Friedman and Anna Jacobson Schwartz:

> The economic collapse from 1929 to 1933 has produced much misunderstanding of the twenties. The widespread belief that what goes up must come down and hence also that what comes down must do so because it earlier went up, plus the dramatic stock market boom, have led many to suppose that the United States experienced severe inflation before 1929 and the Reserve System served as an engine of it. Nothing could be further from the truth. By 1923, wholesale prices had recovered only a sixth of their 1920–21 decline. From then until 1929, they fell on the average of 1 per cent per year. The cyclical expansion from 1927 to 1929 is one of the very few in our record during which prices were a shade lower at the three months centered on the peak than at the three months centered on the initial trough. The stock of money, too, failed to rise and even fell slightly during most of the expansion—a phenomenon not matched in any prior or subsequent cyclical expansion. Far from being an inflationary decade, the twenties were the reverse. And the Reserve System, far from being an engine of inflation, very likely kept the money stock from rising as much as it would have if gold movements had been allowed to exert their full influence.[11]

Mr. A. C. Miller, a member of the Federal Reserve Board, made the following statement to the Senate Committee on Banking and Currency early in 1931:

> In the year 1927 . . . you will note the pronounced increase in

[10] Murray N. Rothbard, *America's Great Depression* (Princeton: D. Van Nostrand Co., Inc., 1963), p. 6.
[11] Milton Friedman and Anna Jacobson Schwartz, *A Monetary History of the United States, 1867–1960,* a study by the National Bureau of Economic Research, New York (Princeton: Princeton University Press, 1963), p. 298.

these holdings [U. S. government securities held by the Federal Reserve banks] in the second half of the year. Coupled with the heavy purchases of acceptances it was the greatest and boldest operation ever undertaken by the Federal Reserve System, and in my judgment, resulted in one of the most costly errors committed by it or any other banking system in the last 75 years![12]

Professor James Washington Bell summarized his view of the causative influences in the following way:

In the light of historical perspective, it is now fairly clear that an understanding of the business cycle history of the twenties, and on into the thirties, lies in the causes and nature of the unusually prolonged period of high investment in producers' and consumers' durable goods. In times past excessive investments and consumption had ultimately been checked by credit limitations, but during the 1920's a new factor, the Federal Reserve System, provided a steady supply of bank credit. Full employment, a high level of income and high propensity to consume, borne of optimism, sustained the demand for goods and a rising tide of speculative fever accounted for enormous fluctuations of new security issues and a boiling stock market.

The "New Era" optimism was reflected particularly in the promotion of new enterprises, real-estate booms, and in the development of a variety of unsound financial practices in both short- and long-term markets. Inflation had taken place more in security values than in commodities and, although a decline in business itself had already appeared in the summer, it was the dramatic break in the stock market in the fall of 1929 which brought on the painful liquidating process and the . . . struggle which our banking and business structure was not designed to meet.[13]

[12] U.S. Congress, Senate Committee on Banking and Currency, *Hearings on S. Res. 71,* 71st Cong., 3d Sess. (January–March, 1931), p. 134.

[13] U.S. Congress, Senate Hearings before a Subcommittee of the Committee on Banking and Currency, March 29–April 1, 1954, *Gold Reserve Act Amendments,* 83d Cong., 2nd Sess., p. 98.

H. Parker Willis, an authority on the Federal Reserve System from the time of its origin, offered the following explanation:

> Negotiations between the Bank of England and the Federal Reserve System, apparently never officially authorized, certainly never officially admitted, developed into the scheme, now well known and recognized, for the maintenance of what is popularly called "easy money" or preferably "easy credit"— low rates of interest and discount—in the New York market. This scheme, at first pursued by indirect and surreptitious methods, gradually came to require more and more positive support, until about three years ago it culminated in an effort to force Federal Reserve rates down to an abnormally low level throughout the United States, nominally in order that there might be no disposition to draw funds to this country from Europe. The Federal Reserve Board at Washington allowed itself to be dragooned into ordering Federal Reserve banks which did not wish to reduce their rates to do so, and the low-rate-and-easy-money philosophy gained ground tremendously. Criticisms and protests were dubbed unpatriotic and plenty of legal reasons were adduced to show that Reserve banks had no rights of their own in regard to the fixing of discount rates, but could always be dictated to by the Board at Washington.

.   .   .   .

> The breakdown of 1929 was as nearly the result of wilful mismanagement and violation of every principle of sound finance as such an occurrence ever has been. It was the outcome of vulgar grasping for gain at the cost of the community.[14]

Freeman Tilden condemned a worldwide "debauch of debt":

What was more clear, and increasingly menacing, was that the

[14] H. Parker Willis, "Who Caused the Panic of 1929?" *North American Review* (February, 1930), pp. 176, 183.

reparation payments and the inter-Allied war debts were causing a stasis of the blood currents of world trade. . . . The complete bankruptcy of Germany in 1923, and the narrow escape
from a similar fate of France in 1926, were unerringly pointing
at a world collapse in 1929. There could have been no other
result: natural laws, if there be no natural morality, demanded
the end of such a debauch of debt. World finance had passed
from the hands of banker-minded economists, through the
hands of broker-minded economists, to come to rest finally in
the grasp of common gamblers. There was no way out of a
financial labyrinth of which the single exit had been stopped by
the refusal of creditors to take payment in the only possible
media of payment; even if it were within the bounds of possibility that the debts could be paid in any manner whatsoever
that would not ruin the creditor as well as the debtor.[15]

Professor John Kenneth Galbraith considers the psychological phenomenon of speculation of great importance:

As already so often emphasized, the collapse in the stock
market in the autumn of 1929 was implicit in the speculation
that went before. The only question concerning that speculation
was how long it would last. Sometime, sooner or later, confidence in the short-run reality of increasing common stock
values would weaken. When this happened, some people
would sell, and this would destroy the reality of increasing
values. Holding for an increase would now become meaning-
less; the new reality would be falling prices. There would be a
rush, pellmell, to unload. This was the way past speculative
orgies had ended. It was the way the end came in 1929. It is
the way speculation will end in the future.

We do not know why a great speculative orgy occurred in
1928 and 1929. The long accepted explanation that credit was
easy and so people were impelled to borrow money to buy

[15] Freeman Tilden, *A World in Debt* (New York: Funk & Wagnalls Company, 1936), pp. 263–64.

common stocks on margin is obviously nonsense. On numerous occasions before and since credit has been easy, and there has been no speculation whatever. Furthermore, much of the 1928 and 1929 speculation occurred on money borrowed at interest rates which for years before, and in any period since, would have been considered exceptionally astringent. Money, by the ordinary tests, was tight in the late twenties.

Far more important than the rate of interest and the supply of credit is the mood. Speculation on a large scale requires a pervasive sense of confidence and optimism and conviction that ordinary people were meant to be rich. People must also have Faith in the good intentions and even in the benevolence of others, for it is by the agency of others that they will get rich.[16]

H. V. Hodson interpreted the boom and its collapse as follows:

The superimposed boom of 1926–29 and its subsequent collapse can be interpreted quite simply in terms of the savings-investment theory. The boom was predominantly an American phenomenon, though in its earlier phases the outflow of American money induced local booms elsewhere. In the United States, investment both at home and abroad was encouraged by the easy-money policy of the Federal Reserve Board, which was initiated in 1927.

.   .   .   .

The volume of construction contracts, which in default of anything better may be accepted as a very fair index of the volume of real investment, increased pretty steadily through 1927 and the first half of 1928. But it is extremely significant that after seasonal fluctuations have been eliminated from it the index touched its maximum level in June, 1928, over a year before the stock market collapse occurred. There were several reasons

[16] John Kenneth Galbraith, *The Great Crash, 1929* (Boston: Houghton Mifflin Company, 1955), pp. 174–75.

for this decline. The earlier investment had diminished the obvious opportunities for more. . . . Second, the effective rate of interest was being raised by the rise of capital values in Wall Street, which was attracting a greater and greater proportion of the country's money savings. High rates of interest were being offered in the frequently justified expectation that the rise of the capital values would outweigh the interest cost altogether. Of course, the rate of saving was probably declining simultaneously—the method of instalment purchase involved, as we have seen, negative saving—but there can be little doubt that the seeds of the subsequent reaction, both in industry and on the stock market, were sown in the autumn of 1928 when the rate of real investment began to fall away and before long to drop behind the rate of saving.

. . . .

The same factors as had inflated the boom, when reversed, accelerated and exaggerated its collapse. The way in which installment buying could do so has already received comment. Those who had spent their capital gains were forced to sell. . . . and were thenceforward constrained to spend less than their current income in order to make up the deficit.

. . . .

It may be legitimately said that the boom and the slump were caused by the alternate domination of greed and fear, and that the one was bound to resign sooner or later in favor of the other, human character being what it is; but the instrument of these emotions in affecting the economic life of millions who may have experienced neither was the relation of saving to investment, of getting to spending.[17]

Professor Alvin H. Hansen, who during the boom had stressed non-monetary aspects of the business cycle, especially the rate of real investment, later declared:

[17] H. V. Hodson, *Economics of a Changing World* (New York: Harrison Smith and Robert Haas, 1933), pp. 158–64.

That the prosperity of the twenties was, at bottom, an investment boom, and that the depression was inevitable once the investment outlets of the postwar period had temporarily become saturated, was in general not recognized by monetary theorists, though many businessmen close to the facts saw quite clearly the real nature of both the boom and the depression.

.   .   .   .

Question is raised whether the monetary weapons designed to check an excessive boom do not inevitably, once they are applied with sufficient vigor to become effective, start a cumulative downward spiral. Lopping off the boom will not automatically fill up the depression gulleys. The monetary weapons can, indeed, be applied effectively to check an expansion. But if the factors making for expansion of investment are vigorous, the monetary brakes have to be applied with great rigor in order to choke off the highly alluring speculative ventures which are driving the economy on toward the boom. If the discount rate is to be raised sufficiently high to choke off the new developments which are the driving force of the investment boom, the more stable segments of the economy will be choked off by a degree of contraction quite incompatible with the aim to level off and stabilize.[18]

Professor Sumner H. Slichter wrote:

The boom which culminated in 1929 was marked by almost no speculative accumulation of inventories. The drop in the demand for housing and automobiles, however, was in large degree responsible for the end of the boom. Although there was no widespread speculation for a rise in commodity prices, the stocks of some raw materials, such as wheat, sugar, cotton, coffee, and rubber, which had been greatly overproduced, were large, and the depression, when it came, was greatly intensified

[18] Alvin H. Hansen, *Fiscal Policy and Business Cycles* (New York: W. W. Norton & Company, Inc., 1941), pp. 70, 71–72.

by the sharp drop in the prices of these and other goods. The boom period was also characterized by enormous speculation in securities. The spending of paper profits made in stock speculation undoubtedly accentuated the boom and the crash in security prices, which followed the recession in business, accentuated the depression.[19]

R. F. Harrod, known especially for his biography of John Maynard Keynes, offered this explanation:

> ... during the boom people were spending more on consumption than they would have done, given their incomes, without the stimulus it provided. They were led on to spend more than they would otherwise have done by a phenomenon which could not continue indefinitely. They were in fact spending more than people with their level of income and their temperament would normally do. There was a lack of balance between saving and spending, consisting of an abnormally high degree of spending. The lack of balance here suggested is in flagrant opposition to that suggested by the production figures. But for the Stock Exchange inflation people would have saved more than they did; but according to the production figures, as things were, they were saving more than was consistent with a proper balance between the output of capital and of consumable goods in industry; they were saving too much in spite of the fact that there was a strong adventitious and temporary influence inducing them to spend more than they would naturally have been inclined [to do]. The conclusion to which these arguments lead is ominous.[20]

Eleanor Lansing Dulles' explanation of the boom, panic, and depression is of special interest because of its broad scope and eclecticism, and also because of her insistence that no single in-

[19] Sumner H. Slichter, *Modern Economic Society* (New York: Henry Holt and Company, 1931), pp. 458–59.

[20] R. F. Harrod, *The Trade Cycle* (Oxford: The Clarendon Press, 1936), p. 211.

fluence or circumstance can account for those developments. Using a "framework of a theory of causes" much like that suggested by Professor Haberler in his study of the business cycle,[21] she analyzed the question of causes by means of a fourfold approach in which the underlying, the precipitating, the continuing, and the cumulative causes were distinguished.

Miss Dulles considered the mistakes made in handling international questions and the "growth in false nationalism" to be the main causes of the depression. Other factors, to which she assigned less weight, were: the speculative boom in real estate and securities; the group of false ideas called the "new era" doctrines; the increasingly artificial situation of American agriculture; excesses in capital equipment production and construction; and errors in judgment and policy stemming from the "new era" psychology. She wrote:

> At the risk of oversimplifying a complex situation, it can be said that from 1927 on two general influences dominated all others. These were the reparation-debt problems and stock market excesses . . . [that] were not completely liquidated even in the dark years of 1932 and 1933. In any case, both the group of problems growing out of reparation—interallied debts and foreign investments on the one hand and the repercussions of the security speculation in the United States on the other—led to continuous and growing distortion in finance.[22]

Professor Chester Whitney Wright briefly summed up the decade of the 1920's as follows:

> In the United States the most deceiving thing was the comparative stability of the price level after the recovery from the

[21] Gottfried Haberler, *Prosperity and Depression*, 4th ed. (Cambridge: Harvard University Press, 1960).

[22] Eleanor Lansing Dulles, *Depression and Reconstruction: A Study of Causes and Controls* (Philadelphia: University of Pennsylvania Press, 1936), pp. 161–62.

1920–1921 reaction. This, on the surface, seemed to belie the warnings as to the danger of inflation, and the action of the Federal Reserve Board showed little evidence that it sensed such a danger. The slow but ominously steady decline of the price level after 1925 went unheeded. Warnings that stock-market values were unjustified were given by some a year or two before the crash, but others insisted that the country was in a "new era" which fully justified them. Banking authorities failed to take any decisive action until the speculative movement was quite out of hand.[23]

R. G. Hawtrey, a British economist, analyzed the situation in the following way:

> Capital outlay had fallen into arrears under war conditions, arrears of upkeep, renewals and extensions, arrears also of improvements and new developments at a time of great technological progress. Revival had been interrupted by the depression of 1921. Enterprise had lagged far behind opportunity.
>
> The need for overtaking these arrears promised in any case a powerful stimulus to the activity of the investment market at a time when a big rise in the value of shares, to correspond with the decline in the wealth value of the dollar, was already overdue.
>
> As the public became more and more alive to the opportunities, investment was reinforced by speculation. A vast mass of advances to speculators in shares came into being in the form of loans to stockbrokers. . . .
>
> These loans for speculation . . . were an extraneous resource provided through the investment market for capital outlay. Any *increase* in this extraneous resource constituted a supplement to the normal supply of investible funds for capital outlay derived from savings. Here was a powerful inflationary force . . . but a precarious one, since the volume of loans for speculation could not go on increasing without limit. Even if it merely

[23] Chester Whitney Wright, *Economic History of the United States*, 2nd ed. (New York: McGraw-Hill Book Company, Inc., 1949), p. 778.

ceased to increase, at however high a level, the inflationary effect would cease; if the volume of loans began to decrease, the effect would become deflationary.

.   .   .   .

The Wall Street crisis of 1929 was not a credit crisis. Great as were the losses sustained by the speculators, the American banks were on the whole well secured and came through unscathed. It was only when the fall in prices of commodities set in, and involved traders in embarrassment, that bank failures began. The crisis of 1929 contributed to hasten the progress of depression, which had already begun, but did not cause any immediate convulsion in the commodity markets.[24]

Carl Snyder, well-known statistician-economist, made this succinct comment:

Never a depression without a preceding boom. Never a boom and high prosperity without an outbreak of speculation. Never such an outbreak that has not ended in a financial crisis. Check the speculation in time, and we shall have no serious depressions. . . .[25]

E. C. Harwood, of the American Institute for Economic Research, described the situation as follows:

The inflationary credit that was slowly poured into the channels of business made possible windfall profits for industry, and invited the speculation that began to grow apace. In 1925 and 1926, the speculative mania found an outlet in the great Florida land boom, but thereafter speculation was centered primarily in the stock market. The increasing marginal purchases became a source of more inflationary credit, which flowed out

[24] R. G. Hawtrey, *Currency and Credit*, 4th ed. (London: Longmans, Green and Company, 1950), pp. 398–99, 404.
[25] Carl Snyder, *Capitalism the Creator* (New York: The Macmillian Company, 1940), p. 229.

into the channels of business and helped to maintain the business boom on which the speculators were gambling.

From 1921 to 1929, the degree of inflation was fluctuating, but was slowly increasing. During most of that period, business activity was maintained at levels well above normal. Commodity prices were supported on a plateau nearly 50 percent higher than prewar levels. . . .

A progressive inflation creates an Alice-in-Wonderland world for the businessman. Speculative risks that, under ordinary circumstances, no sane man would consider, change their character and become safe investments; that is, they are safe for the time being, at least. Men with long experience in the business world, accustomed to evaluating risks . . . are actually handicapped by their knowledge during a period of inflation. . . . The older business virtues, thrift, hard work, and the development of character over a period of years, character of which the hallmark is a fine personal integrity, naturally seem unnecessary adjuncts of business life to those who can obtain success by traveling a much easier route.

.   .   .   .

It is not surprising, therefore, that during the 1920's most people's ideas regarding our economic system became further and further removed from the realities of life. Delusions of grandeur seemed no more than a healthy optimism. Men naturally assumed that they had earned whatever reward they received from the economic system; and all too many individuals accepted the notion that boom-time salaries or profits measured their true worth to society.[26]

A prophetic statement was made early in March, 1929, by Paul M. Warburg, one of the foremost authorities on the Federal Reserve System:

[26] E. C. Harwood, *Cause and Control of the Business Cycle,* 8th ed. (Great Barrington, Mass.: American Institute for Economic Research, 1962), pp. 124–27.

History, which has a painful way of repeating itself, has taught mankind that speculative over-expansion invariably ends in over-contraction and distress. If a Stock Exchange debauch is quickly arrested by prompt and determined action, it is not too much to hope that a shrinkage of inflated stock prices may be brought about without seriously affecting the wider circle of general business. If orgies of unrestrained speculation are permitted to spread too far, however, the ultimate collapse is certain not only to affect the speculators themselves, but also to bring about a general depression involving the entire country.

.   .   .   .

. . . When the savings of the masses are deposited as margins for Stock Exchange speculations, and when the extravagant use of funds for speculative purposes absorbs so much of the nation's credit supply that it threatens to cripple the country's regular business, then there does not seem to be any doubt as to the direction in which the Federal Reserve System ought to exercise its influence quickly and forcefully.

People who express the fear that increase in the Federal Reserve Bank's rediscount rates might hurt business overlook the far greater hurt the country will have to suffer if their advice to permit the situation "to work itself out" were followed. . . .[27]

The variety of explanations of the great boom and panic causes one to suppose that the lessons offered by those destructive episodes are not generally understood or accepted, and so will not be a means of future guidance. Thus it seems reasonable to assume that what happened in the stock market in the autumn of 1929 can happen again—perhaps on a far greater scale.

[27] *The Commercial and Financial Chronicle* (March 9, 1929), p. 1444.

Epilogue

THE STOCK MARKET CRAZE that ended in disaster in 1929 was a misdirection of energy and hopeful expectation. The dreams of wealth evoked by rising stock prices made speculation too tempting for many mortals to resist. The deliberate inflation of credit by the monetary authorities—men who should have understood their responsibilities and known better —and their later reluctance to deflate when the boom began to get out of hand encouraged perhaps a million people to buy stocks on margin, and some millions more to buy them outright, for the most part at unrealistically high prices.

Being in the market was not wicked, nor was it pure folly. Age-old human nature was reacting as it apparently always had under similar conditions. The belief in a New Era, free of panics and depressions, was adhered to and proclaimed by so many of the nation's leaders, intellectuals, and men of affairs that the common man, well-to-do or poor, had little basis for any other opinion. The mass-psychology aspect of it all was due, in part at least, to an indoctrination from the highest levels of academic, financial, and social life.

Once again, in the 1920's, a speculative boom reflected the nationwide belief in a personal and national destiny of wealth—in keeping with the American tradition that faith and the will to believe must lead on to success. When so many looked to the stock market for this wealth, the belief became largely a gambler's illusion. But that same conviction, when it caused the application of common sense to productive activity in the world of reality—and not the world of brokerage accounts, stock quotations, ticker tape, tips, and margins—has helped to make America great and rich and powerful; and it can continue to do so.

BIBLIOGRAPHY

GENERAL REFERENCES

Especially relevant general references for the boom and panic periods, as well as the depression, are certain financial periodicals and leading newspapers of the time, and also publications of the Federal Reserve Board. These include: the *Annalist; Barron's National Business and Financial Weekly*; the *Commercial and Financial Chronicle*; *Federal Reserve Board Annual Reports*; *Federal Reserve Bulletin*; the *New York Herald-Tribune*; the *New York Times*; and the *Wall Street Journal*.

BOOKS

ALLEN, FREDERICK LEWIS. *The Lords of Creation*. New York: Harper & Brothers, 1935.

————. *Only Yesterday: An Informal History of the Nineteen-Twenties*. New York: Harper & Brothers, 1931.

AMERICAN ECONOMIC ASSOCIATION. *Readings in Business Cycle Theory*. Philadelphia: The Blakiston Company, 1944.

ANDERSON, BENJAMIN M. *Economics and the Public Welfare*. New York: D. Van Nostrand Company, Inc., 1949.

ANGLY, EDWARD. *Oh Yeah?* New York: The Viking Press, 1931.

AYERS, LEONARD P. *Turning Points in Business Cycles*. New York: The Macmillan Company, 1939.

BARUCH, BERNARD M., *Baruch: The Public Years*. New York: Holt, Rinehart and Winston, Inc., 1960.

BOARD OF GOVERNORS OF THE FEDERAL RESERVE SYSTEM. *Banking Studies*. Washington, D.C., 1941.

BRATT, ELMER CLARK. *Business Cycles and Forecasting*, 5th ed. Homewood, Ill.: Richard D. Irwin, Inc., 1961.

BRESCIANI-TURRONI, CONSTANTINO. *The Economics of Inflation*. New York: Barnes & Noble, Inc., 1938.

CANTOR, EDDIE. *Caught Short! A Saga of Wailing Wall Street*. New York: Simon and Schuster, 1929.

CASSEL, GUSTAV. *The Crisis in the World's Monetary System*, 2nd ed. Oxford: The Clarendon Press, 1932.

CHANDLER, LESTER V. *Benjamin Strong, Central Banker*. Washington, D.C.: The Brookings Institution, 1958.

COLLMAN, CHARLES A. *Our Mysterious Panics, 1830–1930*. New York: William Morrow & Company, 1931.

COWLES, ALFRED, III, and ASSOCIATES. *Common-Stock Indexes*, 2nd ed. Bloomington, Ind.: Principia Press, Inc., 1939.

DICE, CHARLES A. *New Levels in the Stock Market*. New York: McGraw-Hill Book Company, Inc., 1929.

DULLES, ELEANOR L. *Depression and Reconstruction: A Study of Causes and Controls*. Philadelphia: University of Pennsylvania Press, 1936.

FAULKNER, HAROLD UNDERWOOD. *American Economic History*, 8th ed. New York: Harper & Brothers, 1960.

FISHER, IRVING. *The Stock Market Crash—And After*. New York: The Macmillan Company, 1930.

FLYNN, JOHN T. *Security Speculation, Its Economic Effects*. New York: Harcourt, Brace and Company, 1934.

FRIEDMAN, MILTON and SCHWARTZ, ANNA JACOBSON. *A Monetary History of the United States, 1867-1960*. A study by the National

Bureau of Economic Research, Inc., New York. Princeton: Princeton University Press, 1963.

GALBRAITH, JOHN KENNETH. *The Great Crash, 1929*. Boston: Houghton Mifflin Company, 1955.

GOODBAR, JOSEPH ERNEST. *Managing the People's Money*. New Haven: Yale University Press, 1935.

GRAVES, LLOYD M. *The Great Depression and Beyond*. New York: Press of J. D. McGuire, 1932.

HABERLER, GOTTFRIED. *Prosperity and Depression: A Theoretical Analysis of Cyclical Movements*, new ed. Cambridge: Harvard University Press, 1960.

HANSEN, ALVIN H. *Fiscal Policy and Business Cycles*. New York: W. W. Norton & Company, Inc., 1941.

HARPER, HENRY HOWARD. *After the Stock Market Crash of November, 1929*. Boston: Privately printed, 1930.

HARRIS, SEYMOUR E. *Twenty Years of Federal Reserve Policy*. 2 vols. Cambridge: Harvard University Press, 1933.

HARROD, R. F. *The Trade Cycle*. Oxford: The Clarendon Press, 1936.

HARWOOD, E. C. *Cause and Control of the Business Cycle*. Great Barrington, Mass.: American Institute for Economic Research, 1961.

HAWTREY, R. G. *Currency and Credit*, 4th ed. London: Longmans, Green and Co., 1950.

HEILBRONER, ROBERT L. *The Worldly Philosophers*. New York: Simon & Schuster, 1953.

HIRST, FRANCIS W. *Wall Street and Lombard Street*. New York: The Macmillan Company, 1931.

HODSON, HENRY V. *Economics of a Changing World*. New York: Harrison Smith & Robert Haas, 1933.

————. *Slump and Recovery, 1929–1937*. London: Oxford University Press, 1938.

HOOVER, HERBERT. *The Memoirs of Herbert Hoover: The Great Depression, 1929–1941*. New York: The Macmillan Company, 1952.

JONES, EDWARD D. *Economic Crises*. New York: The Macmillan Company, 1900.

JUGLAR, CLEMENT. *A Brief History of Panics*, ed. by DECOURCY W. THOM. New York: G. P. Putnam's Sons, 1893.

LAWRENCE, JOSEPH STAGG. *Wall Street and Washington*. Princeton: Princeton University Press, 1929.

LEFEVRE, EDWIN. *Reminiscences of a Stock Operator*. Larchmont, N. Y.: American Research Council, 1964.

LEFFLER, GEORGE L. *The Stock Market*. New York: The Ronald Press Company, 1951.

LEONARD, JONATHAN N. *Three Years Down*. New York: Carrick & Evans, Inc., 1939.

LIONBERGER, I. H. *Commercial Crises*. St. Louis: American Credit-Indemnity Company, 1920.

MACAULAY, FREDERICK R. *Some Theoretical Problems Suggested by the Movements of Interest Rates, Bond Yields and Stock Prices in the United States Since 1856*. New York: National Bureau of Economic Research, Inc., 1938.

MCDONALD, FORREST. *Insull*. Chicago: The University of Chicago Press, 1962.

MCNEEL, R. W. *Sick in Bed with Common Stocks*. Boston: McNeel Institute of Investment Education, Inc., 1930.

Major Forces in World Business Depression. New York: National Industrial Conference Board, Inc., 1931.

MITCHELL, WESLEY C. *Business Cycles: The Problem and Its Setting.* New York: National Bureau of Economic Research, Inc., 1959.

————. *What Happens during Business Cycles: A Progress Report.* New York: National Bureau of Economic Research, Inc., 1951.

MOON, THOMAS PARKER (ed.) *Business, Speculation and Money.* New York: The Academy of Political Science, Columbia University, 1930.

MOORE, GEOFFREY H. (ed.) *Business Cycle Indicators.* 2 vols. Princeton: Princeton University Press, 1961.

MORGENSTERN, OSKAR. *International Financial Transactions and Business Cycles.* Princeton: Princeton University Press, 1959.

MYERS, MARGARET G. *The New York Money Market: Origins and Development,* Vol. I. New York: Columbia University Press, 1931.

MYERS, WILLIAM STARR and NEWTON, WALTER H. *The Hoover Administration: A Documented Narrative.* New York: Charles Scribner's Sons, 1936.

NELSON, HARRIS J. *Commonsense Speculation.* New York: Barron's, 1938.

NOYES, ALEXANDER DANA. *The Market Place: Reminiscences of a Financial Editor.* Boston: Little, Brown and Company, 1938.

PECORA, FERDINAND. *Wall Street under Oath.* New York: Simon and Schuster, 1939.

PERKINS, DAVID W. *Wall Street Panics, 1813–1930.* Utica, N. Y.: Utica Printing Company, 1931.

PHILLIPS, C. A., McMANUS, T. F., and NELSON, R. W. *Banking and the Business Cycle: A Study of the Great Depression in the United States*. New York: The Macmillan Company, 1937.

PRICE, WALTER W. *We Have Recovered Before!* New York: Harper & Brothers, 1933.

ROBBINS, LIONEL. *The Great Depression*. London: Macmillan and Co., Ltd., 1934.

ROEPKE, WILHELM. *Crises and Cycles*. London: William Hodge & Company, Ltd., 1936.

ROTHBARD, MURRAY N. *America's Great Depression*. Princeton: D. Van Nostrand Company, Inc., 1963.

RUST, ORTON G. *Roosevelt Takes Hold*. Springfield, Ohio: Shawnee Publishing Company, 1933.

SANDERS, ANNE W. *The Crisis, 1929–*. London: Eric Partridge, Ltd., 1934.

SCHERMAN, HARRY. *The Promises Men Live By: A New Approach To Economics*. New York: Random House, 1938.

SCHUMPETER, JOSEPH A. *Business Cycles*. 2 vols. New York: McGraw-Hill Book Company, Inc., 1939.

SELDES, GILBERT V. *The Years of the Locust*. Boston: Little, Brown and Company, 1933.

SHIRLEY, WILLIAM W. (compiler). *The World Depression, 1929: A List of Books and Pamphlets in the New York Public Library*. New York: The New York Public Library, 1934.

SIMMONS, E. H. H., president of the New York Stock Exchange. *The Principal Causes of the Stock Market Crisis of Nineteen Twenty-Nine*. Address delivered at the Thirty-First Annual Dinner of the Transportation Club, the Pennsylvania Railroad, at Philadelphia, Pennsylvania, January 25, 1930.

SLICHTER, SUMNER H. *Modern Economic Society*. New York: Henry Holt and Company, 1931.

SMITH, EDGAR L. *Common Stocks as Long Term Investments*. New York: The Macmillan Company, 1928.

————. *Tides in the Affairs of Men*. New York: The Macmillan Company, 1939.

SNYDER, CARL. *Capitalism the Creator: The Economic Foundations of Modern Industrial Society*. New York: The Macmillan Company, 1940.

SOULE, GEORGE H. *The Coming American Revolution*. New York: The Macmillan Company, 1934.

SPARLING, EARL. *Mystery Men of Wall Street*. New York: Greenberg Publisher, 1930.

STARCH, DANIEL. *Faith, Fear, and Fortunes*. New York: Richard R. Smith, 1934.

STUDENSKI, PAUL and KROOSS, HERMAN. *Financial History of the United States*. New York: McGraw-Hill Book Company, Inc., 1952.

SULLIVAN, LAWRENCE. *Prelude to Panic*. Washington, D. C.: Statesman Press, 1936.

TILDEN, FREEMAN. *A World in Debt*. New York: Funk & Wagnalls Company, 1936.

U. S. CONGRESS. Senate Committee on Banking and Currency. Hearings on S. Res. 71. 71st Cong., 3d sess. (January–March, 1931).

U. S. CONGRESS. Senate Committee on Banking and Currency. Hearings before the Committee and a Subcommittee, Stock Exchange Practices. 72nd and 73d Cong. (April 11, 1932–September 1, 1932), parts 1–3 and Appendix; (January 11, 1933–

March 2, 1933), parts 4–6; (May 23, 1933–May 4, 1934), parts 1–20 and Index.

U. S. CONGRESS. Senate Committee on Banking and Currency. Hearings before a Subcommittee, Gold Reserve Act Amendments. 83d Cong., 2nd sess. (March 29–April 1, 1954).

U. S. DEPARTMENT OF COMMERCE. Bureau of the Census. *Historical Statistics of the United States, Colonial Times to 1957*. A Statistical Abstract Supplement. Washington, D. C.: U. S. Government Printing Office, 1960.

U. S. TREASURY DEPARTMENT. *Annual Report of the Secretary of the Treasury on the State of the Finances for the Fiscal Year Ended June 30, 1928*. Washington, D. C.: U. S. Government Printing Office, 1928.

WARBURG, PAUL M. *The Federal Reserve System: Its Origin and Growth*. 2 vols. New York: The Macmillan Company, 1930.

WECTER, DIXON. *The Age of the Great Depression, 1929–1941*. New York: The Macmillan Company, 1948.

WHITE, WILLIAM ALLEN. *A Puritan in Babylon*. New York: The Macmillan Company, 1938.

WHITNEY, RICHARD. *Trade Depressions and Stock Panics*. New York: 1930.

WILLIS, H. PARKER and CHAPMAN, JOHN M. *The Economics of Inflation*. New York: Columbia University Press, 1935.

WINKELMAN, BARNIE F. *Ten Years of Wall Street*. Philadelphia: The John C. Winston Company, 1932.

WRIGHT, CHESTER WHITNEY. *Economic History of the United States,* 2nd ed. New York: McGraw-Hill Book Company, Inc., 1949.

PERIODICALS

ADAMS, JAMES TRUSLOW. "Presidential Prosperity," *Harper's Magazine* (August, 1930).

ALLEN, FREDERICK LEWIS. "Financially, Only Yesterday," *Chapters of Business and Finance* (1930).

ANDERSON, PAUL Y. "Sacred Bulls and Sinister Bears," *The Nation* (May 11, 1932).

"Another New High," *World's Work* (May, 1929).

ATWOOD, ALBERT. "The Future of Stock Speculation," *Saturday Evening Post* (September 13, 1930).

———. "The Great Bull Market," *Saturday Evening Post* (January 12, 1929).

———. "Investment and Speculation," *Saturday Evening Post* (December 7, 1929).

———. "Men and Markets," *Saturday Evening Post* (April 27, 1929).

BARMAN, T. G. "Ivar Kreuger: His Life and Work," *Atlantic Monthly* (August, 1932).

BARNARD, EUNICE F. "Ladies of the Ticker," *North American Review* (April, 1929).

BARUCH, BERNARD M. "Bernard Baruch's Own Story; Part One: The 1929 Crash," *Saturday Evening Post* (October 1, 1960).

"Beaux Gestes," *Literary Digest* (November 23, 1929).

"Behind the Credit Battle," *The New Republic* (April 10, 1929).

"Beware of Bear Baiters," *Outlook* (October 14, 1931).

"Broker Broken," *Time* (December 7, 1936).

"Business Must Clean House," *The Christian Century* (May 4, 1932).

"The Call to Order," *The Commonweal* (November 13, 1929).

"Can the Market Be Controlled?" *The New Republic* (November 13, 1929).

CARVER, THOMAS NIXON. "Selling Short," *Atlantic Monthly* (February, 1930).

THE CLEVELAND TRUST COMPANY, Cleveland, Ohio, *Business Bulletin* (October 15, 1929).

COREY, LEWIS. "Who Gains by Speculation?" *The New Republic* (April 17, 1929).

CROWTHER, SAMUEL. "Everybody Ought to Be Rich" (an interview with John J. Raskob), *Ladies Home Journal* (August, 1929).

The Daily Chronicle (London) (October 15–November 15, 1929).

The Daily News and Westminster Gazette (London) (October 15–November 15, 1929).

The Daily Telegraph (London) (October 15–November 15, 1929).

"The Dance of the Billions," *Saturday Evening Post* (December 22, 1928).

DANIELIAN, N. R. "The Stock Market and the Public," *Atlantic Monthly* (October, 1933).

DAYTON, KATHERINE. "This Little Pig Went to Market," *Saturday Evening Post* (March 23, 1929).

DICE, CHARLES A. "Have Stocks Struck a New 'Holding' Zone?" *The Magazine of Business* (November, 1928).

Dun's Review (October 5, 1929).

ECONOMICUS. "The Hatry Scandal," *Review of Reviews* (February 15, 1930).

The Economist (July–December, 1929).

EITEMAN, WILFORD J. "The Economic Significance of Brokers' Loans," *Journal of Political Economy* (October, 1932).

———. "The Relation of Call Money Rates to Stock Market Speculation," *Quarterly Journal of Economics* (May, 1933).

ELLSWORTH, D. W. "Causes of the Stock Market Boom," *Current History* (December, 1928).

FIELDS, M. J. "Speculation and the Growing Instability of Stock Prices," *American Economic Review* (December, 1933).

The Financial World (September–December, 1929).

FLORANCE, HOWARD. "What Really Happened?" *Review of Reviews* (January, 1930).

FLYNN, JOHN T. "The Birthday of the Slump," *Forum* (November, 1930).

———. "How to Make Money in Wall Street," *Woman's Home Companion* (January, 1930).

———. "Mobilizing Deflation," *Forum* (February, 1930).

———. "Riders of the Whirlwind," *Collier's* (January 19, 1929).

———. "Speculation and Gambling," *Harper's Magazine* (January, 1930).

———. "Taming the Great Bull," *Forum* (February, 1929).

———. "The Wall Street Debt Machine," *Harper's Magazine* (July, 1933).

Forbes Magazine (October–December, 1929).

FRASER, LINDLEY. "The Significance of the Stock Exchange Boom," *The American Economic Review* (June, 1932).

FRAZER, ELIZABETH. "The Lady and the Ticker," *Saturday Evening Post* (March 8, 1930).

FREDERICK, J. GEORGE. "Short Selling Loses Caste," *North American Review* (July, 1932).

"From Stock-Gambling to Embezzling," *Literary Digest* (December 7, 1929).

GALBRAITH, JOHN KENNETH. "The Great Wall Street Crash," *Harper's Magazine* (October, 1954).

GAMMACK, THOMAS H. "Scolding by the Federal Reserve," *Outlook* (February 20, 1929).

———. "Six Million Share Days," *Outlook* (December 5, 1928).

GARRETT, GARET. "Speculation," *Saturday Evening Post* (May 4, 1929).

———. "Wall Street and Washington," *Saturday Evening Post* (December 28, 1929).

GARRETT, PAUL W. "The Forces Behind the Fever," *Outlook* (December 26, 1928).

———. "The Jazz Age in Finance," *North American Review* (February, 1930).

"The Great Senate Bear Hunt," *Literary Digest* (May 7, 1932).

GRISWOLD, GLENN. "Definite Reserve Policy—A Business Necessity," *Magazine of Business* (June, 1929).

GWINN, SHERMAN. "Who Said the Day of Railroad Giants Is Over?" *The American Magazine* (July, 1928).

HALL, HENRY. "The Money Market," *The Nation* (June 19, 1929).

"The Halt in the Spring Bull Market," *Literary Digest* (May 17, 1930).

HANEY, LEWIS H. "Who Gets the Money?" *North American Review* (January, 1930).

HANSON, DONALD R. "Taking Advantage of the Bear Market," *Forum* (October, 1931).

"In Praise of Speculation," *Business Week* (March 12, 1930).

"The Inseparable Vans," *Collier's* (May 31, 1930).

JORDAN, VIRGIL. "Our Market Bull and the Foreign China Shop," *Magazine of Business* (July, 1929).

JOSEPHSON, MATTHEW. "The 'New Era': Its Rise and Fall," *The New Republic* (November 4 and 18, 1931).

LEFEVRE, EDWIN. "The Bigger They Are—," *Saturday Evening Post* (January 11, 1930).

———. "Blame the Broker," *Saturday Evening Post* (April 9, 1932).

———. "The Little Fellow in Wall Street," *Saturday Evening Post* (January 4, 1930).

———. "The Long and the Short of It," *Saturday Evening Post* (December 13, 1930).

————. "The New Bears—Normal and Grizzly," *Saturday Evening Post* (December 27, 1930).

————. "Running Past the Signal," *Saturday Evening Post* (February 9, 1929).

————. "Speculation—Both Versions," *Saturday Evening Post* (April 2, 1932).

————"A Trip on the Magic Carpet," *Saturday Evening Post* (February 1, 1930).

————. "Vanished Billions," *Saturday Evening Post* (February 13, 1932).

————. "With Blue Chips This Time," *Saturday Evening Post* (February 2, 1929).

Literary Digest (October, 1928–December, 1929).

LORENZ, ROBERT. "Being Wise after the Event," *The Financial Review of Reviews* (May, 1934).

McCABE, GEORGE. "Wall Street Goes Amateur," *The Commonweal* (December 11, 1929).

McMULLEN, FRANCES D. "Women and Ticker Tape—A Year after the Crash," *The Woman's Journal* (November, 1930).

Magazine of Wall Street (October–December, 1929).

"The March of Events," *World's Work* (June, 1929).

MARCOSSON, ISAAC F. "The Match King," *Saturday Evening Post* (October 12, 1929).

MAUROIS, ANDRÉ. "How You Have Changed!" *Forum* (June, 1931).

"The Men Who Did It," *The Nation* (November 13, 1929).

MERZ, CHARLES. "Bull Market," *Harper's Magazine* (April, 1929).

"Milestones," *Time* (October 23, 1950).

"A Monetary Retrospect," *The Economist* (London) (December 7, 1929).

The Morning Post (London) (October 15–November 15, 1929).

MURPHY, CHARLES J. V. "Wall Street Branches Out," *Outlook* (September 18, 1929).

A NEW YORK STOCK EXCHANGE BROKER. "Inside Pools, Bobtails, and Jiggles," *North American Review* (March, 1930).

NIEBUHR, REINHOLD. "The Speculation Mania," *The World Tomorrow* (January, 1930).

"Nothing to Nothing," *Time* (March 31, 1947).

"Now I've Gone Back to Work," *The American Magazine* (February, 1930).

NOYES, ALEXANDER DANA. "The Conflict over Credit Reaches a Climax," *Scribner's Magazine* (May, 1929).

———. "The Stock Market Panic," *Current History* (December, 1929).

PATTERSON, ROBERT T. "Panics and Politics," *The Wall Street Journal* (November 10, 1954).

PAYNE, WILL. "Deflation," *Saturday Evening Post* (May 3, 1930).

———. "Greatest of Bull Markets," *World's Work* (January, 1929).

———. "A Reformed Speculator," *Saturday Evening Post* (August 10, 1929).

PHILLIPS, H. I. "My Stock Market Operations," *The American Magazine* (March, 1929).

RASCOE, BURTON. "The Grim Anniversary," *The New Republic* (October 29, 1930).

RICHTER-ALTSCHAEFFER, HANS. "Some Theoretical Aspects of Stock-Market Speculation," *Journal of Political Economy* (April, 1931).

RINEHART, MARY ROBERTS. "A Woman Goes to Market," *Saturday Evening Post* (January 31, 1931).

RIPLEY, WILLIAM Z. "Speculation: What to Do About It," *Scribner's Magazine* (October, 1932).

ROBERTS, GEORGE E. "Lessons of the Stock Panic," *Outlook* (January 8, 1930).

ROBEY, RALPH WEST. "Capeadores in Wall Street," *Atlantic Monthly* (September, 1928).

SCROGGS, WILLIAM O. "By-products of the Bull Market," *Outlook* (May 8, 1929).

———. "We Have Changed All That," *Outlook* (December 25, 1929).

SELDES, GILBERT. "Found Money," *The Mentor* (November, 1930).

SHIVELY, CARLTON. "Panics," *Outlook* (November 13, 1929).

SPARKES, BOYDEN. "A Career in Wall Street," *Saturday Evening Post* (March 8, 1930).

SPARLING, EARL. "These Brokers," *Scribner's Magazine* (July, 1930).

"Speculation at the Crossroads," *Review of Reviews* (January, 1929).

"Speculation's Seamy Side," *Saturday Evening Post* (August 10, 1929).

SPRING, SAMUEL. "Whirlwinds of Speculation," *Atlantic Monthly* (April, 1931).

"The Stock-Speculating Mania," *Literary Digest* (December 8, 1928).

"Tale of a Bear," *Saturday Evening Post* (February 18, 25; March 4, 1933).

"Through the Wringer with A. G. & E.," *Fortune* (December, 1945).

"The Tragedy of Insull," *Collier's* (May 12, 1934).

"Two Bankers on the Depression," *The New Republic* (January 21, 1931).

"Two Hours behind the Market," *Popular Mechanics Magazine* (February, 1929).

"Two Years of the Bear Market," *Literary Digest* (October 3, 1931).

UNCLE HENRY. "The Shock Market," *Collier's* (May 4, 1929).

"Van Sweringen Finale," *Newsweek* (November 12, 1951).

VOLKENING, HENRY T. "Wall Street—The Modern Mecca," *The World Tomorrow* (April, 1930).

"Wall Street at Close Range" (a series of articles), *World's Work* (December, 1930–October, 1931).

"The Wall Street Crash, a British Symposium," *The Living Age* (December 1, 1929).

"The Wall Street Crash and the Working Class," *Daily Worker* (October 28, 1929).

"Wall Street Is Placing the Blame," *Business Week* (November 27, 1929).

"Wall St. Lays an Egg," *Variety* (October 30, 1929).

"Wall Street's 'Prosperity Panic,'" *Literary Digest* (November 9, 1929).

"The War against Wall-Street Speculation," *Literary Digest* (April 13, 1929).

"What Bull Market?" *Business Week* (September 7, 1929).

"What Smashed the Bull Market?" *Literary Digest* (November 9, 1929).

"What's behind the Reserve Board's Stand?" *The Magazine of Business* (March, 1929).

"When It's a Man, Wall Street Doesn't Speculate," *Business Week* (January 15, 1930).

WILLIS, H. PARKER. "Who Caused the Panic of 1929?" *North American Review* (February, 1930).

WILSON, EDMUND. "Sunshine Charley," *The New Republic* (June 28, 1933).

WINKLER, MAX. "Paying the Piper," *North American Review* (January, 1930).

WUORINEN, JOHN H. "Kreuger's Vanished Millions," *Current History* (May, 1932).

Index

265